General Editor
Professor Bernard Richards

THE GREATEST BOOKS YOU'LL NEVER READ

A portrait of John Keats reading a book of poetry.

An Hachette UK Company
www.hachette.co.uk

Cassell Illustrated is a division of Octopus Publishing Group Limited
Carmelite House, 50 Victoria Embankment, London EC4Y 0DZ
www.octopusbooks.co.uk

This edition published in 2015

Distributed in the US by Hachette Book Group USA
237 Park Avenue, New York NY 10017 USA

Distributed in Canada by Canadian Manda Group
165 Dufferin Street, Toronto, Ontario, Canada M6K 3H6

The book covers that accompany each entry in this book have been created by contemporary designers to convey to the reader a fictional interpretation of how such a cover might have looked. These are merely creative interpretations of "what might have been." Where the names of real-life individuals appear, there is no intention to denote that such individuals would have proceeded with involvement in the books as depicted in these fictional covers.

ISBN: 978-1-84403-793-3

QSS.TGBN

This book was designed and produced by
Quintessence Editions Ltd.
The Old Brewery, 6 Blundell Street, London, N7 9BH

Senior Editor	Elspeth Beidas
Designers	John Round, Isabel Eeles, Adam Hutchinson
Production Manager	Anna Pauletti
Editorial Director	Jane Laing
Publisher	Mark Fletcher

Color reproduction by Bright Arts
Printed and bound in China by 1010 Printing International Ltd.

10 9 8 7 6 5 4 3 2 1

CONTENTS

INTRODUCTION

In his book *Fear and Loathing on the Campaign Trail '72* (1973), covering the 1972 presidential campaign of the U.S. Democratic Party, Gonzo Journalist Hunter S. Thompson recounts a conversation with a fellow journalist about the threatened fate of Virgil's *Aeneid* (19 BCE):

> "On the morning of election day in Nebraska I was talking to Lydon in the lobby of the Omaha Hilton when he suddenly wrapped off the conversation with: 'You know, Virgil wanted to burn the *Aeneid*.' I stared at him, trying to remember if Virgil was maybe one of McGovern's advance men for Scott's Bluff that I hadn't met yet, or . . . 'You pointy-head bastard,' I said, 'Wait till Wallace gets in. He'll kick your ass all over the street with Virgil.'"

This famous moment in the history of literature is a prime demonstration of the perilous state in which a literary work exists. In the *Aeneid*'s case the threat was from the author, who did not want an imperfect work to survive. Virgil's last wishes were, of course, ignored (see p.12), as, in a later century, were Franz Kafka's (see p.142). But the perfectionism of the author is not only the only danger. There is a whole host of finished works that are unfinished, unbegun, or lost, and today exist as only suggestive fragments or not at all. We dream of these prodigies, knowing that we shall never be able to read them, and their absence makes them all the more tantalizing. Somehow their very non-existence or their incompleteness gives them a kind of virtue and appeal that is often lacking from fully fledged and finished works.

Books look like such reassuringly finished and solid objects, and indeed they are, up to a point. They are the end-product of complex mental and technological processes, and they seem to demand that we place faith in them as final and authoritative works. In fact, though, the situation is not always quite as firm as might be hoped. Between an author's original intentions and the published work, many compromises, adaptations, and revisions will have occurred, not all of them sanctioned by the author. The demands of the marketplace will often have interfered, producing work which is, to an extent, collaborative, between the author and their audience.

Hunter S. Thompson at his typewriter, c. 1976.

Variorum editions of an author's work reveal the elaborate processes a text undergoes as it moves toward its final state, but often the more the details accumulate the more the notion of finality is revealed to be illusion. For some readers this creates despair, but others are more philosophical: French poet Paul Valéry, for instance, said that works of art are "never finished, merely abandoned." In a universe perpetually in a state of flux, concepts of finish and fixity are hard to imagine—especially in something as flowing and evolving as a text. Cancelled and revised proofs can be considered a whole body of lost work in themselves.

One notable case of multiple published versions is the work of Henry James (see p.132). Much of his writing was initially published in magazines. Before reaching book form, James, who was an inveterate tinkerer, revised the texts. Often he would revise when reprints were undertaken, and in the early 1900s there was a massive process of revision as he entirely rewrote the work he wanted to continue in permanent existence for the New York Edition. Strictly speaking, to read James one has to read him two or three times in the various editions, which are so divergent that they are virtually different works.

Another example that raises questions about the stability of a text is T.S. Eliot's poem *The Waste Land* (1922). Eliot showed the early typescripts to Ezra Pound, who suggested numerous cuts. In "The Fire Sermon," for instance, Eliot had the "small house-agent's clerk" delay "only to urinate and spit" after a sexual encounter with a typist, and Pound suggested it was "probaly [sic] over the mark!" Today a facsimile of the typescript with all the emendations is available, so it is possible to see the different roads not taken by the author. For readers interested in the literary process *The Waste Land* manuscript is fascinating, but there is perhaps a danger that the provisional and alternative versions will end up competing for attention with the final work that was selected by Eliot to lay before the public.

The Waste Land also highlights another interesting aspect of the creative process: that Pound's input makes it a collaborative work, challenging the received view of the lonely artist as an individual creator. Although this Romantic myth remains strong in the popular imagination, many works of art in all media have been the result of the collaborative efforts of more than one practitioner. Even Shakespeare—one of the central icons in the annals of individual creation—collaborated with other writers, as he did on his lost play *Cardenio* (see p.28).

Insight into the process of creation can also be found in an author's fragments, which are sometimes gathered together after their death—as Mary Shelley did with as much of her deceased husband Percy's work as she could find. These incomplete fragments of text have an additional allure, because they challenge the reader to imagine more than is there, and to join in the collaborative process of creation.

Revised and fragmented works at least provide us with a text that can be read. At the other end of the scale is a vast corpus of literature that once existed, either in fact or in theory, but that is now lost. Depredations have been especially numerous in the case of classical literature, where there are hundreds of lost works, known only by their titles. Since the advent of printing there is less chance of a work being lost—multiple copies guarantee a degree of survival—but in the contexts where works exist mainly in manuscript form, the chances of survival are much lower. A large gap occurs in literature for Elizabethan and Jacobean drama, for instance, because theater producers tended to regard plays as more stage-events than book-texts. Indeed Shakespeare's works were only gathered together after his death.

Some titles have been more or less complete, only to be lost through accident. Thomas Carlyle's *The French Revolution* (1837) was destroyed by John Stuart Mill's maid, who thought it was trash and used it to light fires. T.E. Lawrence left *The Seven Pillars of Wisdom* (1922) on the train at Reading. Both authors, with considerable courage, set about rewriting their lost works, but we don't know whether they reconstituted them perfectly, and we shall never be able to read the lost originals.

Finally there are the unbegun or incompleted works. Samuel Taylor Coleridge planned many works never executed (see p.36), as did John Ruskin (see p.108). These unachieved schemes suggest considerable energy and ambition, but also point to minds not always focused or disciplined. Honoré de Balzac had enormous ambition—which he largely realized—but nonetheless around 46 of the works he planned for *La Comédie Humaine* were not executed (see p.82). These works begun but not finished are subject to various explanations, including the intervention of death. Their presence often seems to pose a challenge to writers, and many have stepped into the breach to finish them. There have been numerous attempts to finish Jane Austen's unfinished novels (see p.46 and p.240), and Charles Dickens's *The Mystery of Edwin Drood* (see p.98). It is as if writers cannot bear to think of an author they admire leaving behind an incomplete work.

The picture is further complicated by definitions of literature. There is a tendency to think of literature as made up of texts that have gone through the disciplines of construction and publication, and have had audiences in mind. Byron's memoirs (see p.57), Plath's late journal (see p.200), and Philip Larkin's diaries are often mentioned when the corpus of lost works is dwelt on, and yet it is arguable that interesting as they might have been they were never quite literature. These private, personal diaries were not written with the kind of self-conscious aesthetic selection that is associated with literature proper.

All this points to the conclusion that the conditions surrounding the creation and publication of literature greatly complicate and frustrate the drive toward perfection and completion, making it often almost inconceivable. Shakespeare entertained the notion that a perfect finish could be found in nature—"When I consider everything that grows / Holds in perfection but a little moment" (Sonnet 15, 1609)—but it is debatable whether nature, essentially characterized by flux, can truly offer this prospect. Perhaps the best that we can hope for from literature is a constantly evolving series of briefly achieved perfections.

VIRGIL
AENEID

Chapter 1

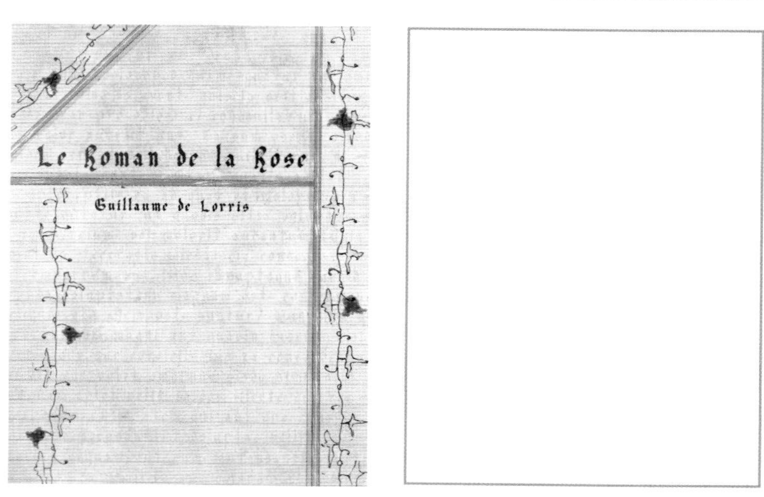
Le Roman de la Rose
Guillaume de Lorris

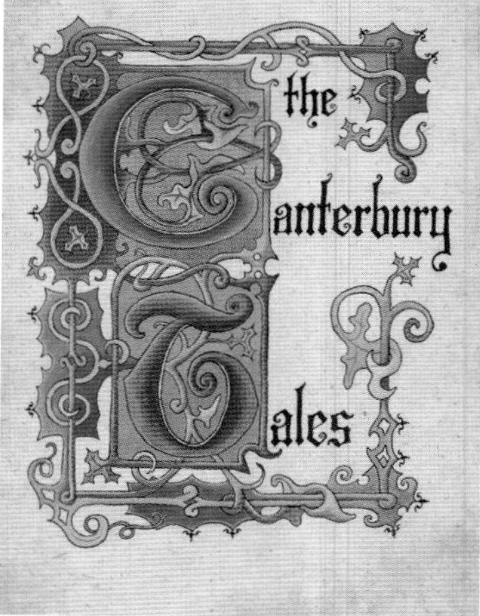
the
Canterbury
Tales

HERO
AND
LEANDER
CHRISTOPHER
MARLOWE

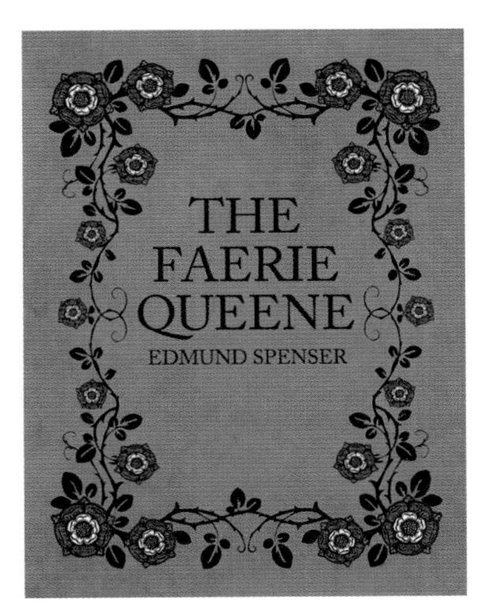
THE
FAERIE
QUEENE
EDMUND SPENSER

Pre-1750
CARDENIO
by
WILLIAM
SHAKESPEARE

AENEID

Author Virgil **Year** 19 BCE **Country** Roman Empire **Genre** Epic poetry

VIRGIL
Regarded by the Romans as their greatest poet, Virgil devoted his life entirely to his poetry and to studies connected with it. Born of peasant stock, he was fortunate in having a rich patron, Maecenas, and an influential friend, Octavian, who in 27 BCE became the Emperor Augustus.

Virgil's *Aeneid* is an epic poem in Latin about the flight of the Trojans after the Greek destruction of their city, their subsequent wanderings around the Mediterranean, and their final triumphal foundation of Rome. Most of its 9,906 lines are complete hexameters—six-foot measures that were to Roman poetry of the Golden Age what iambic pentameters would become to Shakespeare and his contemporaries. However, 57 of these lines are truncated, and it is conventionally agreed that Virgil intended to go back and finish them but that he was prevented by death from so doing.

For this supposition we are indebted to two Roman grammarians. One is Servius, who claimed that Virgil completed another of his short lines extempore while reciting parts of the work in progress to the Emperor Augustus. The other is Donatus, who wrote that in 19 BCE the poet set sail for Greece, where he planned to spend three years polishing his work, but caught a fever en route. On his deathbed in Brindisi he reportedly gave instructions that the imperfect manuscript of the *Aeneid* be destroyed, but his wishes were ignored by order of the Emperor.

Consequently it has been handed down from generation to generation that Virgil had not finished work on the epic, and that if he had lived he would not merely have completed the short lines but perhaps extended them further into epic similes or even longer digressions. However, both Servius and Donatus lived more than 400 years after Virgil, and we have no external corroboration that any of the events they describe ever really occurred.

ERROR OR OMISSION?

Internal evidence is inconclusive: Virgil's previous works—the *Eclogues* (42–37 BCE) and the *Georgics* (37–30 BCE)—contain nothing but complete lines. However, it is possible that in the *Aeneid* the poet was using these half-lines deliberately to heighten effect. Book III line 340, for example, reads:

> "What of the boy Ascanius? Does he survive and
> prosper in heaven,
> He whom in Troy long ago . . .
> Does the boy still feel the loss of his parent?"

Who is to say that this short line is not a dying fall, a deliberate attempt to evoke the sadness of recalling bereavement?

Cover: Tom Howey

The answer to that question is many people, especially during the Italian Renaissance. But the additions made by obscure minor authors of this period are at best contrived and at worst no more than padding. And regardless of their quality, none of them is authentic Virgil.

So the *Aeneid* is a work of a remarkable order: one that may or may not be complete; no one knows the truth. And in that uncertainty lies a challenge for readers, who must decide for themselves whether the material feels in any way lacking.

Most will find that it does not. Nevertheless, encyclopedias and general histories of literature still apply the adjective "unfinished" to the *Aeneid*, and that is why the poem features here. Which raises another matter that will be touched on elsewhere in the present volume: that "uncompleted" may be distinct from "incomplete." **GL**

WHAT HAPPENED NEXT . . .

With the rise of modern languages, the use of Latin declined and most of the literature became neglected or accessible only in translation. The most famous English version of the *Aeneid* was compiled in the 17th century by the first poet laureate, John Dryden. Today, Latin is often described as "a dead language," although it is still studied in schools and at universities around the world, albeit by only a small and usually select minority.

THE
WORKS
OF
VIRGIL:
Translated into
ENGLISH VERSE
BY
Mr. DRYDEN.
Volume the Second.
LONDON:
Printed by Jacob Tonson, MDCCXVI.

WILL IT EVER HAPPEN?

A counter-reformation reinstates Latin in the Roman Catholic church. The language is revived and becomes again widely understood and spoken. There is a renewal of interest in Roman writers of the pre-Christian era. People who speak Latin rather than merely read it have a more reliable sense of whether the short lines in the *Aeneid* sound right. Far-fetched? Perhaps, but never say never.

LE ROMAN DE LA ROSE

Author Guillaume de Lorris **Year** c. 1230 **Country** France **Genre** Poetry

GUILLAUME DE LORRIS
Nothing is known of this man other than that he was an aristocrat from the French village of Lorris, east of Orléans. He is widely and probably correctly supposed to be the author of this poem, but there is no compelling evidence that he was.

The potential for continuation and reimagination which is opened up by an unfinished literary work is perhaps nowhere so generative as in the medieval "best seller" *Le Roman de la Rose* (*The Story of the Rose*). Begun in around 1230 by an otherwise unknown French author, Guillaume de Lorris, the *Rose* is an intricate allegory, narrating a young man's dream of the erotic pursuit of a woman, figured as a rose. Guillaume's narrator passes into a sumptuous walled garden owned by Déduit (Pleasure). In this pleasure-garden, the narrator becomes a lover: hunted and shot by the god of love, he catches his first glimpse of the rose reflected in a fountain pool, and instantly desires her. The rose is surrounded, however, by personifications, some of which represent facets of her own personality, such as Dangier (Resistance), while others represent external forces, such as Jalousie (Jealousy) and Malebouche (Slander). Advised in turn by Ami (an experienced male friend) and Raison (Lady Reason, who counsels him to leave well alone), the lover ultimately finds himself thwarted, the rose well guarded in Jealousy's castle.

De Lorris's first-person narrator repeatedly promises not only to recount his dream, but also to provide a conclusive and authoritative "glose" (gloss/interpretation) of it at the close of the text. Yet this close was never reached: de Lorris's poem breaks off abruptly with the lover in mid-frustrated lament.

A HEAVY SECOND HAND

The inconclusiveness of this ending was exploited by Jean de Meun, a Parisian clerk, in around 1270. De Meun picks up precisely where de Lorris left off in a massive 18,000 line "continuation" that dwarfs the opening 4,000-line portion of the poem. This marks the first of many destabilizing gestures; for instance, how can de Meun possibly continue the narration of someone else's dream? He deliberately highlights this discrepancy, foregrounding the moment of rupture between the two author-figures even as the dream narrative continues. He also responds to de Lorris's promises of a culminating "glose"; his *Rose* is an interpretative reworking of de Lorris's. Yet it subversively turns it on its head. De Lorris's garden of sensory pleasure and desire resurfaces in de Meun's continuation as the "parc de l'agneau" (the heavenly park of the Lamb of God). Ami is reprised, but his advice shifts from

Cover: Gareth Butterworth

being merely politic to downright manipulative—not to mention extremely misogynist. De Lorris's eroticized courtliness has become a cynical infiltration of the castle of Jealousy by characters who embody self-seeking deceit, while the narrator's single-minded sexual conquest of the rose is figured, shockingly, as a pilgrimage to a shrine, culminating in a forced entry that is tantamount to rape. Such is the audacity of de Meun's "glose" that critics have wondered if de Lorris were not an invention of de Meun's, designed to allow him to experiment with continuation as a theme.

Whatever the truth, unfinishedness and multiple authorship are key elements of the poem's transmission. The Middle English translation of the poem, for example, is *also* unfinished, and was itself undertaken by more than one person. LR

WHAT HAPPENED NEXT . . .

In 1402–03, Christine de Pisan, the first female professional author of the late Middle Ages (depicted in blue below), engaged in an epistolary debate with a group of Parisian chancery notaries about the text's deeply problematic sexual and ethical politics. She critiqued its misogyny in resolute terms, and stood her moral and intellectual ground in the face of an all-male, clerkly elite—hardcore fans of the *Rose* largely affronted by her intervention.

WILL IT EVER HAPPEN?

5/10

From one perspective, it already has happened. But the question of whether Jean de Meun wrote all of the *Rose* or merely the continuation remains a matter of debate. Not much of one, admittedly: most scholars accept that Guillaume de Lorris was a real person, but without any concrete proof his existence remains a matter of speculation.

THE CANTERBURY TALES

Author Geoffrey Chaucer **Year** 1400 **Country** England **Genre** Story collection

GEOFFREY CHAUCER
Chaucer worked at the royal courts of Edward III and Richard II and ended his life as Controller of the Port of London. When he died he was buried in the part of London's Westminster Abbey that has since become known as Poets' Corner.

Are *The Canterbury Tales* unfinished by accident, or by design? Geographically, they stop short of their stated destination. The pilgrims who set out from the Tabard Inn in Southwark never reach the shrine of the martyred archbishop Thomas Becket in Canterbury Cathedral. The narrative schedule is not completed either. At the Tabard, the innkeeper Harry Bailey appoints himself governor of the group and devises a program of entertainment to while away the journey. He proposes, and the pilgrims agree, that each of them should tell two tales on the way out and two more on the return. Half of these tales remain untold. There can be no return if the pilgrims never arrive. Several pilgrims—the Yeoman; two of the nameless priests; the Ploughman, and the five guildsmen—never get to speak. The only pilgrim who could be said to tell two tales on the outward journey is Chaucer. Harry interrupts his first tale, a romance, complaining that its atrocious rhyme is not worth a turd. Perhaps to get his own back, Chaucer's second offering is a stolid morality in prose. The Cook almost tells two tales. The first comes to an abrupt halt with the description of a prostitute. His later attempt never gets off the ground because he is so drunk that he falls off his horse. If we include Chaucer and the Host among the 29 pilgrims fallen serendipitously into company in Southwark, of the 124 tales promised, fewer than a fifth of these are delivered.

DID CHAUCER MEAN WHAT HE SAID?

Incomplete then; but unfinished? While it is still claimed that Chaucer died before he could finish *The Tales*, a more plausible explanation is that Chaucer poses the question of whether they could ever have lived up to their billing. Under Harry Bailey's governance, narrative and social decorum yields to all manner of unruliness. Given that the Knight is the highest-ranking pilgrim, it is seemly that he tells the first tale. His appointment, however, results from drawing straws. Is he meant to be pre-eminent, is his first place an accident, or did Harry rig the poll? When Harry, as is fitting, invites the Monk to speak next, the drunken Miller brushes them both aside and brazenly usurps the churchman's place. The Miller's Tale not only calls the chivalry of the Knight's into question, but it also tilts spectacularly at Church practices and beliefs. The order of the subsequent tales is governed by spite and revenge

Cover: Isabel Eeles

EASTBOUND BAND

This 19th-century painting of Chaucer's Canterbury pilgrims leaving the Tabard Inn in Southwark (now a district of London) is by British artist Edward Henry Corbould. Known primarily as a watercolorist, Corbould produced illustrations for an 1854 edition of *The Canterbury Tales* as well as for the works of Spenser and Shakespeare.

as much as aesthetic principle. The Reeve's revenges the Miller's, and later, the Summoner swipes at the Friar's. Pilgrims refuse to hear each other out: the Knight puts an end to the Monk's gloomy tragedies because he can bear no more misery, and the Franklin patronizingly calls a halt to the young Squire's interminably chivalric flights of fancy. Narrative order is literally overtaken when a Canon and his Yeoman unexpectedly assail the company at Boughton in the Blee. The Yeoman delivers a long prologue and tale that were never foreseen in Harry Bailey's designs. It is hard to determine where "tales" begin and where they end. Lengthy prologues, such as the Canon's Yeoman's, or those of the Pardoner and the Wife of Bath, may be considered "tales" in their own right. The Friar observes waspishly that the Miller's Alison has delivered a "long preamble of a tale" even before she has embarked on her "tale" proper. Interjections, and the conversations in and between the tales, are dramatic narratives in themselves.

This narrative incontinence has a spiritual resonance; it questions the devotional motivations of pilgrimage. The opening of the General Prologue makes it clear that the pilgrims' inspiration comes, not so much from spiritual devotion, as from a springtime rejuvenation that reawakens sexual sap. Zest for bawdry abounds: buttocks thrust out of windows branded with red-hot pokers (the Miller); marital strife, sexual fantasy, and deceit (the Reeve, the Wife of Bath, the Merchant, and the Franklin); prostitution (the Cook); and prodigious farting (the Miller again—and the Summoner). Theft and fraud are rife (the Pardoner, the Shipman, the Summoner, the Friar, and the Canon's Yeoman). A father murders his child (the Physician); three revellers poison each other (The Pardoner). In the anti-Semitic tale of the Prioress, Jews murder a little Christian boy, and in the Manciple's, a cuckolded husband, goaded by a pet crow, kills his wife with a crossbow. The Nun's Priest tells of chickens strutting around as members of the gentry who double up as Adam and Eve in a reenactment of the 1381 Peasants' Revolt. Is this appropriate preparation for pilgrims to fall on their knees at St. Thomas's shrine?

¶ The tale of the chanons yeman

¶ And begynneth the tale

With this chanon I duellyd vij yere
And of his science am I neuer the nere
Al that I had I haue lost ther by
And god woot so haue mo than I
Ther as I was wont to be right fressh & gay
Of clothynge and of other good array
Now may I were an hose vp on myn hed
And where my colour was both fressh & rede
Now it is wan and of a ledyn hewe
Who so it vsith sore shal he rewe
And of my swynk y blent is myn eye
Lo suche auauntage it is to multiplye
That slydyng science hath made me so bare
That I haue no good where that euer I f
And yet I am endettid so sore therby.
Of gold that I borowed trewly

CAXTON EDITION

William Caxton, the first British book printer, produced an edition of *The Canterbury Tales* in 1476 (above). Before that, the work had been reproduced by scribes: that there are so many early versions of the work suggests that it was always a best seller.

And yet, the last tale in the sequence would appear to restore order and religious decorum. At four o' clock in the afternoon, with the shadows beginning to fall, the Host observes that his ordinance for the storytelling competition is almost complete. He invites the Parson, the parish priest who is the only speaking pilgrim apparently above reproach, to tell a tale. The Parson makes it clear that he will do no such thing. If the assembly does not want to hear morality and virtuous matter, then they should not give him audience. The pilgrims agree that devotional substance is timely and the Parson preaches a resounding sermon on the Seven Deadly Sins. A fitting conclusion perhaps? But when the Parson falls silent, there is no response from his audience. Readers cannot tell whether the pilgrims are moved to repentance and to devotion by his words.

In most manuscripts of *The Canterbury Tales*, the sermon is followed by a passage of prose, in which Chaucer appears to speak in his own voice to take leave of his book. *The Retractions*, as they are known, are a moral commentary on Chaucer's oeuvre. Chaucer urges his readers to pray for his soul, and to forgive any trespasses he may have incurred in the writing of his works. The last words of *The Canterbury Tales* narrate the author's determination to spend his time in penance in the hope that on the Day of Judgment his soul may be saved. Chaucer may not have got his pilgrims to Canterbury, but his own personal ending is enveloped in spiritual repentance. Given the chameleon performance of this shape-shifting author, however, narrating the voices and inhabiting the persons of all those pilgrims, can readers be sure that this final sentence is not just one more deftly orchestrated narrative exercise? It is decorous to end thus, but also a consummate performance of doing so. Does the author abjure all the tales, or only those that wallow in sin? This is an appropriate "end," but not the end of the matter. As ever in Chaucer's poetry, it is impossible to be confident that the narrative means what it seems to say. While The Parson's Tale and *The Retractions* provide a decorous holy close to the storytelling, the preceding unruliness, purposefully or not, casts doubt on their sincerity. In a perfect world *The Canterbury Tales* could be "finished." With its interleaving of play and devotional earnest, Chaucer's narrative delivers a world that is fallen. HB

"This is a long preamble of a tale!"

The Friar, *The Canterbury Tales*

WHAT HAPPENED NEXT . . .

Two of many "completions" pre-empt the Canterbury pilgrimage. *The Prologue and Tale of Beryn* (c.1420) occurs in the midst of a unique manuscript. Even before we hear all of Chaucer's stories on the way to Canterbury, the pilgrims visit Becket's shrine, and the Merchant tells a tale as they set off for London. John Lydgate's *Siege of Thebes* (c.1420, below) also stages the return journey. The author (a monk), usurps Chaucer's place to tell a prequel to *The Knight's Tale* that leaves it in ruins.

WILL IT EVER HAPPEN?

0/10

Although *The Canterbury Tales* is still readable without too much difficulty by modern readers, the English language has changed so much in the 600 years since it was written that any writer eager to continue it would be faced with an impossible task.

HERO AND LEANDER

Author Christopher Marlowe **Year** 1593 **Country** England **Genre** Poetry

CHRISTOPHER MARLOWE
It is known for certain that Marlowe was educated at Cambridge University, wrote half a dozen plays, including *Doctor Faustus* (c.1592), and was murdered in a brawl. He may also have been an atheist, a spy, a homosexual, and the author of Shakespeare's plays—but that is largely speculation.

A celebration of the famous lovers of Greek mythology, Christopher Marlowe's poem *Hero and Leander* was left unfinished when he died in a brawl at a lodging house in Deptford, London, in 1593. A quarto edition was published in 1598, which has survived in only one copy, now in the Folger Library in Washington, DC.

CLASSICAL BACKGROUND

Marlowe's sources for his poem were most likely the Roman poet Ovid and Musaeus (a Greek poet of the 6th century), who both composed treatments of the Greek myth. Leander is a young man living on Abydos, on one side of the Hellespont (the stretch of water separating Europe from Asia next to what is now Istanbul, between the Aegean and the Black Sea). He falls in love with Hero, who lives in Sestos, on the other side, and is a nun for Venus, sworn to chastity. The pair meet at the feast of Venus and declare their attraction for each other. To reach her for their subsequent romantic assignation Leander must swim across the treacherous stretch of water, guided by a light in her tower. While he is swimming he is seen by Neptune, god of the sea, who mistakes him for Ganymede (the most beautiful of mortals) and carries him down to the bottom of the ocean. Neptune eventually releases him and Leander reaches Hero's tower, where he and Hero consumate their love. Marlowe's poem comes to a halt with morning breaking, Hero's nakedness revealed, and the "loathsome carriage" of Night "dang'd down to hell." In the myth, the couple's trysts continue over the summer but Leander is drowned on a winter night when the light in the tower is blown out and he loses his way. Overwhelmed with grief, Hero throws herself from the tower to join him in the afterlife.

Hero and Leander is an odd and intriguing work. It is an example of what is called an *epyllion* (little epic). Marlowe brings the mythological scenes to life with a richness reflective of the Elizabethan golden age in which he was writing. It is as if the concept of the Renaissance—the rebirth of the classical spirit—is fully and literally realized. And yet what is given by Marlowe with one hand is taken away with another, because there is a facetiousness in its tone, a distanced lightness of touch, a spirit of irony at a far remove from anything approaching reverence and seriousness. It is in

HERO AND LEANDER

CHRISTOPHER MARLOWE

Cover: Rebecca Richardson

FALSE DEATH

Did Marlowe actually die in the brawl at Deptford? Conspiracy theorists like to believe he did not, and survived to go on to write Shakespeare's plays. The main proponent of the theory was the US theater critic Calvin Hoffman, who popularized the notion in his book *The Man Who Was Shakespeare* (1955). This idea has even found acceptance in Westminister Abbey, where a stained-glass window commemorating Marlowe has "1593?" as his death date (below).

the rhymes especially that this irreverence is apparent. Many of them take the poem dangerously in the direction of doggerel, especially when they are polysyllabic. One vivid example is:

> "At last, like to a bold sharp sophister,
> With cheerful hope thus he accosted her."

It is not just the sound that is disruptive here, but the reference: a "sophister" is not only a specious arguer, but also a second- or third-year Cambridge undergraduate in Marlowe's time.

> *"Whoever loved that loved not at first sight?"*
>
> *Hero and Leander*

There is not much substance to the story, but Marlowe fleshes it out with elaborate references to the classical gods and goddesses and their amours, and complex philosophical arguments about virginity and its loss, relating to the *carpe diem* theme (anticipating the quirky complexities of John Donne's metaphysical poetry.) There is a powerful eroticism, not only heterosexual, but also homosexual, when Neptune falls for Leander.

Hero and Leander was popular and influential. It contains the line "whoever loved that loved not at first sight?" which is notably quoted in *As You Like it* (1598–1600) by the character of Phoebe—one of the rare occasions when Shakespeare resorts to a literary allusion.

AN ATTEMPT AT COMPLETION

Marlowe's success as a writer meant that it was always going to prove a temptation to someone to continue where he left off, and make some literary and financial capital out of it. The challenge was taken up by George Chapman, a dramatist and well-known translator of Homer. He added 1,300 lines to Marlowe's 818, divided the poem into six "sestiads," and wrote cryptic little introductions to each of them. This edition, published in 1598,

HERO AND LEANDER IN ART

The tragic tale of Hero and Leander has proved as fruitful a source of inspiration to artists as it has to writers. This painting of the pair done by Domenico Fetti in 1622–3 is almost contemporary with Marlowe's poem. Later artworks to take the story as their subject include *The Parting of Hero and Leander* (1837) by J.M.W Turner, which hangs in the Tate Gallery in London, and *Hero and Leandro (To Christopher Marlowe)* (1985) by the American artist Cy Twombly.

WHAT HAPPENED NEXT . . .

The poem continued to haunt English literature, and make its influence felt in pastiches and travesties. In *Bartholomew Fair* (1614, right), Ben Jonson burlesques the poem in a puppet show; his Hellespont is the Thames, and his Leander is a dyer's son in Puddle-wharf. In *Lenten Stuffe* (1599), Thomas Nashe makes the caustic comment: "Two faithfull lovers they were, as everie apprentice in Paules church-yard will tell you for your love, and sel you for your money," and he summarizes the story in a knockabout style. And the skeptical Rosalind in *As You Like It* also refers to the myth: "Leander, he would have lived many a fair year though Hero had turned nun if it had not been for a hot midsummer night, for, good youth, he went but forth to wash him in the Hellespont and, being taken with the cramp, was drowned . . . But these are all lies. Men have died from time to time, and worms have eaten them, but not for love." A poem based to some extent on Marlowe's text was set to music around 1628 by Nicholas Lanier; this may have been one of the earliest recitative works in English. (There is a discredited theory that Nicholas's aunt Emilia Lanier was Shakespeare's "Dark Lady.")

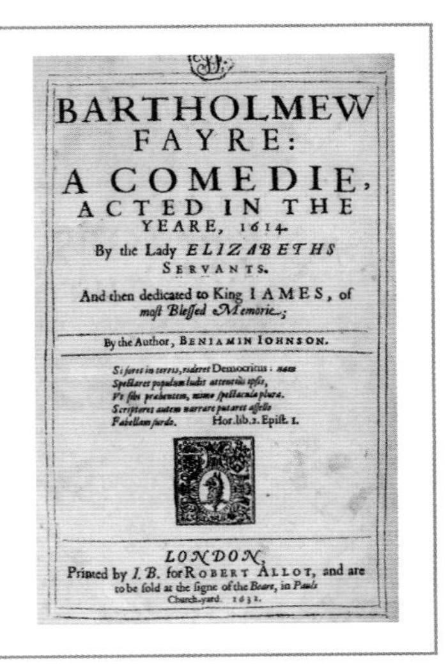

BARTHOLMEW
FAYRE:
A COMEDIE,
ACTED IN THE
YEARE, 1614.
By the Lady *ELIZABETHS*
SERVANTS.
And then dedicated to King IAMES, of
most Blessed Memorie;

By the Author, BENIAMIN IOHNSON.

Si foret in terris, rideret Democritus: *nam*
Spectaret populum ludis attentius ipsis,
Vt sibi praebentem, mimo spectacula plura.
Scriptores autem narrare putaret asello
Fabellam surdo. Hor. lib. 2. Epist. 1.

LONDON,
Printed by *I. B.* for ROBERT ALLOT, and are
to be sold at the signe of the *Beare*, in *Pauls*
Church-yard. 1631.

survives in two copies, one in the British Library in London and the other in the Huntington Library in San Marino, California.

Inevitably Chapman has attracted some criticism for having the temerity to "finish" Marlowe. He is not in the same league as Marlowe for poetic genius, and his completion operates at an altogether lower temperature. However, he is part of the English Renaissance, and thus has a similar understanding of the concepts that lie behind the classical revival. He uses the same medium as Marlowe, the five stress line in couplets, and also includes rhymes so bad that they must deliberately be part of the effect. At one point he builds into the poem reflections on the activity he is engaged in, a combination of a kind of inspiration from "spirits immortal" and "th' eternal clime / Of his [Marlowe's] free soul. Whose living subject [his bodily manifestation] stood / Up to the chin in the Pierian flood." Chapman finishes with the beautiful image of the souls of Hero and Leander transformed into goldfinches, "Which we call thistle-warps, that near no seas / Dare ever come."

After Chapman another attempt to capitalize on Marlowe was made by Henry Petowe in *The Second Part of Hero and Leander, Conteyning their Further Fortunes* (1598). In this version, the lovers are transformed into pine trees at the end. Petowe's text also contains the phrase "the stricken deer," which later appeared in *Hamlet*. BR

WILL IT EVER HAPPEN?

1/10

Hero and Leander is the product of a particular time and place, and of a particular epoch in the history of the English language, the history of poetry, and the history of ideas. Poets now operate under a different regime, and no one could effectively complete Marlowe's work. After all, even Chapman, a contemporary five years older than Marlowe, failed.

THE FAERIE QUEENE

Author Edmund Spenser **Year** 1599 **Country** England **Genre** Epic poetry

EDMUND SPENSER
Born in 1552 or 1553, Spenser was a Londoner who served the English government in Ireland for several years but returned to his native city in 1590 to promote this newly published masterwork. He was buried next to Chaucer in Poets' Corner, Westminster Abbey.

Edmund Spenser's epic poem *The Faerie Queene* is composed of six books, which were published in two instalments in 1590 and 1596. Appended to the first volume was a "Letter" addressed to Sir Walter Raleigh, in which Spenser revealed his plan to write 12 books in total. Two new cantos and a fragment (the "Mutability Cantos") appeared posthumously in 1609, suggesting that Spenser did intend to continue the poem, but Books VII–XII never materialized. During the 17th century many assumed that Spenser had in fact completed the poem: some claimed that the manuscript was thrown overboard by a disgruntled servant charged with conveying it from Ireland (where Spenser lived and worked); others held that the manuscript was burned in the Irish rebellion that drove Spenser back to London. It is now thought highly unlikely that Spenser composed six more books between 1596 and his death in 1599, particularly given that in his sonnet sequence *Amoretti* (1595) he had voiced his weariness with the epic.

In the "Letter" to Raleigh, Spenser explains that the 12 books will to have 12 knights as their heroes, each of whom will allegorically represent a different virtue; Prince Arthur will appear throughout, embodying the chief virtue, "Magnificence." Spenser's moral purpose, he claims, is to "fashion a gentleman"—that is, Arthur and the 12 knights will together exhibit all the qualities of the perfect courtier. Book I begins in the middle of the story, but in Book XII, Spenser assures Raleigh, it will be revealed that the knights have been sent on their adventures by the Fairy Queen (who represents Queen Elizabeth I) to address specific injustices throughout Fairy Land, a mystical chivalric realm that borders Britain.

SQUARING THE ROUND TABLE

This seems to leave little doubt about how Spenser would have continued, but the scheme outlined in the "Letter" maps poorly on to the six extant Books. Only Book I (just about) lives up to its dictates: Redcrosse, the Knight of Holiness, undertakes the majority of the action, and succeeds in his goal of slaying the dragon, with appropriate help from Christian artifacts. As the poem progresses, it becomes less straightforward. Scudamour is dispatched to rescue Amoret, but he proves so hopelessly susceptible to enemy enchantments that the female Knight of Chastity, Britomart, belatedly

Cover: Jayne Evans

A GENTLE KNIGHT
The illustration below, taken from the 1598 edition of *The Faerie Queene*, depicts the climactic episode of Book I, in which the Red Cross Knight (St. George, the patron saint of England) slays the dragon that has laid waste to Eden. He then marries Una, but continues his errantry in later books.

takes over as the hero of Book III. Cambel and Telamond are the designated protagonists of Book IV, but they ultimately prove relatively minor characters. Guyon, the Knight of Temperance, successfully completes his allotted task in Book II—by laying waste to the indolent Acrasia's Bower of Bliss, he eliminates a potent symbol of excess—but in doing so he unleashes the "tempest of his wrathfulnesse," disconcertingly revealing his intemperance.

A similarly unsettling inversion takes place in Book V, when the Egalitarian Giant receives short shrift from Arthegall, Knight of Justice. The Giant complains that the world is fundamentally unequal, and proposes that mountains and valleys be leveled, and wealth be redistributed; after a heated debate, Arthegall's henchman Talus throws the Giant from a cliff top to his death. Although it is revealed that the Giant's followers were seeking to redress the balance of power only to gain more for themselves, Spenser's condemnation of the social chaos of collectivism is subtly equivocal: Arthegall's ruthlessness shows that the hero has an equally self-serving interest in retaining his privileged role as dispenser of Justice. This episode is a reminder that Spenser had an uneasy relationship to the Elizabethan court: while he depended on it for patronage, in poems like *Mother Hubberds Tale* (1591) and *The Shepheardes Calendar* (1579), he was an overt and fierce critic of the system of preferment.

Readers should therefore be wary of taking too seriously the neat scheme earnestly rehearsed in the "Letter" to Raleigh. Within the poem itself, Spenser is characteristically candid about the moral flexibility necessary to succeed at court. Spenser was a profound moralist, but he relentlessly interrogated his own claim that it was possible to "fashion a gentleman," ultimately revealing that the "perfect courtier" was an unobtainable ideal. Considered in this light,

QUEEN OF ARTS
The Fairy Queen herself is Gloriana (Glory). She represents Queen Elizabeth I of England. Spenser honors her in the poem, but is much more ambivalent and equivocal about her courtiers and the spirit of the age in which he lived.

WHAT HAPPENED NEXT . . .

Few have taken up the pen Spenser so unceremoniously threw down. It is a problem seldom confessed in criticism that, at over 4,000 stanzas long, *The Faerie Queene* is difficult to finish reading, let alone writing (T.S. Eliot regarded those who finish it as an "eccentric few"). Nonetheless, in the 1630s Ralph Knevet supplied Books VII–IX, introducing Knights of Prudence, Fortitude, and Liberality, but his efforts went unpublished. Others picked up incomplete strands from earlier in the poem. Spenser himself had played the continuer, attempting to finish Chaucer's "Squire's Tale" in Book IV; in 1616 John Lane extended this tale, and in 1785 Joseph Sterling revived it again, by which point Cambuscan and Cambel were embroiled in exploits far removed from those envisaged by Chaucer and Spenser. Like Lane and Sterling, later writers continued specific subplots rather than tackling the poem whole. Claims that Books VII–XII had been lost inspired antiquarian ruses, such as Samuel Croxall's tongue-in-cheek publication of two cantos he "discovered" in an attic (1714). Those who remained concerned about the poem's unfinished state found that a simple solution was to shorten it. In *Prince Arthur* (1779), Alexander Bicknell translated Books I and II into prose, removing hints that the story continued; Lucy Peacock did the same by selecting only the material pertaining to Guyon for her prose adaptation, *The Knight of the Rose* (1793). In the 19th century Spenser appeared trimmed and tidied in several publications for children. Byron and Shelley revived the Spenserian stanza, and Tennyson and Scott plundered the poem for Arthurian imagery. Romantics and medievalists were untroubled by fragments, and indeed often relished them.

THE FAERIE
QVEENE.

Diſpoſed into twelue books,
Faſhioning
XII. Morall vertues.

LONDON
Printed for William Ponſonbie.
1590.

the unfinished nature of *The Faerie Queene* becomes part of its meaning. Numerous story lines are put on hold for several cantos, or even Books; others remain incomplete. Some characters, like Una's Dwarf, drop silently out of the story all together. Others resurface unexpectedly: the villain Archimago has a single-stanza cameo appearance in Book III. Spenser's preference for pronouns over proper names creates deliberate confusion about who is doing or saying what, to comic, sinister, or erotic effect. As at the Elizabethan court, there is not room for everyone. Characters jostle for space and edge each other out. To go back and pick up all the loose threads would be to impose a fantasy of fair play on the poem that Spenser himself was pointedly reluctant to indulge.

> *"The generall end therefore of all the booke is to fashion a gentelman . . ."*
>
> Edmund Spenser

Fittingly, *The Faerie Queene* ends at its most inconclusive moment. Throughout Book VI, Calidore hunts the Blatant Beast, a many-tongued monster that spreads scandalous rumors. Calidore finally muzzles the Beast, but it breaks free again in the Book's penultimate stanza. The final stanza contains a bitter aside in which, far from looking forward to his poem's completion, Spenser imagines it torn to shreds by "wicked tongues" and "venemous despite." While the "Mutability Cantos" (usually tacked on to the end of the poem) contain a more philosophical investigation of change and instability, their fragmentary condition prevents them from fully ameliorating the hopeless vision of Book VI. HW

WILL IT EVER HAPPEN?

0/10

Although the "Letter" to Raleigh provides a clear scheme for anyone wishing to complete *The Faerie Queene*, Spenser surely considered it unfinishable. This is hinted at as early as Book II, when Guyon picks up a book called the "Antiquitie of Faerie lond," a thinly veiled analogue for *The Faerie Queene* itself. While Guyon peruses it, King Arthur spends two cantos reading a history of Britain, until it breaks off in mid-sentence; we then return to Guyon, who has not finished the "Antiquitie of Faerie lond," and never will, "for it was a great / And ample volume." With these two imagined books, one incomplete and the other unreadable, Spenser shows that chronicles of national history, albeit fictionalized ones, can never truly be finished. And the chances of a 21st-century author reproducing Spenser's pattern of thought and mode of expression are nil.

CARDENIO

Author William Shakespeare **Year** 1613 **Country** England **Genre** Verse drama

WILLIAM SHAKESPEARE
It is often said that Shakespeare died on the same day as Cervantes, whose work was the source of *Cardenio*. However, the given date of Shakespeare's death is April 23, 1616, at which time England used the Julian calendar while Spain used the Gregorian: there was in fact an 11-day difference between two.

There are a number of missing Shakespeare plays. This fact is not entirely surprising, since the energies of Elizabethan and Jacobean drama went more into stage production than book publication. The most intriguing lost Shakespeare play is *Cardenio*, which was staged as one of the 20 or so plays put on for the daughter of James I, Princess Elizabeth, and the Elector Palatine, as part of their wedding celebrations in 1612–13. It was also staged for the Duke of Savoy's ambassador to England and possibly presented at Blackfriars and the Globe in London.

The plot came from an incidental story in *Don Quixote* (1605–15) by Miguel de Cervantes. (Thomas Shelton's English translation of the First Part appeared in 1612.) No copy of this play—either handwritten or printed—survives, and it is not heard of again until September 1653 when *The History of Cardenio* was entered in the Stationers' Register by Humphrey Moseley. The play is there stated to have been written "by Mr. Fletcher. & Shakespeare." If it was genuine, it is likely to have been similar to other works that Shakespeare produced in collaboration with John Fletcher, such as *The Two Noble Kinsmen* (1612–14) and *All is True* (*Henry VIII*) (1613).

There is no further record of *Cardenio* until December 13, 1727, when a version of it by Lewis Theobald, entitled *Double Falsehood; or, The Distrest Lovers*, was put on at the Theatre Royal in Drury Lane. Theobald claimed to have possessed various manuscripts of the play, but the version of *Double Falsehood* printed in 1728 was, it seems, heavily edited and rewritten.

TESTS OF AUTHENTICITY

Theobald probably did not know that the play was mentioned in the royal chamber accounts of May 1613, in which it is recorded that John Heminge was paid for staging entertainments. Neither is it likely that he knew about the Moseley record, so that if he were going to forge this play from scratch he would have had no idea where to begin. Is it likely that, even had he known of the collaboration, Theobald would have been capable of forging a text showing the hand of both writers which could satisfy 20th-century stylometric tests? Possibly not.

The Cardenio story in *Don Quixote* is roughly the same as the one in the play. Cardenio's friend Fernando has betrayed him by stealing his lover

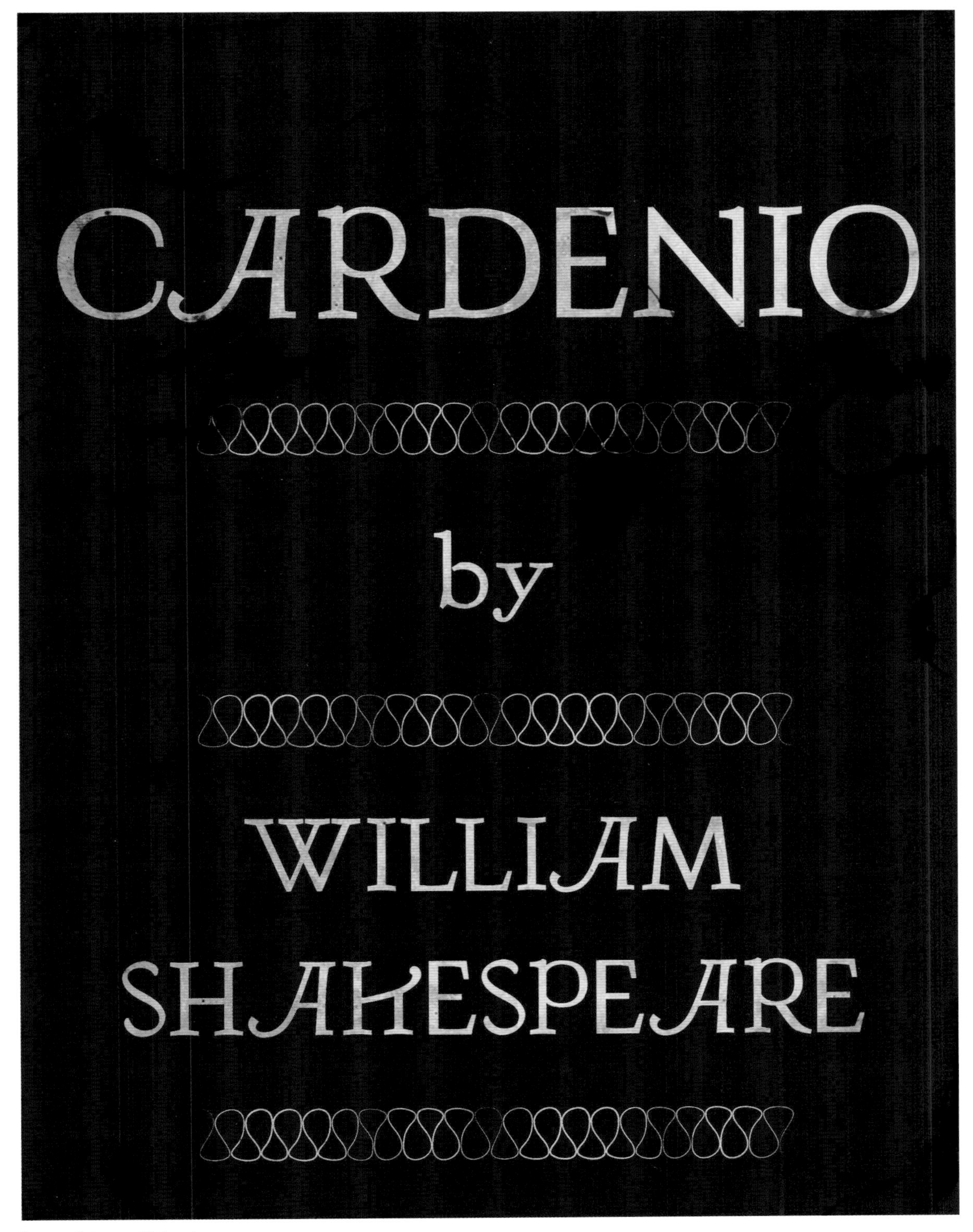

Cover: Rebecca Richardson

AUTHENTIC SHAKESPEARE OR IMITATION?

Which lines sound particularly Shakespearean? When Henriquez attempts to seduce Violante it sounds as if he has been reading Shakespeare: "Nay, your perfume, / Which I smell hither, cheers not my sense / Like our field-violet's breath."

Several critics think these lines of Julio's sound like authentic Shakespeare: "Till, like a credulous fool, / I showed the treasure to a friend in trust, / And he hath robb'd me of her." It is exactly like Claudio committing in *Much Ado about Nothing* (1598–99) the "flat transgression of a schoolboy, who, being overjoyed with finding a bird's nest, shows it his companion, and he steals it." And this lament by the ravaged Violante recalls Valentine in *Two Gentlemen of Verona* (1589–91):

"I am not become
The tomb of my own honor, a dark mansion
For death alone to dwell in. I invite thee,
Consuming desolation, to this temple,
Now fit to be thy spoil. The ruin'd fabric,
Which cannot be repair'd, at once o'erthrow."

"You must be grafted into noble stocks" resembles the horticultural image in *The Winter's Tale* (1609–11), and the "clouds that now / Bear such a pleasing shape and now are nothing" recall "Sometimes we see a cloud that's dragonish" in *Antony and Cleopatra* (1606). The problem, though, is that lines which sound Shakespearean might not be Shakespeare, since it is easier to imitate than to innovate.

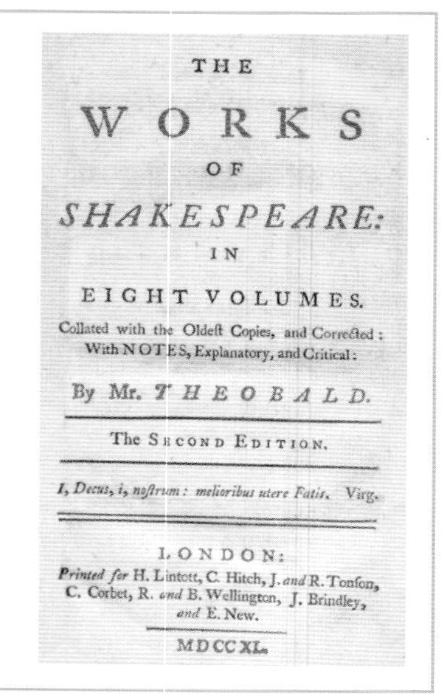

THE WORKS OF SHAKESPEARE: IN EIGHT VOLUMES. Collated with the Oldest Copies, and Corrected: With NOTES, Explanatory, and Critical: By Mr. THEOBALD. The SECOND EDITION.

I, Decus, i, nostrum: melioribus utere Fatis. Virg.

LONDON: *Printed for* H. Lintott, C. Hitch, J. *and* R. Tonson, C. Corbet, R. *and* B. Wellington, J. Brindley, *and* E. New. MDCCXL.

Luscinda. She escapes from a forced marriage to a nunnery. Fernando, at the same time, has betrayed his lover Dorotea, who ventures into the wilderness. All the characters find themselves together for the ultimate reconciliations and resolutions. Shakespeare and Fletcher developed the parents of Cardenio and Luscinda into full figures, and changed many small details, but in broad terms the main lineaments of the original plot survive, and *Double Falsehood*, whatever complicated processes it went through to reach the version available to us, was almost certainly not modified beyond recognition.

There is, however, a mystery: Cardenio does not appear under that name in the play as it was printed in 1728. He has been renamed Julio. All the other characters have been renamed too: Fernando becomes Henriquez, Luscinda becomes Leonora and Dorotea becomes Violante. This is not particularly surprising. When dramatists adapted sources, names were often changed. What is more surprising is that despite this the play was called *Cardenio*. Perhaps this is because it was a convenient working title, attached to the manuscripts. The other possibility is that the names of the characters in the original production were the same as those in Cervantes, and were changed later, possibly during the Restoration, possibly by Theobald.

CHANGES FROM THE ORIGINAL

Double Falsehood is very short as a play, and it is possible that Theobald cut out a whole comic subplot involving Lopez and Fabyan. Moreover, there are various points in the narrative where there seem to be gaps. There is a report of Henriquez raping Violante, but we do not see it presented. This scene exists in Cervantes, though it is not particularly graphic. It may have existed in the original version of the play, and been cut by Theobald for reasons of propriety. The combination of moral, religious, and tasteful probity in plays

THE DUNCIAD

Lewis Theobald is famous, or rather notorious, as one of Pope's victims in *The Dunciad* (1728). However, he was in some ways a pioneering figure as a textual scholar of Shakespeare.

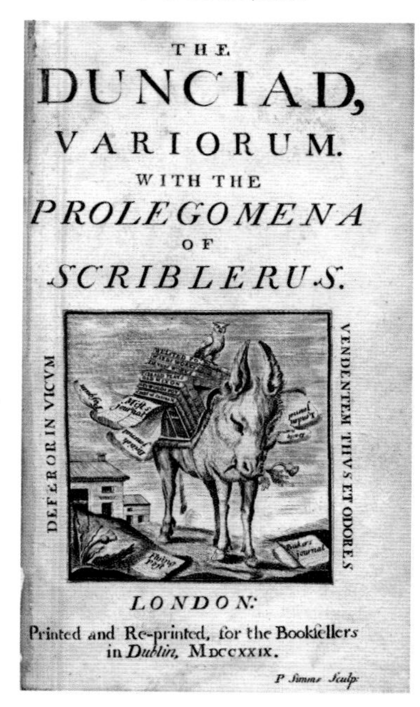

THE DUNCIAD, VARIORUM. WITH THE PROLEGOMENA OF SCRIBLERUS.

DEFEROR IN VICUM VENDENTEM THUS ET ODORES

LONDON: Printed and Re-printed, for the Booksellers in *Dublin*, MDCCXXIX.

P Simms Sculp.

addressed to early 18th-century bourgeois audiences did occasion a change in theater practice. For instance, when *The Two Gentlemen of Verona* (1590–94) was revived by Benjamin Victor in 1762–63, Proteus's line as he was about to rape Silvia ("I'll force thee yield to my desire") was dropped. Leaders of opinion in this prudish cultural movement were Jeremy Collier (author of *Short View on the Immorality and Profaneness of the English Stage*, 1698) and Joseph Addison (co-founder and first editor of *The Spectator*, 1711–12).

Later, Leonora is abducted from a nunnery, possibly in the same coffin that Henriquez used to enter it. This recalls Iachimo's chest scene in Shakespeare's *Cymbeline* (1611), when he is smuggled into Imogen's chamber. In Cervantes, she is simply snatched away by violence.

> *"I do not see that fervour in the maid,*
> *Which youth and love should kindle."*
>
> Julio, *Double Falsehood*

There is no question that this play is interesting, even if not on a par with the great major works. It ties Shakespeare and Fletcher to a major contemporary European work, and the quality of much of the writing is good. Violante disguising herself as a shepherd boy continues the cross-dressing traditions of Renaissance romantic comedies. The broken male friendship theme between Henriquez and Julio resembles that between Valentine and Proteus in Shakespeare's *The Two Gentlemen of Verona* (1590–94). The big elaborate reconciliation scene at the end is reminiscent of authentic Shakespearean drama. The play does not add anything very much to the vision we already have of the early 17th-century psyche, but it complements

LIVING TEXT

The full story of the reconstructions of this play and the complex textual problems surrounding it is told in *The Quest for Cardenio* (2012).

This extensive work, edited by David Carnegie and Gary Taylor, contains essays by 20 experts. Among the matters examined are the influence of Cervantes, the theatrical tradition of cross-dressing and gender-swapping, and the authenticity of the extant text.

This volume has helped to revitalize *Cardenio*, not only as a topic for scholars but also as a work that can be reimagined anew in modern productions, of which there have recently been several, including the one shown here by the Royal Shakespeare Company in 2011.

much of what we already know about Shakespeare and Fletcher, and adds just a little more to a complete picture. The writing is very much in line with a great deal of Elizabethan and Jacobean drama, so that at one end of the spectrum is the world of ideal romantic love, phrased in poetic blank verse, and at the other end is the more banal and down-to-earth prose world of everyday characters. The play has a rich and varied texture, and is lively and briskly moving.

INTERNAL EVIDENCE

Shakespeare's verse appears most in evidence at the beginning of the play, which bears a resemblance to the openings of his other dramatic works. These lines from Julio sound particularly Shakespearean:

"I do not see that fervour in the maid,
Which youth and love should kindle. She consents,
As 'twere to feed without an appetite;
Tells me she is content, and plays the coy one,
Like those that subtly make their words their ward,
Keeping address at distance. This affection
Is such a feigned one, as will break untouched;
Die frosty, e'er it can be thawed; while mine,
Like to a clime beneath Hyperion's eye,
Burns with one constant heat."

However, one plausible Shakespeare-sounding speech was confessedly written by Theobald, although it is noteworthy that not a single one of these lines is a regular iambic pentameter:

"But touch the strings with a religious softness;
Teach sound to languish through the night's dull ear,
Till melancholy starts from her lazy couch
And carelessness grow convert to attention."

The most authentic relic of the original play is possibly "Woods, rocks and mountains," a song by Robert Johnson, an English composer and lutenist who is known to have provided music for some of Shakespeare's later plays:

"Woods, rocks and mountains and ye desert places
Where nought but bitter cold and hunger dwells,
Hear a poor maid's last will, killed with disgraces.
Slide softly whilst I sing, you silver fountains.
And let your hollow waters like sad bells
Ring to my woes, whilst miserable I,
Cursing my fortunes, drop a tear and die.

"Griefs, woes, and groanings, hopes and all such lies
I give to broken hearts that daily weep;
To all poor maids in love, my lost desiring.
Sleep sweetly while I sing my bitter moaning,
And last, my hollow lovers that ne'er keep

ANTI-STRATFORDIANS

If a copy of the *Cardenio* manuscript is ever discovered it will be subjected to the kind of controversy that occurs every time Shakespeare's authorship is considered. There is a whole body of people—"the anti-Stratfordians"—who believe Shakespeare did not write any of his plays. This viewpoint has reached popular exposure in Roland Emmerich's film *Anonymous* (2011), in which the 17th Earl of Oxford is proposed as "the onlie begetter" of the works. It would have been difficult for him to have penned *Cardenio*, as he died before it was first staged. Such uncomfortable details seldom deter conspiracy theorists, however.

WHAT HAPPENED NEXT . . .

Theobald's published edition of 1728 survived, becoming the subject of much scholarly scrutiny with regard to its authenticity. In 2010 Brean Hammond published *Double Falsehood* in the Arden Shakespeare series, despite some critics holding that the play was a Theobald forgery. The consensus is that slight traces of the original survive his heavy reworking. In 1994 Charles Hamilton published *The Second Maiden's Tragedy* as the lost *Cardenio*, but most scholars dismiss the claim and assign that play to the Jacobean playwright Thomas Middleton.

In 2011 Royal Shakespeare Company director Greg Doran opened the refurbished Swan Theater in Stratford-upon-Avon with a production of *Cardenio*. Drawing on the works of Cervantes, Shakespeare, Fletcher, Shelton, and Theobald he reimagined the whole, adding the scene where Henriques rapes Violante, and giving it a more Spanish feel.

Truth in their hearts; while miserable I,
Cursing my fortunes, drop a tear and die."

The lyrics of "Woods, rocks and mountains" may or may not be by Shakespeare, but they are indubitably Shakespearean.

A MYSTERIOUS DISAPPEARANCE

So what became of the original *Cardenio* manuscript? There is no record of Theobald selling any Shakespeare manuscripts in his lifetime, and they weren't included in his estate at his death in 1744. One of the last known references to a copy is in 1770, when an advertisement for a revival of *Double Falsehood* mentioned it as one of the treasures in the "Museum of Covent Garden Playhouse." If one did reside there, it was probably burnt in the fire of September 19, 1808. For those who disbelieve Theobald's claim to have ever possessed a copy, there are alternate theories. One is that it was a victim of the fire at the Globe Theatre on June 29, 1613. Another is that it was lost during the Great Fire of London in 1666, when books and scripts stored for safekeeping in a stone vault underneath St. Paul's Cathedral were set alight by molten lead from the roof. Was *Cardenio* among the lost works in one of these conflagrations? We will never know. BR

WILL IT EVER HAPPEN?

3/10

There is always a hope that a manuscript of *Cardenio* will turn up, but it is unlikely. (A novel by Jennifer Lee Carrell, *The Shakespeare Secret* (2008), deals with the sensational hunt for the manuscript.) Doubtless other authors will come along and attempt a reconstruction. It is very difficult to imitate Shakespearean blank verse for a decent length, however, so an essential element will almost inevitably be lacking. It appears that there was a comic subplot which has disappeared, and that will be impossible to re-envisage.

Chapter 2

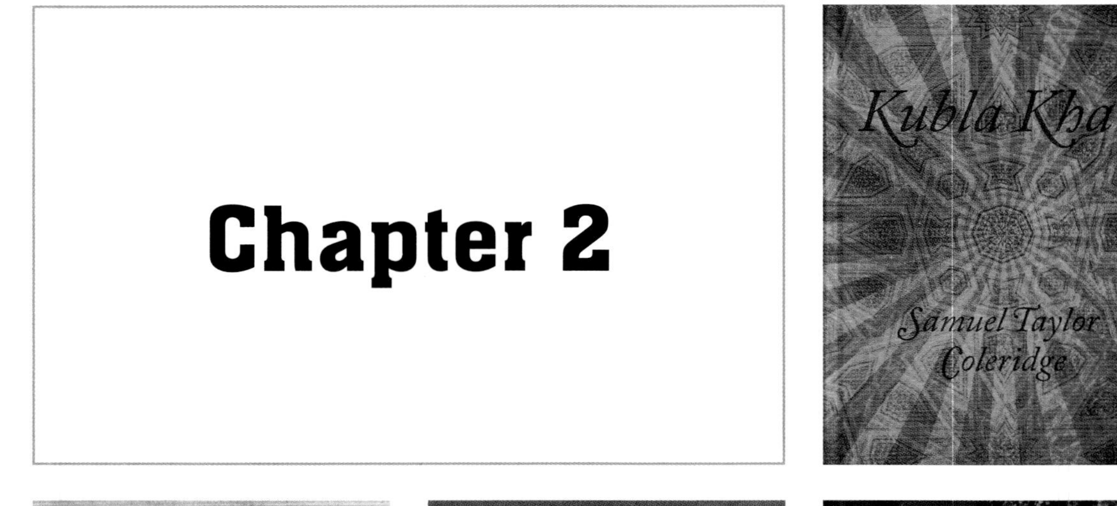
Kubla Khan
Samuel Taylor Coleridge

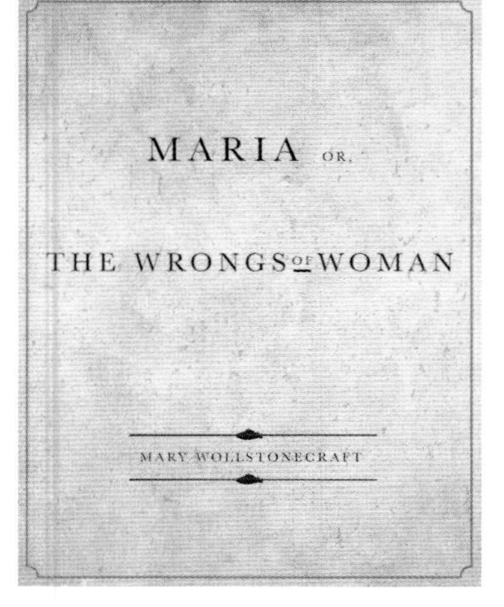
MARIA OR,
THE WRONGS OF WOMAN
MARY WOLLSTONECRAFT

HEINRICH VON OFTERDINGEN
NOVALIS

Jane Austen
SANDITON

HYPERION
by John Keats

DON JUAN

BY LORD BYRON.

"DIFFICILE EST PROPRIE COMMUNIA DICERE."

HOR. EPIST. AD PISON.

1824

Lucien Leuwen

Stendhal

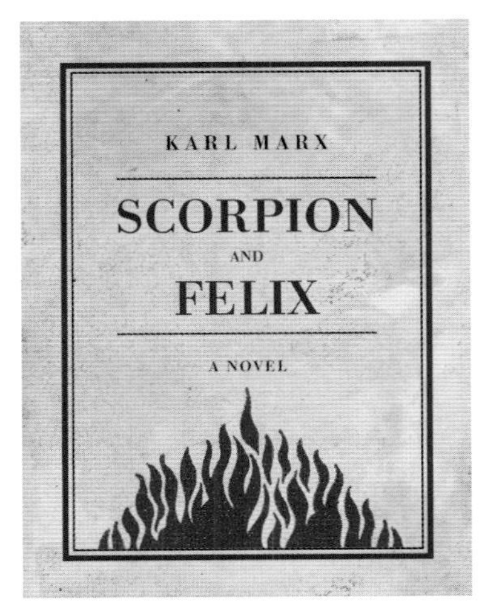

KUBLA KHAN

Author Samuel Taylor Coleridge **Year** 1797 **Country** England **Genre** Poetry

SAMUEL TAYLOR COLERIDGE
Coleridge was an English poet whose contributions to *Lyrical Ballads* (1798), a joint publication with William Wordsworth, included "The Rime of the Ancient Mariner." He was also an accomplished critic, and his *Biographia Literaria* (1817) remains influential today.

One of the most famous unfinished works in literature, "Kubla Khan" is a beautiful poem describing a visionary experience, full of suggestive and cryptic details. When Coleridge published it in 1816 it came with a preface—now almost as well known as the work itself—in which the poet describes the circumstances in which it was written.

In the summer of 1797, while staying in a farm house somewhere between Porlock and Linton in the West Country of England, he felt unwell, took some medicine, and fell asleep in his chair while reading Samuel Purchas's *Purchas his Pilgrimage* (1613), a collection of reports by travelers to foreign countries. He then had a vivid dream inspired by the subject matter, and awoke convinced that he had a poem in his mind of around 200 to 300 lines. He at once began writing, but he had not got very far with his transcription when "a person on business from Porlock" came to the house and "detained him by above an hour." On returning to his study, Coleridge found "to his no small surprise and mortification," that though "he still retained some vague and dim recollection of the general purport of the vision," the rest of it had "passed away like the images on the surface of a stream into which a stone has been cast."

BEHIND A DREAM

It is not certain precisely where Coleridge wrote his poem, but he later told his nephew Henry Nelson Coleridge that it was "in Brimstone Farm between Porlock and Ilfracombe—near Culbone." There is no such place, but there is a Broomstreet Farm in the area, and it's quite possible that he misremembered the name. (Given Coleridge's interest in matters diabolical, "Brimstone" was a fitting invention.)

"Kubla Khan" is a mysterious sequence of images: "caverns measureless to man," "gardens bright with sinuous rills," a "deep romantic chasm," "a mighty fountain," "a lifeless ocean," a "woman wailing for her demon-lover," and "ancestral voices prophesying war." Each one is clear enough, but it is not easy to see how they all add up to a coherent meaning, and that is part of the endless fascination of the poem.

The circumstances of the poem's composition tie it to the long tradition of religious vision in poetry, of which the most famous example is John Milton's

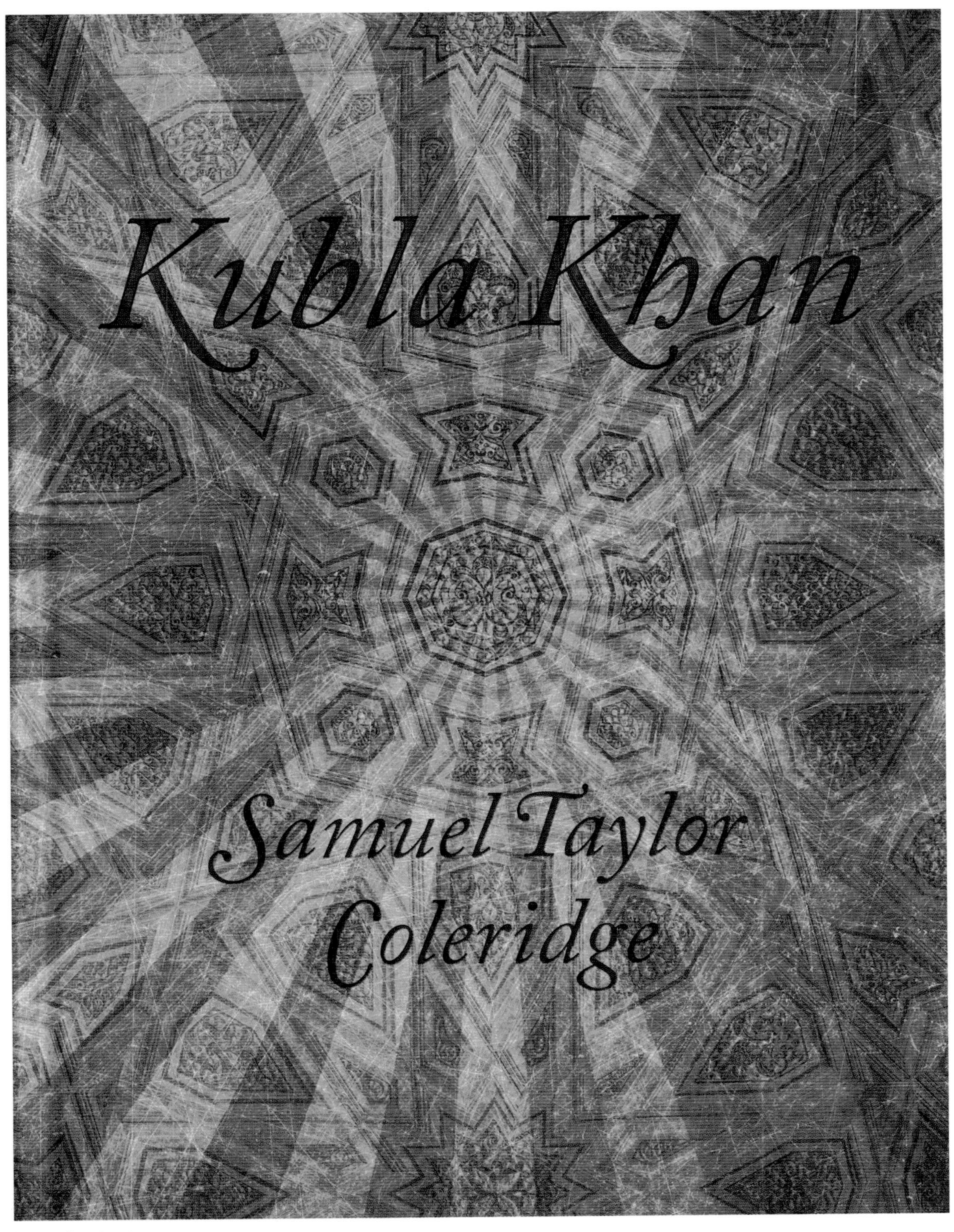

Cover: Damian Jaques

TOWERING AMBITION

In Orson Welles's *Citizen Kane* (1941), the title character (played by the director, right), a newspaper magnate based on William Randolph Hearst, has a palace named Xanadu. At the start of the movie, the voice over the newsreel covering his death directly quotes from *Kubla Khan*:

> "Legendary was the Xanadu where Kubla Kahn decreed his stately pleasure dome—'Where twice five miles of fertile ground, with walls and towers were girdled 'round.' Today, almost as legendary is Florida's Xanadu—world's largest private pleasure ground . . . Here in a private valley, as in the Coleridge poem, 'blossoms many an incense-bearing tree.' Verily, 'a miracle of rare device.'"

Paradise Lost (1667), whose "celestial patroness" dictated to him in his sleep and inspired his "unpremeditated verse." Coleridge's contemporary William Blake also has lines about heavenly inspiration: "My fairy sat upon the table, and dictated Europe [*Europe: A Prophecy*, 1794]." In Blake's *Jerusalem*, "the Savior" is heard "dictating the words of this mild song," although the message comes across as a "Monotonous Cadence" and Blake realizes he has to perform some revisions of his own. Visionary poems, therefore—even if inspired by divine sources or subconscious mental processes—need conscious, industrious artistry to bring them onto the page.

> *"When composition begins, inspiration is already on the decline."*
>
> Percy Bysshe Shelley, *A Defense of Poetry*

Many have questioned Coleridge's account of the origination of the poem and are skeptical that there was a longer poem, irretrievably lost. Another piece of evidence relating to the composition of the poem supports this view. It is a short postscript to the Crewe Manuscript, which has been in the British Library since 1934. This handwritten copy of "Kubla Khan" was composed sometime before the poem was published in 1816. It contains some small variations to the published poem, and also features a note on the back from Coleridge that reads:

> "This fragment with a good deal more, not recoverable, composed, in a sort of Reverie brought on by two grains of Opium, taken to check a dysentery, at a Farm House between Porlock and Linton, a quarter of a mile from Culbone Church, in the fall of the year, 1797."

It is not known who "the person from Porlock" was, but in *Confessions of an English Opium-Eater* (1821) essayist Thomas De Quincey suggested it was his physician Dr. P. Aaron, who supplied Coleridge with his drugs. With this in mind, the reference to "a sort of Reverie" conjures up an entirely different picture of the poem's origination from the "profound sleep" of the Preface.

THE DIFFICULTIES OF MEDIATION

When Coleridge writes in the Preface "If that indeed can be called composition in which all the images rose up before him as *things*, with a parallel production of the correspondent expressions," he is referring to a mental process in which there was little or no distinction to be made between the "images" and the ancillary "expressions" which brought them to life. In other words, he achieved something like the Holy Grail of Romantic poets: a situation in which the vision was direct and unmediated. Once he awoke, the difficulties of mediation must have started to assert themselves, and he found himself in the state outlined by Percy Shelley in *A Defense of Poetry* (1840): "when composition begins inspiration is already on the decline, and the most glorious poetry that has ever been committed to the world is probably a feeble shadow of the original inspiration of the Poet."

The differences between the published version and the Crewe Manuscript raise further issues about the poem's composition. For instance, the published version makes reference to "Mount Abora," whereas the Crewe manuscript refers to it as "Mount Amara." This suggests that the poet went on working on the poem after the original vision—contradicting, to some extent, the notion of complete and final visionary experience. He also speaks in the poem about attempts at recapture: "Could I revive within me / Her symphony and song." This could not have been part of the original vision, since the original vision was happening and there was no need for "revival."

Unfinished the poem may have been, but it was sufficiently arresting to have impressed Lord Byron. English essayist and critic Leigh Hunt recalled that Byron came away from a reading of "Kubla Khan" by Coleridge, "highly struck with his poem, and saying how wonderfully he talked," and he persuaded John Murray to publish it. BR

WHAT HAPPENED NEXT . . .

The poem appeared in Coleridge's *Complete Works* with *Christabel* (below), another unfinished poem that was published alongside *Kubla Khan* in 1816. This violates the tradition that demands that works of art should be perfect, crystalline, and finished. However, it fits readily into Romantic movement aesthetics, in which incompleteness was regarded as a sign of spontaneity and authenticity. This collides head-on with another Romantic assumption: that works of art are organic. Organicism implies completion. Coleridge's notebooks suggest that he hoped to finish the poem, which undermines the concept of divine inspiration, and substitutes a more unromantic view of art: that it involves conscious effort and hard work.

WILL IT EVER HAPPEN?

5/10

A notable critical effort was expended on the poem by J. Livingston Lowes in *The Road to Xanadu* (1927), and in theory the material that he gathered could provide inspiration for a possible continuer. Taking drugs ought in theory to put one in a position to imitate the Coleridgean creativity, but the record of drug-induced works, "Kubla Khan" aside, is not impressive. Drugs alone cannot produce significant works out of thin air; what is needed is a well-stocked mind and a highly attuned sensibility. What could put the final nail in the coffin of the enterprise of aiming to finish "Kubla Khan" is the possibility, which a number of critics entertain, that—contrary to Coleridge's claims—it is not a fragment at all, but a finished poem!

MARIA: OR, THE WRONGS OF WOMAN

Author Mary Wollstonecraft **Year** 1797 **Country** England **Genre** Novel

MARY WOLLSTONECRAFT
The daughter of a farmer, Mary Wollstonecraft worked as a teacher, a governess, and a translator. In 1792 she went to Paris to witness the French Revolution first hand. On her return to England she joined a group of radical thinkers that included her future husband.

Mary Wollstonecraft's most famous work is her revolutionary treatise *A Vindication of the Rights of Woman* (1792). It struck a weighty blow in the campaign for the liberation of women and their rights to equality. She died in 1797, having given birth to her second daughter Mary (who would go on to be another prominent figure in the history of revolutionary thought, as well as marry the poet Percy Bysshe Shelley and write *Frankenstein*, which was published in 1818). At the time of her death she was working on a novel titled *Maria: or, The Wrongs of Woman*, which was posthumously published in 1798 by Wollstonecraft's husband William Godwin.

TALE OF EXPLOITATION

The novel concerns the story of Maria Venables, imprisoned in an insane asylum by her husband, George. It criticizes the patriarchal institution of marriage in 18th-century Britain, and identifies a number of sources for the subjugation of women, including the tyranny of unsympathetic brothers and the appalling conditions in hospitals and workhouses. In a society where divorce was almost impossible, there was no prospect of escape for women.

Not only has George condemned Maria to live in an insane asylum, but he has also taken their child away from her. She befriends one of her attendants in the asylum, an impoverished, lower-class woman named Jemima, who, after realizing that Maria is not mad, agrees to bring her a few books, some of which have notes scribbled in them by Henry Darnford, another inmate. Maria falls in love with Darnford at a distance. The two begin to communicate and eventually meet. Darnford reveals that he has led a debauched life.

Jemima tells her life story to Maria and Darnford, explaining that she was born a bastard and forced to become a servant in her father's house. She was apprenticed to a master who beat her, starved her, and raped her. When the man's wife discovered that Jemima was pregnant with his child she was thrown out of the house. Unable to support herself, she aborted her child and became a prostitute. After the death of a gentleman keeping her, she was employed as an attendant at the asylum where Maria is imprisoned.

In chapters 7 to 14 (about half of the completed manuscript), Maria relates her own life story in a narrative she has written for her daughter. She starts by confessing that her husband was discovered to be a libertine. The malign

MARIA OR,

THE WRONGS OF WOMAN

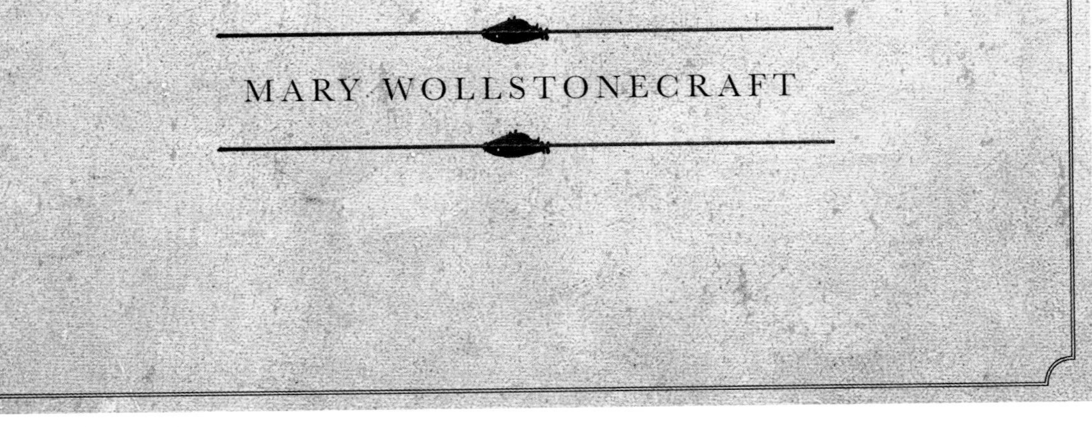

Cover: Gareth Butterworth

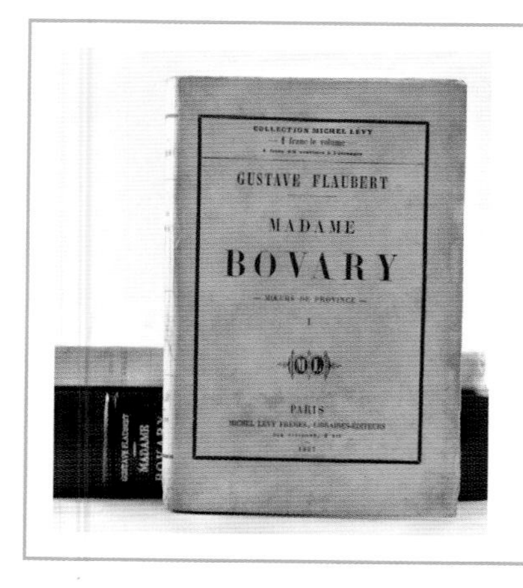

THE INFLUENCE OF NOVELS

To what extent do novels influence behavior and attitudes? Some say that fictions have no influence whatsoever, but the consensus seems to be that some influence does take place, if only in the matter of lifestyles and habits of expression. The danger is that novels can promote unreal expectations and romantic attitudes, which are harmful if translated into behavior or even into habits of thought. Flaubert's *Madame Bovary* (1856) is the classic treatment of the theme. Closer to Wollstonecraft's time is Jane Austen, whose *Sense and Sensibility* (1811) interrogates the possibly pernicious effects of extreme forms of sensibility (emotional self-indulgence) that connect to the political theories of Jean-Jacques Rousseau. Wollstonecraft is closer to Rousseau than to Austen, but she warns that sensibility can be used to justify the subjugation of women.

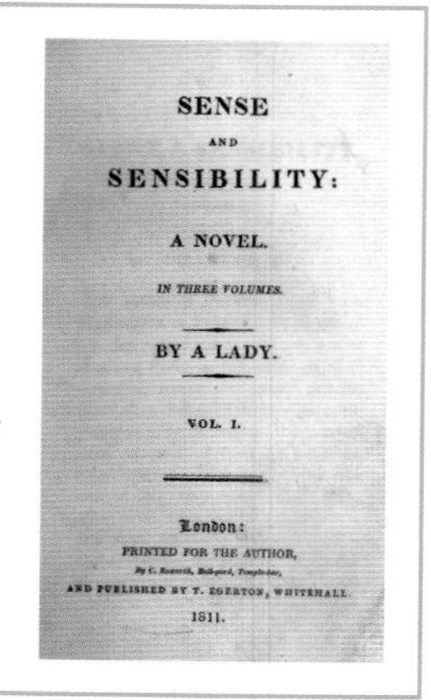

aspect of libertinage is explored in the novel, in contrast to the highly civilized and sophisticated mode of behavior it was often thought to represent. Readers learn that Maria's life became impossible when her mother died and her father took the housekeeper as his mistress. A rich uncle who was fond of Maria, unaware of Venables's true character, arranged for her to be married to him, giving her a dowry of £5,000. Her husband misused the fortune. Wollstonecraft is anxious to demonstrate that the rights of husbands over their wives' property was a manifest injustice. Maria holds that marriage laws turn a wife into an "idiot, or perpetual minor, for ever in bondage."

Maria became pregnant after unwanted sexual encounters with her husband. As Maria's uncle is leaving for the continent, he tells her that women have the right to separate from their husbands. After Venables attempts to prostitute Maria to one of his friends, Maria tries to leave him, but she fails. She initially escapes and manages to live in several different

CULT OF THE SUPREME BEING

Wollstonecraft was in France in 1794 for the Fête of the Supreme Being, shown here in a celebrated painting by Pierre-Antoine Demachy. The Cult of the Supreme Being was established by French revolutionary Maximilien Robespierre, and Wollstonecraft seems to endorse it in her novel when she speaks of "impartial lawgivers" ideally following "the existence of an *être suprême*." Her 600-page work *An Historical and Moral View of the Origin and Progress of the French Revolution* (1795) does not get as far as the worst obscenities of the Terror, but they were a traumatic shock for her, especially the shooting of 300 men in Lyon in the name of "Reason."

lodgings, often with other women who have also been wronged by their husbands, but he always manages to trace her. When she tries to leave England with her newborn child and the fortune her now deceased uncle has left them, her husband seizes the child and imprisons Maria in the asylum. At this point the manuscript breaks off.

WHAT MIGHT HAVE COME NEXT

The notes for the remainder of the novel point to a number of different possibilities for the plot. George Venables wins a lawsuit against Darnford for seducing his wife; Darnford then abandons Maria, flees England, and takes another mistress. When she discovers this treachery, Maria loses the child she was carrying by him (either through abortion or miscarriage). In one ending, Maria commits suicide (something that Mary Wollstonecraft herself attempted). In another possible ending Maria is saved from suicide by Jemima, who has found Maria's first daughter, and decides to live for her child.

This is a strong work, driven by powerful convictions, but since most of it is in the form of autobiographical report, it often does not read like a novel. Wollstonecraft has a tendency to tell rather than show.

"Marriage has bastilled me for life."

Maria, *Maria:or, The Wrongs of Woman*

The novel sometimes approaches the extremes of Gothic fiction, but many painful contemporary conditions were close to the apparent improbabilities of that genre. Wollstonecraft draws heavily on the rhetoric of subjugation: during her lifetime slavery was a pervasive evil in the world, and the abolition movement was only in its early infancy. Another form of slavery was the unjust repression associated with the *ancien régime* in France, coming under the heading "Bastillism." Yet another form of slavery was marriage in its crudest patriarchal manifestations, and in the novel Maria connects the two, saying "Marriage has bastilled me for life."

Mary Wollstonecraft was what today would be called a left-wing intellectual, a trailblazer in the promotion of equal rights for women. Proper education was one of the pillars of the program for female emancipation, and although the novel endorses romanticism and imagination, it is also alert to their dangers. BR

WHAT HAPPENED NEXT . . .

Wollstonecraft's husband William Godwin (below) published the novel after her death, with some additions of his own. In certain quarters it was reviled as recommending innovatory lifestyles that threatened the fabric of conservative society and even supported prostitution. There was resistance to the idea that women had independent rights to the pleasures of sexuality. Godwin's editorial work is a model of how to proceed, making it clear where the original ends and interventions begin. These are all visible in the World's Classics edition (2007), edited by Gary Kelly. Godwin in the "Advertisement" has interesting and intelligent thoughts on the business of incomplete works: "The fastidious and cold-hearted critic may perhaps feel himself repelled by the incoherent form in which they [the broken paragraphs and half-finished sentences] are presented. But an inquisitive temper willingly accepts the most imperfect and mutilated information, where better is not to be had."

WILL IT EVER HAPPEN?

3/10

No one has attempted to finish *Maria*, and it is unlikely that anyone will. It cannot be expected that anyone will discover further notes as to where the novel's plot was to proceed. It has, however, enjoyed a lively history in the ongoing debates about the rights of women, providing at once arguments in the text and dramatized situations which are exemplary. It is what might be called a "thesis novel," and many novelists nowadays are reluctant to write such things.

HEINRICH VON OFTERDINGEN

Author Novalis **Year** 1801 **Country** Germany **Genre** Novel

NOVALIS
Born in 1772 in Prussian Saxony, Novalis died of tuberculosis in 1801, aged 28. His blue flower has become an emblem of Romanticism, being referenced by, among others, the critic Walter Benjamin, C.S. Lewis in his autobiography *Surprised by Joy* (1955), and John le Carré in his novel *A Small Town in Germany* (1968).

Novalis was the pseudonym of Georg Philipp Friedrich Freiherr von Hardenberg, an aristocratic poet, author, and philosopher—a major figure in the history of early German Romanticism. Romantics are often thought of as dreamy, arty, and impractical, but Novalis was of a strain that was scientific and philosophic. He studied law, biology, and mathematics, which brought him into contact with a range of writers and philosophers, including Goethe, Herder, Schelling, and the Schlegel brothers.

Novalis viewed philosophy as a wide-ranging activity of thought and imagination—the whole of human mental effort—rather than a form of narrow and hard-headed reasoning. This attitude is exemplified by his frequently quoted phrase: *"Philosophiren ist dephlegmatisiren vivificiren"* (to philosophize is to rid oneself of inertia, to come to life). He was an idealist who hoped for the evolution of a Romantic Christianity that would oppose what he regarded as the twin catastrophes of rationalist Enlightenment philosophy and the French Revolution.

As a poet, Novalis was famous for his collection *Hymnen an die Nacht* (*Hymns to the Night*, 1800), which offered a romantic interpretation of life and death. This work was heavily influenced by the death of his fiancee, Sophie von Kühn, in 1797; the pair had become engaged in 1795 when Sophie was 13, but she died of tuberculosis before the marriage could take place. Upon his death in 1801 Novalis left behind two novel fragments: *Heinrich von Ofterdingen* and *Die Lehrlinge zu Sais* (*The Novices of Sais*). *Heinrich von Ofterdingen* was written in opposition to Goethe's *Wilhelm Meister's Apprenticeship* (1795–96), which Novalis thought unpoetical.

DREAM SEQUENCE OF EVENTS

Heinrich von Ofterdingen is set in an idealized vision of the Middle Ages and concerns a young poet. The title character goes to bed and has a fantastic dream in which he sees a blue flower, but he is disturbed and wakes up. He talks about dreams with his parents. His father tells him that he once had a dream that inspired him to propose to his mother, but adds that he does not attach any importance to dreams. His mother takes him to Augsburg, hoping that he will find a girl and collect new experiences, because he has never left his home town. There he meets a beautiful young maiden, Mathilde. After

Cover: Gareth Butterworth

WHAT HAPPENED NEXT . . .
Novalis's friend, Ludwig Tieck, published the novel posthumously. He said that Novalis had intended to continue the story with Heinrich, after Mathilde's death, setting out on a philosophical journey, visiting Pisa, Rome, and Jerusalem and finally finding a blue flower that turns when plucked into a living Mathilde.

The cult of Novalis began shortly after his death. He is celebrated in Penelope Fitzgerald's *The Blue Flower* (1995).

their encounter, he thinks: "Do I not feel as I felt in that dream about the blue flower? What peculiar connection is there between Mathilde and that flower?" The novel abruptly ends shortly after Heinrich's wedding with Mathilde.

Discussion of *Heinrich von Ofterdingen* often concentrates on its importance for the Romantic movement as a fragment. The value of this form was stressed in the 18th century by philosopher Johann Gottfried von Herder, who thought that it prevented philosophy from hardening into a repressive and fixed system, allowing for spontaneity of thought and the cross-fertilization of art and the more disciplined intellectual spheres. Since the work of Novalis is largely made up of fragments, it is easy to see the application of this approach, but perhaps had he lived longer he would have constructed systems that were more disciplined and concentrated. BR

WILL IT EVER HAPPEN?
The philosophical legacy of Novalis continues to cumulate interest, so it is always possible that one of his readers may be inspired to attempt a continuation. The worldwide success of Jostein Gaarder's popular history of philsophy *Sophie's World* (1991)—in which Novalis and *Heinrich von Ofterdingen* receive a mention—suggests that there could be an audience for one.

SANDITON

Author Jane Austen **Year** 1817 **Country** England **Genre** Novel

JANE AUSTEN
Jane Austen was born in Hampshire in 1775. Showing a love of writing from an early age, she completed six novels in her lifetime. Her work has received praise ever since it was first published—contemporary admirers included the Prince Regent (later George IV).

Jane Austen began writing *Sanditon* in January 1817 and abandoned it on March 18 of that year, four months before her death at the age of 41. The novel concerns the development of a little fishing village on the south coast of England into a fashionable resort, a process that was happening with a vengeance at the beginning of the 19th century in places such as Sidmouth, Weymouth, Worthing, Bognor Regis, Eastbourne, and Brighton, among many others. She called the novel *The Brothers*, possibly for three of the main characters, but it was named *Sanditon* by her niece Anna Lefroy in 1869. The original manuscript includes only the first 11 chapters of the story, around 26,000 words. It is now in King's College, Cambridge, where Jane Austen's grand-nephew, Augustus Austen-Leigh, was Provost from 1889 to 1905.

CAST AND PLOT

The novel's heroine is Charlotte Heywood, the eldest daughter of a country gentleman. She meets the Parkers, who with Lady Denham plan to develop Sanditon. They take her there as their guest.

Mr. Parker gives an early indication of his plans: "Everybody has heard of Sanditon. The favorite—for a young and rising bathing-place—certainly the favorite spot of all that are to be found along the coast of Sussex; the most favored by nature, and promising to be the most chosen by man."

Charlotte meets the inhabitants of the town, of whom the most important is Lady Denham, who has profited enormously from outliving two husbands, the first of whom left her a substantial fortune, the second her aristocratic title. Lady Denham's nephew and niece, Sir Edward Denham and Esther Denham, also live in Sanditon; they have little money of their own and are thought to be keen to get their hands on their aunt's.

The Parkers soon receive an unexpected visit from Mr. Parker's two sisters and his younger brother. All three of them claim to be unwell, but they seem so active that Charlotte suspects they are imaginary invalids.

One of the sisters says that she is looking on behalf of a rich family from the West Indies for a house in Sanditon. She also mentions a party of schoolgirls that is looking for a summer residence in the town. This is all good for Mr. Parker's plans to promote Sanditon as a bathing resort.

Cover: Hortense Franc

Gradually, however, Charlotte discovers that the family from the West Indies and the school party are not two groups of people, but just one.

The next character to arrive is another Parker brother, Sidney. Charlotte is impressed by his manners and good looks.

Mrs. Parker and Charlotte visit Lady Denham at her home, where they encounter Sir Edward and Clara Brereton, Lady Denham's impoverished niece. It is evident that these two have an intimate rapport.

Sanditon is fascinating because it shows an increased awareness in Jane Austen of a sense of place—an awareness that can be seen developing in *Mansfield Park* (1814) and *Persuasion* (1817). She shows the vanity and

> *"The library . . . afforded everything: all the useless things in the world that could not be done without."*
>
> *Sanditon*

tastelessness of the ambitions of the developers, just as in *Mansfield Park* she is critical of the modish "improvers" of country estates (such as the landscape designer Humphrey Repton), but she was also prepared to enjoy the positive elements that a resort could offer: circulating libraries, assembly rooms (Austen was a keen dancer), billiard rooms, smart shops, bathing machines, esplanades, clean streets with pavements, and more. For Austen a word such as "improvement" often needed to be hedged in with heightened inverted commas, as it does for many people today. There is almost a touch of Oscar Wilde as she contemplates the library in Sanditon, which "afforded everything; all the useless things in the world that could not be done without."

ANOTHER LADY

One challenge facing continuators of *Sanditon* is to identify the young man with whom Charlotte will end up via subtle linguistic signals (the kinds of subtle signals which put Frank Churchill out of the running in *Emma* and foiled Henry Crawford in *Mansfield Park*). The 1975 attempt by "Another Lady" is surprising in its choice. In Austen's novels we are asked to identify a possible final partner for the heroine, and all kinds of false leads are thrown in our way—in Another Lady's *Sanditon*, Sidney Parker is presented as the obvious candidate who will finally turn out to be a false lead, yet it is he who emerges as eligible in the end.

In addition to the immediate difficulty of what to do about plot, there is another element which is invariably problematic when attempting to complete a work from a previous century: language. Anachronisms are the very death of any bid for authenticity, because they immediately alert the reader to the fact that what is in front of him or her is simply not genuine. In Another Lady's completion of *Sanditon* there is no shortage of them. She does, however, fully admit to her faults, and at the end of the novel is a note of contrition:

"What was there left to worry about in completing Jane Austen's last manuscript? Only the way she wrote it. Her language, her integrity, and her painstaking methods of work—that terrifyingly accurate and meticulous technique—combine to give us the same sense of serenity and assurance in the six novels in which she brought her world to life and made it real for us. None of these things can be faithfully copied. And for their deficiencies in this seventh novel, I do apologize."

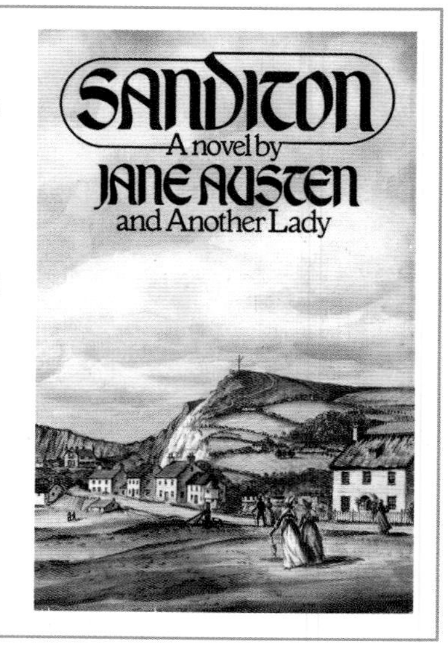

SEA BATHING
Thomas Rowlandson's *Summer Amusement at Margate, Or a Peep at the Mermaids* (1815) pokes gentle fun at the practice of sea bathing. Lauded by some doctors for its health-giving benefits, others voiced concern that the activity encouraged moral depravity.

The south coast towns were becoming fashionable in the early 19th century because of the popularity of sea bathing, which was believed to be good for health. Austen herself was suffering from serious illness while working on *Sanditon*, but this did not prevent her from administering a characteristically tart stylistic dose to hypochondriacs in the novel.

One of the best parts of the novel is Charlotte's meeting with Sir Edward, in which vacuous conversation is larded with the cheap intellectual commerce of the Romantic movement, whose absurdity Austen readily identified: "He began, in a tone of great taste and feeling, to talk of the sea and the sea shore—and ran with energy through all the usual phrases employed in praise of their sublimity, and descriptive of the *undescribable* emotions they excite in the mind of sensibility." His unstoppable monologue condemns him—as it condemns all unendorsed characters in Austen.

Sanditon would not, probably, have been Austen's best work, because it seems to be going in the direction of local, small-town specificities rather than the broader sweep of her earlier work, but its loss is still to be mourned. There is another incomplete Austen work, *The Watsons*, which she worked on between 1804 and 1807 but never finished. It too promises well, and has slightly more of that delightful vintage Austen acerbity. BR

WILL IT EVER HAPPEN?

5/10

Continuations have already happened and will most likely continue. The popularity of the numerous pastiches of Jane Austen's work—such as *Pride and Prejudice and Zombies* (2009) and P.D. James's *Death Comes to Pemberley* (2011)—demonstrates that there is clearly an audience for novels based around her oeuvre. However, it's inconceivable that any continuation could ever truly compare to the real thing.

WHAT HAPPENED NEXT . . .
Attempts to finish *Sanditon* began in the 19th century and have continued ever since. The novel first became available to the public when R.W. Chapman produced an edition in 1927, titled *Fragment of a Novel*. Anna Lefroy, Austen's niece, attempted a continuation and "Another Lady" finished it in 1975. Other continuations include those by Juliette Shapiro, Anne Toledo, D.J. Eden, Donald Measham, and Julia Barrett.

HYPERION

Author John Keats **Year** 1819 **Country** England **Genre** Epic poetry

JOHN KEATS
Keats abandoned a promising medical career to devote himself to writing, and although he had scant success in his lifetime, since his death in 1821 at the age of 25, he has become one of the most revered English poets. Also acclaimed are his often brilliant letters.

Keats worked on *Hyperion* from late 1818 until the spring of 1819, at the dawn of what would be his most creatively fertile year. The subject of the poem is the defeat and fall of the Titans of Greek mythology by the Olympians. The Titans are a pantheon of gods who include Saturn (king of the gods), Ops (his wife), Thea (his sister), Enceladus (god of war), Oceanus (god of the sea), and Hyperion (god of the sun). The poem opens with Saturn bemoaning the loss of his power as he is supplanted by Jupiter. Thea leads him to a place where the other Titans sit, similarly miserable, and they discuss whether they should fight back against their conquest by the new Olympian gods. The debate is reminiscent of that of the Fallen Angels in John Milton's *Paradise Lost* (1667). Hyperion's palace is then described, and we first see Hyperion himself, the only Titan who retains power. He is addressed by Uranus (old god of the sky, father of Saturn), who encourages him to go to where Saturn and the other Titans are. We leave the Titans with the arrival of Hyperion. The scene changes to Apollo (the new sun god, also god of music), weeping on the beach. Here Mnemosyne (goddess of memory) encounters him and he explains to her the cause of his tears: he is aware of his divine potential, but is as yet unable to fulfill it. By looking into Mnemosyne's eyes, he receives knowledge which transforms him fully into a god. Here the poem breaks off.

THE FALL OF HYPERION

Keats did not entirely abandon the project, however. Later in 1819 he made a second attempt at the poem, this time titled *The Fall of Hyperion*. This is a totally different poem, which casts the events as a dream vision. It shows a greater influence from Dante's *Purgatorio* (Purgatory), part two of *The Divine Comedy* (c.1308–21), which Keats had been reading in Henry Francis Cary's blank verse translation of 1814.

The Fall of Hyperion opens with the narrator stumbling on a post-Edenic feast scene. After enjoying these pleasures, he is compelled to partake of a "cool vessel of transparent juice" that causes him to fall into a deep sleep. Upon waking, the poet finds himself before a temple, with the gates to the East shut. He is challenged by a mysterious figure, Moneta, to climb the stairs, and experiences a painful death that is reminiscent of Apollo's pain

Cover: Angharad Burnard

THE ELGIN MARBLES

There are a number of literary influences behind both poems, but in addition Keats was very struck by the Elgin Marbles, which he saw in 1817 and which inspired him to compose a sonnet. They provided Keats with a fresh image of classical divinities from a more primitive and sublime period than later Roman derivatives, and he registered "a dizzy pain / That mingles Grecian grandeur with the rude / Wasting of old time."

when "dying into life" in *Hyperion*. The poet narrator has to overcome the desire not to suffer and the desire not to dwell in spiritual pleasure in order to transcend the mistakes of false poets. Once the poet has climbed the steps, he is lectured by Moneta on the nature of poetry and visions:

> "Art thou not of the dreamer tribe?
> The poet and the dreamer are distinct,
> Diverse, sheer opposite, antipodes.
> The one pours out a balm upon the world,
> The other vexes it."

After the poet has passed a test, Moneta allows him to witness a vision of the Titans and of Hyperion. This scene ends with the image of Hyperion rising, which leads to the beginning of the previous fragment, *Hyperion*.

The Fall of Hyperion is some of the most arresting and challenging poetry from the Romantic movement. It further develops *Hyperion*'s consideration of the nature of beauty and art by exploring the nature of the poet, continuing the self-consciousness about the role of poetry that Keats had previously expressed in "Sleep and Poetry" (1817). Keats here suggests that the true poet must not rest in poetical dreams but must share the sorrows of humanity in order to comfort man.

THE INFLUENCE OF MILTON

The problem for Keats with both *Hyperion*s was that the shadow of Milton hung over them. Milton was the great predecessor, and whenever an English poet dealt with gigantic struggles between warring divinities, the influence of *Paradise Lost* (1667) was bound to be present. This need not be a great problem, except that the Romantic movement placed great stress on the criterion of originality, more so than in previous epochs. A few years earlier when Keats found himself being derivative and unoriginal as he was composing "Calidore" he gave it up.

There was another problem, perhaps more serious: that Keats's chosen form was blank verse. His two major forerunners with this style were

Shakespeare and Milton, and as he composed he found Miltonic tics difficult to forget. The use of the Miltonic "horrid" in particular stands out. In a letter to his brother in September 1819, Keats wrote that "I have but lately stood on my guard against Milton. Life to him would be death to me." But he eventually admitted defeat: in a letter of the same month to his friend John Hamilton Reynolds, he declared: "I have given up *Hyperion*—there were too many Miltonic inversions—in an artful or rather artist's humor."

It is interesting that Keats, for some a key weapon in the armory of aestheticism, here rejects aestheticism. There is no shortage of the inversions (where an adjective follows a noun) that he mentions: "alteration slow," "influence benign," "metal sick," "stride colossal," "nadir deep," and "plumes immense" are just a few. Even the second *Hyperion* is plagued with them: "elixir fine," "roof august," "pavement cold," "utterance sacrilegious," "dreamers weak." These lines from *Hyperion* could easily have been written by Milton, and are typical of the writing that explains the failure of the poem:

> "Next Cottus: prone he lay, chin uppermost,
> As though in pain; for still upon the flint
> He ground severe his skull, with open mouth
> And eyes at horrid working."

> *"I have given up Hyperion—there were too many Miltonic inversions."*
>
> John Keats

POETIC SUCCESSES

Keats was much preoccupied during the composition of the first *Hyperion* with his brother Tom, who was dying of tuberculosis. Although he failed to complete either version, the year was not a total poetic failure: in 1819 Keats also wrote "Lamia," "The Eve of St. Agnes," and his great odes, "On Indolence," "On a Grecian Urn," "To Psyche," "To a Nightingale," "On Melancholy," and "To Autumn". Milton continued to haunt and impress Keats, and on board ship traveling to Italy, where he died in 1821 also from tuberculosis, he thought of writing a long poem based on Sabrina in Milton's *Comus* (1634). Another poem we shall never be able to read. BR

WILL IT EVER HAPPEN?

1/10

It is all too easy to write Miltonic blank verse, as Keats found to his cost. There have been countless parodies and pastiches of *Paradise Lost* from John Philips's "The Splendid Shilling" (1701) onward. It is theoretically possible that *Hyperion* could be completed, as there is at least a story that a potential author could continue. *The Fall of Hyperion*, however, is another matter. It is so intricately bound into Keats's subtle and original thought that it would be impossible for a continuation to do it justice.

WHAT HAPPENED NEXT . . .

Hyperion was published in an edition of Keats's *Poems of 1820*. It was titled *Hyperion: A Fragment*, in line with the Romantic movement's taste for fragments. *The Fall of Hyperion: A Dream* was published in 1857, shifting the emphasis from epic to vision. This was during the period when there was increased interest in Keats, following the publication of his letters (below) in 1848 by Richard Monckton Milnes.

as it happens I have just received the Book which contains the only copy of the verses in question. I have asked for it repeatedly ever since I promised Mr. Haydon and could not help the delay,

John Keats

DON JUAN

Author Lord Byron **Year** 1824 **Country** England **Genre** Narrative poetry

GEORGE GORDON, LORD BYRON
The publication in 1812 of *Childe Harold's Pilgrimage*, like *Don Juan* a long narrative poem, made Byron a literary star overnight. But rather than bask in its glory he was forced by sexual scandal into exile on mainland Europe, where he spent the rest of his life.

Lord Byron completed 16 cantos of his narrative poem *Don Juan*, leaving the 17th unfinished when he died fighting for Greek independence from the Ottoman Empire in 1824. Published in parts from 1818, it is more than 16,000 lines long and offers ample testimony of the poet's skill. It is not merely a narrative poem; as the story unfolds Byron interjects himself at every point to give us his tart opinions. These keep the story moving and are, in many ways, the most enjoyable parts of the work. Byron is very conscious of what he is up to, and builds this awareness into the writing:

"Prose poets like blank-verse, I'm fond of rhyme,
Good workmen never quarrel with their tools;
I've got new mythological machinery,
And very handsome supernatural scenery."

As he races along he also takes the opportunity to make some amusing satirical swipes at his poetic contemporaries, particularly the Lake Poets:

"Thou shalt not set up Wordsworth, Coleridge, Southey;
Because the first is crazed beyond all hope,
The second drunk, the third so quaint and mouthey."

A LIVELY INTELLIGENCE

Byron has been called "a mere versifier" by British scholar Hugh Trevor-Roper, but the way that the poet draws information and a wide range of emotions together demonstrates a lively and skeptical intelligence. *Don Juan* is a powerful gravitational field which draws all kinds of material into its orbit. Canto XI features lines about his rival Keats:

"'Tis strange the mind, that very fiery particle
Should let itself be snuffed out by an article . . ."

He also includes an observation on the way in which aristocrats hanged from street-lights in the French Revolution are symptomatic of the intellectual illumination of the Continental Enlightenment:

"A row of gentlemen along the streets
Suspended may illuminate mankind
As also bonfires made of country seats;
But the old way is best for the purblind."

DON JUAN

BY

LORD BYRON.

"DIFFICILE EST PROPRIE COMMUNIA DICERE."

HOR. *EPIST. AD PISON.*

1824

Cover: Joseph Bisat Marshall

PUBLISHING MOGUL
John Murray founded the publishing house that bore his name in 1768. His son John Murray II (above) took over the business in 1804, establishing a list that included the works of Jane Austen and later Charles Darwin and Arthur Conan Doyle. But Byron made him the most money. In 2004, the company became an imprint of the French publisher Hachette.

One further example of Byron's skill as a poet is in his superb control of the difficult verse form he chooses: *ottava rima*, an eight-line stanza with the rhyming pattern abababcc. Some of the rhymes are ambitiously absurd, such as "intellectual/hen-pecked you all." "Plato" is made to rhyme with "Cato," and also with "potato."

THE RAKE'S MAKEOVER

Don Juan challenges the received picture of the Romantic hero, and offers readers something more speculative and intellectual. In Canto VII Byron lists the worthies in whose company he feels he belongs, including Dante, Niccolò Machiavelli, Martin Luther, Miguel de Cervantes, François de La Rochefoucauld, Jonathan Swift, John Wesley, and Jean-Jacques Rousseau.

Byron's take on Don Juan modifies the archetypal figure of a libertine and seducer (mainly exemplified in Mozart's *Don Giovanni*) and presents him not as a womanizing rake, but as one easily manipulated by women—as Byron himself was, to some extent. Don Juan has a series of picaresque adventures. At age 16 he has an affair with the married woman Donna Julia. When it is discovered, his mother sends him away to improve his morals. He is shipwrecked, occasioning some superb caustic poetic writing from Byron. One comedic passage describes the fate of the crew after they cannibalize Don Juan's tutor Pedrillo, following the exhaustion of their food supplies:

> "By night chill'd, by day scorch'd, thus one by one
> They perish'd, until wither'd to these few,
> But chiefly by a species of self-slaughter,
> In washing down Pedrillo with salt water."

Landing ashore in the Cyclades as the sole survivor of the journey, Don Juan is discovered by Haidée, a pirate's daughter, with whom he falls in love. The environment is celebrated in the inset poem "The Isles of Greece." Haidée's father sends Don Juan to a slave market in Constantinople, where, disguised as a girl, he is purchased for a seraglio. There he meets the beautiful Sultana Gulbeyaz, who becomes jealous of his relationship with Dudù, a young odalisque. Don Juan escapes and arrives in Ismail, which is under siege. He rescues a ten-year-old Muslim girl, Leila. He then goes to St. Petersburg, where the nymphomaniac Catherine the Great lusts after him. He is despatched on a mission to England. Before reaching London he has an encounter with a highway robber, whom he kills. (This episode enables Byron to show off his love of modish slang, which he picked up socializing with the boxing fraternity.) Don Juan then befriends Lord and Lady Amundeville. He falls in love with the 16-year-old Aurora Raby, but at a country-house party he attracts the Duchess Fitz-Fulke, who appears at night disguised as a Friar.

> *"But—Oh! ye lords of ladies intellectual,*
> *Inform us truly, have they not hen-pecked you all?"*
>
> Lord Byron, *Don Juan*, Canto I

Canto XVI comes to an abrupt halt:

"Back fell the sable frock and dreary cowl,
And they revealed—alas! that e'er they should;
In full, voluptuous, but not o'er grown bulk,
The phantom of her frolic grace—Fitz-Fulke."

There is a fragmentary Canto XVII, of 112 lines, written in Genoa on May 8, 1823, in which it seems that Don Juan did not sleep with the Duchess Fitz-Fulke.

FORWARD PLANNING

Byron had no idea of the direction the plot would take, but it seems there was not going to be a reprise of the famous final scene in Mozart's *Don Giovanni*, in which the title character descends into hell. There was a possibility that Don Juan would die in the French Revolution. After the first two cantos had been issued, Byron wrote to his publisher John Murray:

> "You ask me for the plan of Donny Johnny; I have no plan—I had no plan; but I had or have materials . . . You are too earnest and eager about a work never intended to be serious. Do you suppose that I could have any intention but to giggle and make giggle? A playful satire, with as little poetry as could be helped, was what I meant."

In a further letter to Murray, Byron wrote:

> "I meant to have made him a Cavalier Servente in Italy, and a cause for a divorce in England, and a Sentimental 'Werther-faced' man in Germany, so as to show the different ridicules of the society in each of these countries, and to have displayed him gradually gâté and blasé, as he grew older, as is natural. But I had not quite fixed whether to make him end in Hell, or in an unhappy marriage, not knowing which would be the severest."

Don Juan is not the only work of Byron's that it will never be possible to read, at least not in its entirety. There is a scene infamous in the annals of philistinism when John Murray burned his memoirs at 50 Albemarle Street, London, a month after the poet's death, because they were felt to be too scandalous and obscene. Only the Irish poet Thomas Moore (Byron's literary executor) opposed the destruction, but his protests were in vain, and he divulged none of their contents in his *Letters and Journals of Lord Byron* (1830). Since then, the lost work has acquired a legendary reputation for salaciousness that it is hard to believe it would have merited. BR

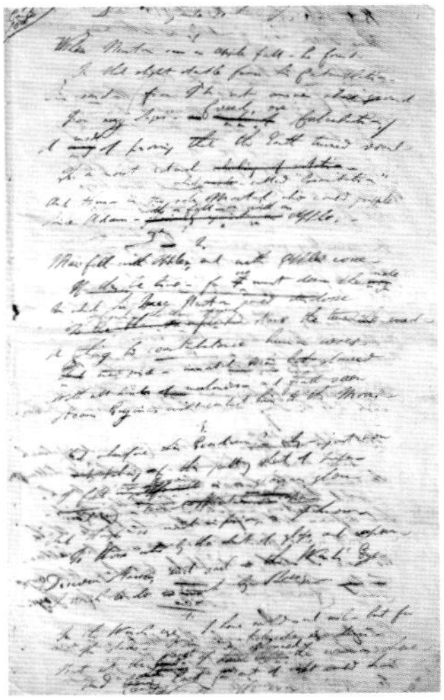

7/10

WILL IT EVER HAPPEN?

Ill-advised poets are likely to continue to attempt a finish. Since there is no information regarding the direction in which the plot was intended to go, no continuation will or can be satisfactory or convincing. In 1864 Harry W. Wetton wrote that to attempt to complete *Don Juan* "savors strongly of egregious madness, and appears the acme of all possible presumption." However, this did not stop him from attempting to complete the work.

WHAT HAPPENED NEXT . . .

There have been many attempts to finish *Don Juan*, some of them even within Byron's lifetime. Writers to try their hand at the work include I.S. Clason, Junus Secundus, Charles Clark, G.R. Baxter, William Cowley, H.W. Wetton, and G.N. Byron. In August 2010 playwright Ranjit Bolt had a continuation of Canto XVII published in *The Times Literary Supplement*. Byron's fragmentary Canto XVII (below) was first published by Murray in 1903.

LUCIEN LEUWEN

Author Stendhal **Year** 1834 **Country** France **Genre** Political novel

STENDHAL
Marie-Henri Bayle wanted to be a playwright, became an army administrator, and ended as one of the greatest French novelists. He wrote under numerous pseudonyms, the best known of which is Stendhal, which he first used in a travel book of 1817.

Stendhal (the pen name of Marie-Henri Beyle) is famous as the author of two highly regarded novels, *Le Rouge et Le Noir* (*The Red and the Black*, 1830) and *La Chartreuse de Parme* (*The Charterhouse of Parma*, 1839). He came to novel writing late in life, after a rich and varied career in the French army during the Napoleonic period and various administrative posts. Consequently he had a wealthy body of material on which to draw—including intense love affairs. He began writing *Lucien Leuwen* in 1834 when he was consul at Civitavecchia, a port outside Rome. The novel was to chart the history of a wealthy banker's son, a member of the middle classes which benefited under the conditions afforded by the regime that came to power after the July Revolution of 1830. Although the armed mob had won the fighting in Paris and the Bourbon Charles X had been overthrown, power was retained in the hands of the wealthy under the "July Monarchy" of the slightly more liberal Orléanist, Louis-Philippe (Philippe Égalité): a true republic remained elusive. Unfortunately the novel was never finished, and as its theme was political Stendhal was discouraged from pursuing it. Publication would almost certainly have got him into trouble with the authorities—this was an era in which Delacroix's iconic painting *Liberty Leading the People* (1830) was consigned to an attic after being considered too inflammatory to be allowed on display.

LEADING THE TROOPS

In the first volume, *The Green Huntsman*, Lucien Leuwen is expelled from the École Polytechnique for daring to air mild republican views. He joins the Lancers, cutting a dash in his glamorous uniform. He is sent to the city of Nancy, where he embarks on a love affair with the chaste widow Bathilde Chasteller. The title of the volume is taken from the name of a café-haus in the romantic woods of Burelviller, where a woodwind band plays excerpts from Mozart's *Don Giovanni* and *The Marriage of Figaro*, providing the soundtrack to Lucien's. Lucien is, relatively, an innocent ("a naive soul with no self-knowledge") alongside the older and more worldly-wise narrator, but as the novel progresses he draws closer to the standpoint of the narrator.

One of the tasks of Lucien's regiment is to put down the rebellious weavers of Nancy who are trying to form trades unions. But the expedition

Cover: Gareth Butterworth

RESTRICTED VIEW
Eugène Delacroix's *Liberty Leading the People* was painted in the year of the event it depicts, the July Revolution of 1830. On completion, the work was purchased by the French state, which then banned it from public display because it was judged too subversive.

is not efficiently provisioned. As someone who had witnessed the retreat of Napoleon's army from Moscow in 1812, Stendhal was in a good position to know about a catastrophically mismanaged campaign. After a merciless struggle, the troops eventually prevail and the weavers are arrested. The trials of the weavers in April 1834 are mentioned in chapter 67, when in the middle of a dramatic love scene Lucien remembers that Madame Grandet "did not blink an eyelid" when told of the sufferings of the prisoners "dying of cold and misery in their carts."

AWAKENING SOCIAL CONSCIENCE

Lucien is not ideologically completely sympathetic to the republican cause, and hates the democratic America which he has not visited, but he is sufficiently perceptive to register the suffering of the oppressed classes, assaulted by an army theoretically organized for the defense of the nation. He receives a vivid impression of what the wretches feel, living in a village where the windows are covered in "old writing paper soaked in oil" and the brook runs blue with the effluence of dye-works. Nancy is presented as a boring and provincial (words that are used scores of times) city, and is made to seem worse than it actually was. Stendhal gives a detailed presentation of the banality, pretentiousness, commonplaceness, and stupidity of the inhabitants, and lashes them with the same sort of energy expended against the same targets shown later by Flaubert in *Bouvard et Péchuchet* (see p.104). Truth and sincerity are almost impossible to find: "The age has contracted a marriage with hypocrisy." There is a documentary authenticity about the novel, in line with Stendhal's comment that "There's no originality of truth except in details."

Stendhal presents a society in which spying and control from the top leave little room for freedom of maneuver. Owing to the insecurity of the regime, bribery and corruption are rife and elections are all about vote rigging. This novel is perilously realistic, and a very thin partition separates it from the actual world of the 1830s.

The second volume is titled *The Telegraph* and concerns Lucien's job in the office of the Comte de Vaize. He goes to supervise elections, on a trip to places based on Blois, Bourges (appropriately since it gives us the word "bourgeois"), Niort, and Caen, and the "infernal" telegraph enables him to keep in touch with his boss and to facilitate fraudulent financial transactions. It was not an electric telegraph (that had not yet been invented), but a semaphore system, first demonstrated by Claude Chappe in 1792.

> *"There is no originality of truth except in details."*
>
> Stendhal

Lucien is the still center in a maelstrom of corruption, self-seeking, and chicanery. In the words of French essayist Michel de Montaigne, he "grapples with necessity." One of the most powerful scenes in the novel finds Lucien at the hospital bedside of Kortis, whom the government wants poisoned by opium. In the darkness and stench Lucien manages with dignity and persistence to foil the plot. He "handles his ship well," but misses the opera he had planned to see. By now he is separated from the love of his life (who, he believes wrongly, has given birth to an illegitimate child), and his father recommends that he have an affair with a rich married woman, Augustine

THE RED AND THE BLACK

First published in 1830, Stendhal's greatest novel shows mastery in several forms, most notably comedy, satire, affecting lyricism, and ultimately tragedy. It charts the life and death of Julien Sorel, who endures an impoverished childhood and is then torn between a career in the army (the red) and entering the church (the black). On reaching adulthood he faces other tough choices: between the provinces and Paris, between true love and promiscuity, between worldly success and spiritual self-fulfillment. He makes numerous misjudgments, but finally learns to distinguish between worthwhile pursuits and vanity. Stendhal's depiction of the historical background—a time of hideous upheaval in France—has been criticized for inaccuracies, but no one can doubt the quality of his insights into human psychology.

Grandet, so that he can avoid accusations of being a Saint-Simonian—a supporter of Henry de Saint-Simon, the left-wing reformer and advocate of a form of technological and scientific socialism. All of Stendhal's famed amatory expertise is brought to bear on this shallow and unsatisfactory affair. When his father proposes it he says, "*Pater meus, transeat a me calix iste!*" ("O my father, if it be possible, let this cup pass from me")—a blasphemous allusion to Matthew 26.39.

The volume ends with Lucien about to go off to a post in Rome. Plans have survived in which Lucien would be reunited with Bathilde. Stendhal is unable to show the relationship as happy and fulfilled because that would, he admits, make the readers jealous and, worse, bored, so that they cry out "Good Lord, how dull this book is!" He was fully alive to the dangers of boredom in erotic encounters, and records in the notes for the novel: "Last night I was bored to death with the prettiest, youngest, richest, and, for me, most well-disposed young woman in Rome, whom I left at one o'clock in her bed." His philosophy of love is famously expounded in *De l'amour* (*On Love*, 1822), which draws on an unrequited love affair with Countess Mathilde Dembowski, whom he met in Milan in March 1818. Stendhal has been accused of negativity and cynicism, but he defended himself by saying that he was merely holding up a mirror to nature.

WHAT MIGHT HAVE BEEN

There is much in the novel to inspire regret that it is incomplete, but perhaps not as much as if either of Stendhal's other two great novels had not been finished. *Lucien Leuwen* can be very slow and laborious, and is heavy with the names of real people that mean little or nothing to readers with little knowledge of them, especially readers nearly 200 years distant from the events. Real events are there too, such as the claim of U.S. President

LES MISÉRABLES

Victor Hugo's novel *Les Misérables* (1862)—about the spiritual redemption of ex-convict Jean Valjean—begins in 1815 and culminates in the 1832 June Rebellion in Paris. It was turned into a musical in 1980 by Claude-Michel Schönberg with lyrics by Alain Boublil and Jean-Marc Natel. The musical had a poor initial reception, but after English journalist Herbert Kretzmer wrote an English-language version it became an award-winning smash hit with record-breaking runs all over the world. A movie adaptation starring Hugh Jackman, Russell Crowe, and Anne Hathaway received comparable acclaim when it went on general release in 2012.

WHAT HAPPENED NEXT . . .

The novel was not published in Stendhal's lifetime. In 1855 Stendhal's cousin Romain Colomb published the first part as Le Chasseur Vert (The Green Huntsman). In 1894 there was an edition by Jean de Mitty, but it was not until 1927 that Henry Debraye produced a scholarly text. The manuscripts of Lucien Leuwen are now in Grenoble Municipal Library, and one page is visible online, as is a page of Stendhal's other unfinished novel, Lamiel.

Stendhal left behind prefaces and notes for the novel. There are full descriptions of a gay Englishman called Milord Link, and he noted down as chronological "scaffolding" a scheme in real time, from April 1833 to January 1835. There are several gaps, inconsistencies, and slips which Stendhal would have corrected had the novel been prepared for publication. It is not known whether he would have persisted with the envisaged chapters on the hero's diplomatic life in Rome.

What happened next in real history after Stendhal's death were further episodes in the protracted nightmare of French politics in the 19th century: the deposition of Louis-Philippe in July 1835, the Revolution of 1848, the enthronement of Napoleon's nephew Napoleon III, the horrors of the Franco-Prussian War, and the Commune of 1871.

Andrew Jackson for reparations from the Napoleonic Wars, which almost brought the United States and France to war in 1834. There is too much about the political activities of Lucien's father, the banker. It is also packed with fictional people, some of whom it is hard to grasp. The description of the election in Caen feels as long drawn out as following an election live—Charles Dickens's depiction of the Eatanswill election in the almost contemporary *Pickwick Papers* (1836) may not be quite as real, but it is arguably more readable and amusing. (Although in fairness Stendhal was probably limited by the dangers of dealing with politics in the novel, of which he was well aware.)

Nonetheless, there is much to admire in *Lucien Leuwen* compared to Victor Hugo's *Les Misérables* (1862), which covers some of the same period in French history but is committed to a narrower and more partial political spectrum. Stendhal set out to study his world with merciless detachment. Had *Lucien Leuwen* been finished it would have been one of the major political novels of all time. BR

WILL IT EVER HAPPEN?

0/10

It is difficult to decide the extent to which the novel available in modern editions approaches the finished state Stendhal planned. In the notes there are abandoned schemes, which the author could perhaps have come back to. It is highly unlikely that anyone would possess the skill now to finish the work in a plausible manner, or the historical tact to enter convincingly into the political and erotic life of the French 1830s. Stendhal envisaged that someone might finish the novel, but he didn't want it to be Honoré de Balzac. He said it could be his friend Prosper Merimée—most known as the author of *Carmen* (1845)—but added that Merimée didn't even finish his *own* works.

SKORPION UND FELIX

Author Karl Marx **Year** 1837 **Country** Germany **Genre** Humorous novel

KARL MARX
After abandoning his attempts at humor, Marx wrote *The Communist Manifesto* and then *Das Kapital*, two works that had greater influence than any others on the history of the 20th century.

The legacy of Karl Marx's two most famous written works, *The Communist Manifesto* (1848, with Friedrich Engels) and *Das Kapital* (Volume I, 1867, Volumes II and III published posthumously), is well documented. What is less well known is that prior to embarking on a career as a revolutionary thinker, Marx harbored aspirations of a more literary inclination. In 1837, at the age of 19, he wrote a comic novel called *Skorpion und Felix* (*Scorpion and Felix*). At this time he looked like a pomaded dandy—quite unlike the hirsute grandee that he is familiarly pictured as. Written while he was studying law and philosophy at the University of Berlin, the work remains unpublished. It was composed after reading Laurence Sterne's *The Life and Opinions of Tristram Shandy* (1759), which in many respects can be considered an unfinished work of literature itself.

WHIMSICAL FAILURE

Those readers hoping for a repeat of *Tristram Shandy*, however, will likely find themselves disappointed. *Skorpion und Felix* is widely dismissed by commentators as an exercise in fatuous attempts at humor. In his 1999 biography of Marx, Francis Wheen characterizes the work as "a nonsensical torrent of whimsy and persiflage." As it now exists only in fragments it is difficult to get a sense of the novel as a whole, and the most that it offers is the opportunity to analyze certain observations that deal with politics and philosophy. As in his later writings, Marx tried to penetrate to a deeper reality beyond superficial appearances.

Told by a first-person narrator, the plot concerns three main characters—Merten (a tailor), Scorpion (his son), and Felix (his apprentice)—and their quest to uncover their origins. The characters' fireside chat not only touches on the philosophical ideas of Hegel, Locke, Fichte, and Kant, but it also references the works of Ovid, Goethe, and Shakespeare, and makes numerous allusions to the Bible. Marx was an avid reader, and his intellectual explorations as a student covered a broad spectrum. In chapter 21 he leads the protagonists of *Skorpion und Felix* into the realm of philology (the study of language as used in literature), as the narrator meditates on the origins of Merten's name:

Cover: Steve Panton

> "This warrants a new hypothesis: partly because he is a tailor, partly because his son's name is Scorpion, it is highly probable that he is descended from *Mars*, the god of war, genitive *Martis*, Greek accusative *Martin*, *Mertin*, *Merten*, since the craft of the god of war, like that of the tailor, consists in cutting, for he cuts off arms and legs and hacks the happiness of the earth to pieces. The scorpion, further, is a poisonous animal which kills with a glance, whose wounds are fatal, whose eyes discharge annihilating lightning, a fine allegory of war, whose gaze is lethal, whose consequences leave scars on the victim which bleed internally and are past healing."

Skorpion und Felix also provides a link to the early stirrings of Marx's political consciousness. While at university in Berlin he joined the Young Hegelians, a group of German intellectuals who used elements of Hegel's philosophy to argue for reform of the Prussian political system. This desire for social change can be seen in chapter 29, as the narrator analyzes the laws of entail and the practice of giving the lion's share of any inheritance to the first-born offspring:

> "I sat deep in thought . . . and gave myself up to profound reflection to discover what a wash-closet could have to do with the right of primogeniture, and suddenly it came to me like a flash, and in a melodious succession of thoughts one upon the other my vision was illuminated and a radiant form appeared before my eyes.
>
> "The right of primogeniture is the wash-closet of the aristocracy, for a wash-closet only exists for the purpose of washing. But

TRISTRAM SHANDY

Sterne's greatest work was an anti-novel almost 200 years before Jean-Paul Sartre coined the term. It is ostensibly the life story of the title character, but there are so many digressions that it never really gets going along its biographical path. *Tristram Shandy* is at the head of a category of literary works whose influence is much wider than their readership: very few people claim to have read this book from cover to cover, but many of its incidents and stylistic traits have been adopted by subsequent authors of numerous nationalities, from James Joyce and Virginia Woolf to Carlos Fuentes and Milan Kundera. Another prominent work of this kind is Robert Burton's *The Anatomy of Melancholy* (1621), a repository of stories. Sterne knew this book and despised it for its sermon-like solemnity: even at its most serious, *Tristram Shandy* is lighthearted.

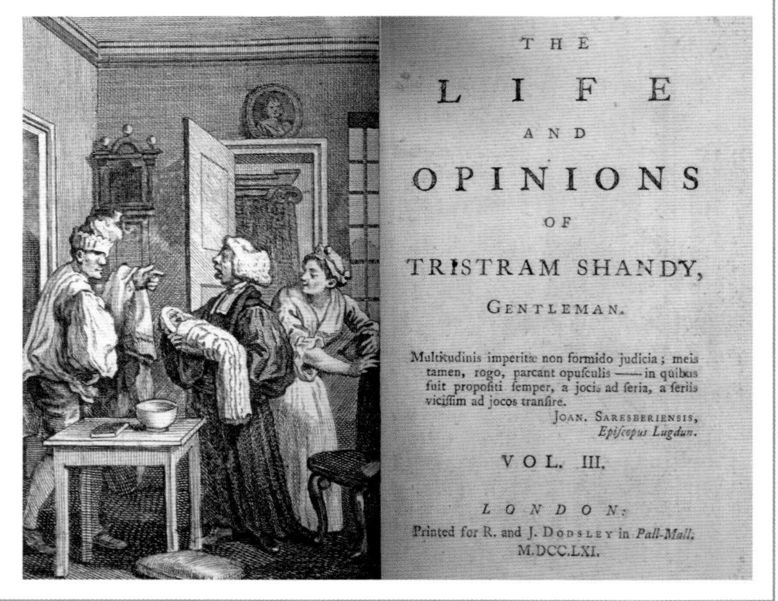

THE
LIFE
AND
OPINIONS
OF
TRISTRAM SHANDY,
GENTLEMAN.

Multitudinis imperitæ non formido judicia; meis tamen, rogo, parcant opuſculis —— in quibus fuit propoſiti ſemper, a jocis ad ſeria, a ſeriis viciſſim ad jocos tranſire.

JOAN. SARESBERIENSIS,
Epiſcopus Lugdun.

VOL. III.

LONDON:
Printed for R. and J. DODSLEY in *Pall-Mall.*
M.DCC.LXI.

washing bleaches, and thus lends a pale sheen to that which is washed. So also does the right of primogeniture silver the eldest son of the house, it thus lends him a pale silvery sheen, while on the other members it stamps the pale romantic hue of penury . . .

"The ordinary mortal, i.e., he who has no right of primogeniture, fights the storms of life, throws himself into the billowing sea and seizes pearls of Promethean rights from its

> *"Every giant . . . presupposes a dwarf, every genius a hidebound philistine, and every storm at sea—mud."*
>
> *Skorpion und Felix*

depths, and before his eyes the inner form of the Idea appears in glory, and he creates with greater boldness, but he who is entitled to primogenital inheritance lets only drops fall on him, for fear he might strain a limb, and so seats himself in a wash-closet."

Additionally, there can be found in *Skorpion und Felix* a foreshadowing of one of Marx's most oft-quoted observations—"History repeats itself . . . first as tragedy, then as farce"—which appeared in his essay *The Eighteenth Brumaire of Louis Napoleon* (1852). (The title of this later work alludes to Napoleon's seizing of power in the month known as the Eighteenth Brumaire in the French Revolutionary calendar, and his nephew Louis Napoleon becoming Emperor after the Revolution of 1851.) The germ of this dictum can be seen in chapter 37: "Every giant ... presupposes a dwarf, every genius a hidebound philistine, and every storm at sea—mud, and as soon as the first disappear, the latter begin, sit down at the table, sprawling out their long legs arrogantly."

FORESAKEN AMBITION

At around the same time that he composed *Skorpion und Felix*, Marx was also writing a verse drama titled *Oulanem* (influenced by Goethe's *Faust*) and experimenting with lyric poetry. However, it appears that none of these works could measure up to the aesthetic ideals that he had evolved while writing them, leading him to abandon the writings and foresake his literary ambitions. In a letter to his father of November 1837, he confided: "Suddenly, as at the touch of a magic wand—oh, the touch was shattering at first—the kingdom of true poetry glistened toward me like a distant fairy palace, and all my creations crumbled into nothing." BR

WHAT HAPPENED NEXT . . .

Marx underwent some sort of physical breakdown, after which he burnt many of his poems and novellistic fragments in order to prevent himself from writing anything further. A certain number of chapters of *Skorpion und Felix* survived, however, and he published fragments in his *Book of Verse* (1837). Surviving fragments were published in English for the first time in Volume I of *Marx–Engels Collected Works* (1975).

WILL IT EVER HAPPEN?

6/10

Marx's later writings have had a persistent and irrepressible life, so it is always possible that this minor and obscure literary episode will be resurrected in some reimagined form.

EL DIABLO MUNDO

Author José de Espronceda **Year** 1842 **Country** Spain **Genre** Epic poetry

JOSÉ DE ESPRONCEDA
Among the many contradictions in Espronceda's short but eventful life was his political affiliation: he began as a revolutionary but later became a member of the Spanish parliament and secretary of his nation's diplomatic legation to The Hague.

José de Espronceda started off as a nature poet, rather in the manner of John Keats, and matured into a "gloomy egoist" with deeply radical politics. He became known as the Spanish Lord Byron. This transformation was completed in *El Diablo Mundo* (*Devil World*), an epic poem that was left unfinished at the poet's death. The surviving fragment consists of six cantos, only the first three of which are complete. In Canto I, Espronceda mocks his own desire for literary immortality. In Canto III he expresses misgivings about and sometimes contempt for romantic love, which is depicted as little more than the vanity of the participants. Sandwiched between these reflective, analytical, and often sardonic segments is the "Canto a Teresa" (Canto II), a straightforward paean to the woman with whom Espronceda had a long and tempestuous affair.

At the beginning of *El Diablo Mundo* we encounter an elderly man who is tired of life, which he finds incomprehensible. A beautiful woman appears before him and offers him the choice between death (after which he will learn the ultimate truth) and reincarnation as Adán (Adam), who will thereafter wander the world, innocent and naked, forever. The old man takes the latter option.

The influence of *Faust* (Part I, 1808; Part II, 1832) is acknowledged in the prose Prologue. However, unlike in Goethe's work, the bargain here contains no forfeit: Adán is no lost soul buying time until perdition, but an observer of social mores and a philosopher who reflects on metaphysical questions. When he encounters Satan, he finds that the devil is a projection of the human mind, full of uncertainty about himself and God.

Maintaining continuity with his youthful work, Espronceda describes Adán's birth and love for a woman named Salada in terms of the beauties of nature, particularly flowers. But later, when Adán rejects her, he is likened to the wind—a destructive force. Symbolism in literature is often protean: it cannot be relied on always to represent the same thing throughout a single work. In *El Diablo Mundo*, the flowers and the wind gradually cease to stand merely for love and rejection, respectively, but increasingly represent, again respectively, Spain and Fernando VII, the king who opposed the forces of Napoleon. (In common with many writers, artists, and musicians of the Romantic movement—at least for a while—Espronceda regarded Napoleon as a liberator and a savior.)

Cover: Gerry Fletcher

WHAT HAPPENED NEXT . . .

Espronceda wrote in the same manner as Byron but, unlike the author of *Don Juan* (see p.54), he never achieved celebrity abroad. (It is commonly reported that, after Shakespeare, Byron is the most popular classic English poet in translation in non-Anglophone countries.) Espronceda remains further from the limelight than he perhaps deserves to be.

El Diablo Mundo is an ambitious work that encompasses emotion, philosophy, and politics. It confirmed Espronceda as the greatest Spanish poet of his generation. Perhaps if he had completed the poem he would have gained greater fame abroad, but he was overtaken by events. In 1826 his revolutionary leanings forced him to flee Spain. He went first to London, where he fell in love with Teresa Mancha (the woman apostrophized in the poem), and then to Paris, where he participated in the July Revolution of 1830. After the death of Fernando VII in 1833, Espronceda returned to his homeland, where he helped to found the Republican Party of Spain and was imprisoned several times for his trouble. He died of diphtheria in Madrid in 1842, aged 34. **GL**

5/10

WILL IT EVER HAPPEN?

Today the existence and nature of God are not as widely debated as they were in the early 19th century. This means less interest in works like *El Diablo Mundo*, and less chance of anyone trying to finish it. However, budding poets could do worse than imitate Espronceda's style, perhaps by taking up where he left off.

THE LIGHTHOUSE

Author Edgar Allan Poe **Year** 1849 **Country** United States **Genre** Short story or novel

EDGAR ALLAN POE
One of the first Americans to make a sole living (albeit not much of one) by writing, Poe wrote poetry before turning his hand to short prose fiction. His "The Murders in the Rue Morgue" (1841) is sometimes credited as the earliest detective story.

When Edgar Allan Poe died in 1849 he had written very little of *The Lighthouse*—only about four pages. It is unclear whether it was intended to be a short story or a novel. The text that we have is written as a series of diary entries, the first being New Year's Day, 1796. The setting is Scandinavia, 190 or 200 miles (304 or 320 km) from Norland—presumably Norrland in northern Sweden.

IMPENDING PARANOIA

The plot concerns an aristocratic misanthrope who gets a job as a solitary lighthouse keeper—ideal for someone who shares Jean-Paul Sartre's view that hell is other people:

> "It never would have done to let Orndoff accompany me. I never should have made any way with my book as long as he was within reach of me, with his intolerable gossip."

On January 1 the narrator records that a storm is in progress, and that the cutter that brought him "had a narrow pass." He looks forward to being alone so that he can get on with writing his book, in the company of his dog Neptune, who "is not to be taken into consideration as society." There is an ominous premonition of dramas to follow in the acoustics of the interior:

> "It is strange that I never observed, until this moment, how dreary a sound that word has—'alone'! I could half fancy there was some peculiarity in the echo of these cylindrical walls—but oh, no!—this is all nonsense. I do believe I am going to get nervous about my insulation. *That* will never do."

On January 2 he describes the sea as being calm and uneventful, the wind having "lulled about day-break." On January 3 the day is calm, and he resolves to explore the lighthouse. The building is 160 feet (49 m) tall from the shoreline, but it goes down 20 feet (6 m) into the ground and the narrator thinks it should have been reinforced "with solid masonry." The walls are 4 feet (1.2 m) thick and "solid-iron-riveted," but since the foundations are on chalk there are hints of foreboding. There are similarities to Poe's short story "A Descent into the Maelström" (1841), which is also set in Scandinavia and tells the tale of a sailor caught in a giant whirlpool. There are glimpses of impending paranoia.

Cover: Jayne Evans

A heading for January 4 follows, but there is no further text. And that is all there is to it. It is possible, but far from likely, that *The Lighthouse* was complete, and the blank page was put there intentionally to indicate that the narrator died. BR

WILL IT EVER HAPPEN?

0/10

Poe left no notes or drafts behind, so it is impossible to know how the story was intended to finish. He continues to be an intriguing and enigmatic character, and although numerous writers have attempted continuations of the tale, it remains a mystery as to whether any of them have come close to the plotline that was originally envisaged.

WHAT HAPPENED NEXT . . .

Robert Bloch (best known as the author *of Psycho*, 1959) completed Poe's tale with a version of his own in 1953. Richard Selzer included his short story, "Poe's Lighthouse," in *Imagine a Woman and Other Tales* (1990). In *Poe's Lighthouse* (2006, below), edited by Christopher Conlon, 23 authors continue the narrative (or entirely reimagine it). Joyce Carol Oates includes "Poe Posthumous, or The Lighthouse" in her collection *Wild Nights!* (2008), moving the date to October 7, 1849, the day of Poe's death. Leigh M. Lane's *Finding Poe* (2012) explores the role Poe's own works, including *The Lighthouse*, may have played in his mysterious death—he died four days after being found lying semi-conscious in the gutter outside a public house, dressed in shabby second-hand clothes.

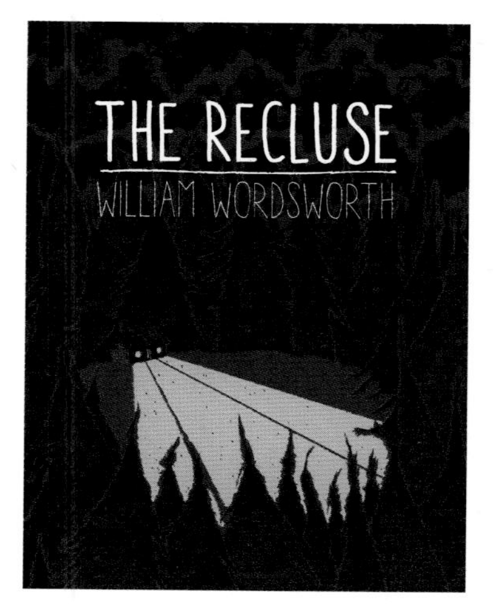
THE RECLUSE
WILLIAM WORDSWORTH

ARTHUR H. CLOUGH
DIPSYCHUS

LA
COMEDIE
HUMAINE
HONORÉ
DE BALZAC

Chapter 3

МЁРТВЫЕ
ДУШИ
Н. В. ГОГОЛЬ

THE
ISLE OF THE
CROSS
BY
HERMAN MELVILLE

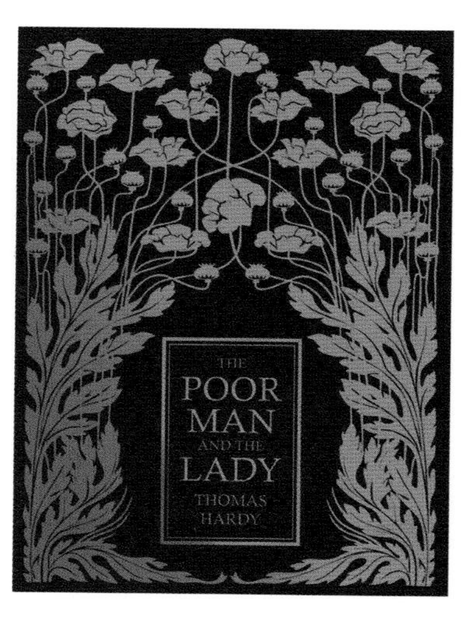
THE
POOR
MAN
AND THE
LADY
THOMAS
HARDY

the mystery of
Edwin Drood

BOUVARD
ET PÉCUCHET
GUSTAVE FLAUBERT

1850–99

PRAETERITA
JOHN RUSKIN
AN AUTOBIOGRAPHY

GASTON
DE LATOUR
Walter Pater

Leopold von Sacher-Masoch
Das
Vermächtnis
Kains

Jean
Santeuil
Un roman de
Marcel
Proust
3 Volumes

THE RECLUSE

Author William Wordsworth **Year** 1850 **Country** England **Genre** Poetry

WILLIAM WORDSWORTH
The poet's first publication, *Lyrical Ballads* (1798), written with Samuel Taylor Coleridge, helped to launch the English Romantic movement in literature.

The Recluse is a poem that Wordsworth planned, but never finished. What we have of it is *The Prelude*, in itself a long impressive blank verse poem charting the growth of the poet's mind, and *The Excursion*. The unwritten third part survives only in fragments. Wordsworth planned to write this work in collaboration with his friend Samuel Taylor Coleridge, their aim being to surpass Milton's *Paradise Lost* (1667). Had *The Recluse* been completed, it would have been approximately three times longer than *Paradise Lost* (33,000 lines as opposed to 10,500).

In the introduction to *The Prelude* (published posthumously in 1850), Wordsworth explains that the original idea was "to compose a philosophical Poem, containing views of Man, Nature, and Society, and to be entitled *The Recluse*; as having for its principal subject, the sensations and opinions of a poet living in retirement." Composition of the work began in 1798–99, but got off to a slow start. In September 1799, Coleridge wrote to Wordsworth:

> "I am anxiously eager to have you steadily employed on 'The Recluse' . . . I wish you would write a poem, in blank verse, addressed to those who, in consequence of the complete failure of the French Revolution, have thrown up all hopes of amelioration of mankind, and are sinking into an almost Epicurean selfishness, disguising the same under the soft titles of domestic attachment and contempt for visionary philosophies. It would do great good, and might form a Part of 'The Recluse.'"

Wordsworth pays tribute to Coleridge in his introduction, saying that the work is "addressed to a dear friend, most distinguished for his knowledge."

A LIFETIME'S AMBITION

Wordsworth was seriously at work on *The Recluse* until about 1808, but toiled on it for decades afterward, and was disappointed that he could not manage to finish it. No single explanation can account for his failure to finish the work, but it is the case that constantly evolving conditions, both external and internal, meant that the central motives could never gel.

The Prelude or, Growth of a Poet's Mind; An Autobiographical Poem is a revealing autobiographical work on the key details of Wordsworth's life. Like the whole of *The Recluse* it is in Wordsworth's distinctive form of blank verse.

THE RECLUSE

WILLIAM WORDSWORTH

Cover: Josse Pickard

HOME AT GRASMERE

This extract from *The Recluse* describes the environment in the English Lake District where the work was being conceived (right). It is representative of Wordsworth's lifelong tendency to relish description rather than philosophical abstractions:

"But I would call thee beautiful, for mild,
And soft, and gay, and beautiful thou art
Dear Valley, having in thy face a smile
Though peaceful, full of gladness. Thou art pleased,
Pleased with thy crags and woody steeps, thy Lake,
Its one green island and its winding shores;
The multitude of little rocky hills,
Thy Church and cottages of mountain stone
Clustered like stars some few, but single most,
And lurking dimly in their shy retreats,
Or glancing at each other cheerful looks
Like separated stars with clouds between.
What want we? have we not perpetual streams,
Warm woods, and sunny hills, and fresh green fields,
And mountains not less green, and flocks and herds,
And thickets full of songsters, and the voice
Of lordly birds, an unexpected sound
Heard now and then from morn to latest eve,
Admonishing the man who walks below
Of solitude and silence in the sky?"

As with so much of Wordsworth's writing, *The Prelude* is not plain sailing textually. The poet kept tinkering with it, and there is a 1799 draft and an 1805 one, as well as numerous variations. He never gave the work a title; he called it the "Poem (title not yet fixed upon) to Coleridge" and in his letters to his sister Dorothy Wordsworth referred to it as "the poem on the growth of my own mind." The poem was unknown to the general public until published three months after Wordsworth's death in 1850, its name suggested by his widow Mary.

The Prelude is one of the mountain peaks of poetic achievements in English literature. Beginning in his boyhood and continuing to 1798, it has memorable passages on Wordsworth stealing a boat, studying in Cambridge, spending time in London, encountering the French Revolution in both its benign and malign aspects, crossing the Alps, and, finally, climbing Mount Snowdon at night. (It doesn't, however, contain an account of his affair with Annette Vallon, whom he met in Orléans in December 1791, and the illegitimate daughter he fathered with her, Anne-Caroline Wordsworth.) The poem conveys a circular journey, ending with Wordsworth returning to his childhood home of the Lake District.

The Excursion was published in 1814, and it came with a long explanatory preface in which Wordsworth stated that it was "the second part of a long and laborious Work." He explains in the Preface that the poem is growing slowly like a cathedral, and various poems are "little cells, oratories, and sepulchral recesses, ordinarily included in these edifices." *The Prelude* was "the Ante-chapel." The longest of Wordsworth's poems to be published in his lifetime, *The Excursion* is arranged into nine books which record the conversation and debate among four characters—a Poet, Wanderer, Solitary, and Pastor—over a period of five days. It also included a poetic "Prospectus" to *The Recluse*, a 107-line poem in which Wordsworth laid out the structure and intention of the whole work.

The Excursion was poorly received upon publication. Critic and essayist William Hazlitt commented: "I shed tears because I couldn't praise it as I wanted." Francis Jeffrey's assessment of the poem for the *Edinburgh Review* notoriously opened with the sentence "This will never do." Many readers, such as Mary Shelley and Lord Byron, felt betrayed by what they viewed as Wordsworth's U-turn toward a more politically conservative stance.

ESTABLISHED REPUTATION

Wordsworth suffered many such critical attacks in the course of his career, but eventually the tide began to turn and by the mid-1830s his reputation had been established with both critics and the reading public. In 1843 Wordsworth was named Poet Laureate. Upon his death in 1850, at the age of 80, poet Matthew Arnold declared that "the last poetic voice is dumb."

Some of *The Recluse* survives in the poem "Home at Grasmere," the latest version of which was first published in 1888, although early manuscripts have survived. It provides a picture of the setting in which composition took place. Other poems written for *The Recluse* include "The Tuft of Primroses" and the short blank-verse poem "St. Paul's," whose concluding lines show great promise for the quality of work:

> "Pure, silent, solemn, beautiful, was seen
> The huge majestic Temple of St. Paul
> In awful sequestration, through a veil,
> Through its own sacred veil of falling snow."

There is also a poem composed in 1826 when Wordsworth was threatened with having to leave his house at Rydal Mount.

Why was *The Recluse* never finished? Perhaps because Wordsworth was more at home, so far as poetic creation goes, with vivid epiphanic moments than a large philosophical structure. BR

WHAT HAPPENED NEXT . . .
The Prelude came to be viewed by many as Wordsworth's masterpiece. Today it is possible to read parallel text editions of *The Prelude*, with the earlier version on the left hand page and the later version on the right. The magisterial Cornell Wordsworth (below) was concluded in 2007, a 21-volume series of editions of Wordsworth's poems in which one can attempt to follow the intricate wanderings of his creative mind.

WILL IT EVER HAPPEN?

There are now more and more manuscript materials available online for Wordsworthians to see the poet at work. We now know more about what *The Recluse* might have been like, but it is inconceivable that anyone should attempt to write it, and difficult to imagine that anyone should manage to reproduce the particular timbre of Wordsworthian blank verse. In addition, the whole nexus of attitudes to the environment, the central concern of *The Recluse*, has shifted away from Romantic movement sacramentalism toward a more scientific book-keeping assessment.

DIPSYCHUS

Author Arthur Hugh Clough **Year** 1850 **Country** England **Genre** Poetic drama

ARTHUR HUGH CLOUGH
Clough's unexpected failure to get a first-class degree at Oxford made it convenient for biographers and critics to call his life and work a disappointment and gloss over his poetry, some of which is among the finest of the Victorian age.

Arthur Hugh Clough is a Victorian poet who many of his readers would argue is not as well known as he should be. His poem "Say not the Struggle nought Availeth" was given a measure of fame in the Second World War when Winston Churchill quoted it in one of his speeches. And "The Latest Decalogue," which contains the lines "Thou shalt not kill; but needst not strive / Officiously to keep alive," is sometimes cited in euthanasia debates. But the bulk of his work is ignored, and he is known *about* because of Matthew Arnold's poem "Thyrsis" (1865, which celebrates him and his undergraduate association with the pastoral countryside around Oxford) rather than *known*.

Nonetheless, his long poems *The Bothie of Tober na Vuolich* (1848) and *Amours de Voyage* (1858) are of sufficient quality to hold their own among more famed poetic works of the 19th century—such as Alfred Tennyson's *Maud* (1855) and Gerard Manley Hopkins's "Wreck of the Deutschland" (written in the mid-1870s and published posthumously in 1918)—and are arguably better than some of Robert Browning's longer works. And the short poem "Natura naturans" evokes a sexuality that is surprising in relation to the popular view of the Victorians as highly sexually repressed. Clough's great poetic drama *Dipsychus*, however, remains unfinished.

OPPOSITION AND IRREVERENCE

A Faustian drama that debates issues of belief and morality, *Dipsychus* to some extent anticipates T.S. Eliot's "The Love Song of J. Alfred Prufrock" (1915). Clough began writing the poem on a trip to Venice in the fall of 1850, during one of his most productive periods. He spent the following years revising the drafts that he brought back with him, but had failed to complete the task by the time that he died of malaria in 1861, aged only 42. The poem was left behind as a series of disjointed fragments, so the intended order of the scenes is unclear. Posthumously published editions of *Dipsychus* vary in their structure, and the version released by Clough's wife in 1869 divides the poem into two parts.

Dipsychus (called Faustulus in an early draft) is a priggish young Englishman who encounters in Venice a Mephistophelean spirit who tries to persuade him out of his puritanical state of mind. The Spirit is Hyde to

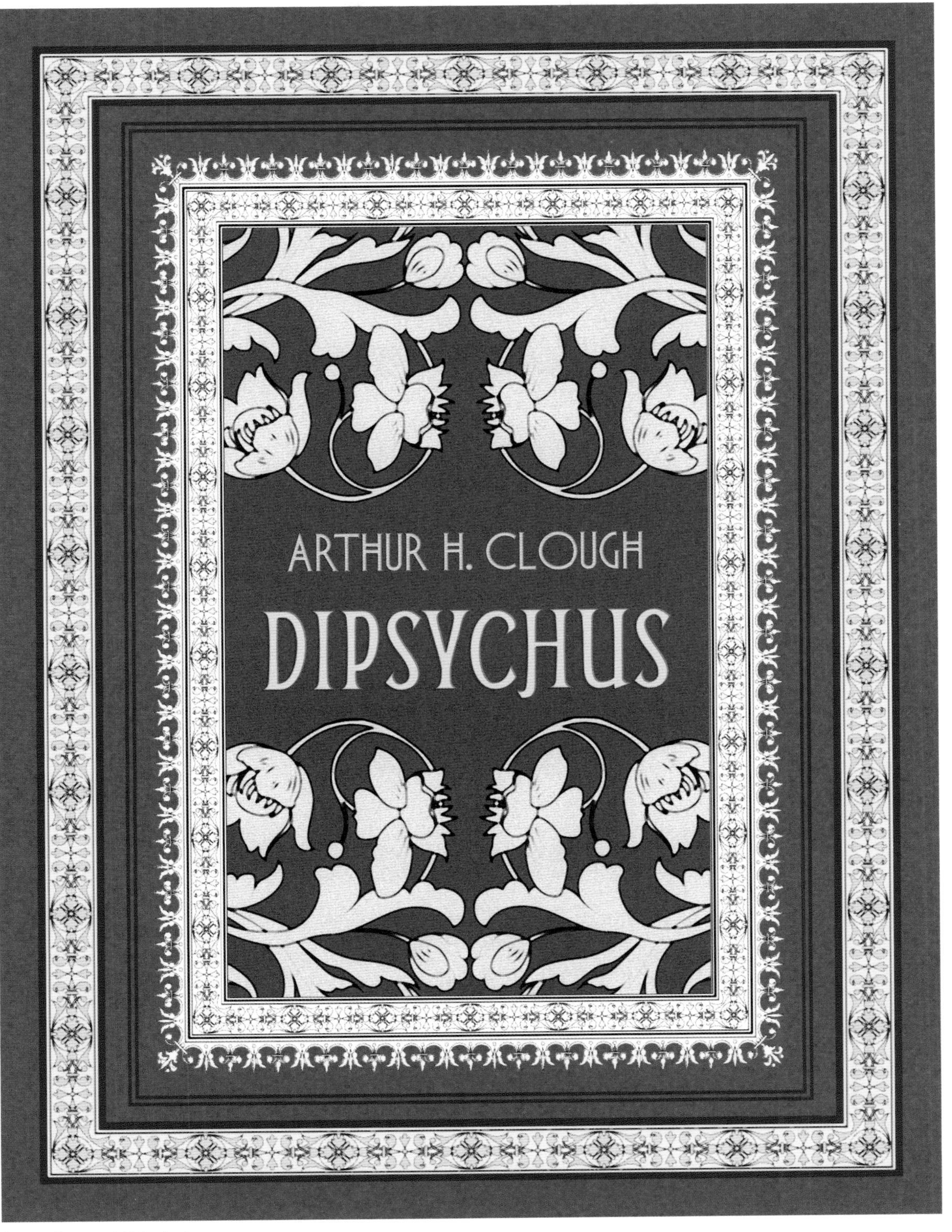

Cover: Emanuel Zahariades

the hero's Jekyll—"Dipsychus" means "split soul." The poem is "framed" by a Prologue and Epilogue as the poet reads it to his 70-year-old uncle, who doesn't understand it all. The Spirit in the poem is cynical, urbane, and amusing, and represents an opposition and irreverence that is relatively rare in the strict outlook of Victorian England—Clough is one of the very few Victorians who keeps the facetious spirit of Byron alive. This lightheartedness can be seen in the opening scene of the poem, in St. Mark's Square, with its "red flaunting streamers on the staffs," where Dipsychus guiltily recalls some "old verses" he wrote in Naples. The Spirit tells him to subdue his guilt and:

"Enjoy the minute,
And the substantial blessings in it;
Ices, *par exemple*; evening air;
Some pretty faces here and there."

The "old verses" written in Naples refer to Clough's poem "Easter Day" (1848), which was a determined denial of the resurrection of Jesus. Clough had many doubts about religion, a skepticism that the Spirit voices openly:

"And almost every one when age,
Disease, or sorrows strike him,
Inclines to think there is a God,
Or something very like Him,"

The poet is similarly open about sexual matters in *Dipsychus*, and the Spirit speaks frankly about prostitution and the realities of sex:

"There's not a girl that by us goes
But mightn't have you if she chose:
No doubt but you would give her trouble;
But then you'd pay her for it double."

NO PLACE LIKE ROME

As evidence of Clough's modernity, these lines from Canto I of *Amours de Voyage* (1849) are compelling:

"Rome disappoints me much;
I hardly as yet understand it, but
Rubbishy seems the word that
most exactly would suit it."

In an age when most poets, artists, and critics extolled the ancient world in high-flown terms, this sentiment—and the mode of its expression—look forward to the 20th century, when colloquial terms such as "rubbishy" became increasingly acceptable—and ultimately almost indispensible—in literature.

In the Victorian age, a man who admitted that the Pantheon and the Colosseum left him cold might have been derided as a philistine; here Clough daringly states something that was almost unthinkable. He was ahead of his time.

These comments were shocking to Victorian sensibilities, and Clough's widow Blanche censored many such passages in her 1869 edition. Clough was well aware of the potential for outrage, and while Blanche was his fiancée he wrote a letter begging her not to read the manuscript of *Dipsychus*: "Dear Blanche, please don't read *Dipsychus* yet—I wish particularly not. You shall see it sometime—but now, not, please—dear, I beg not, please."

Clough's aversion to the Victorian worship of Gothic—promoted most prominently by John Ruskin in *The Seven Lamps of Architecture* (1849) and *The Stones of Venice* (1853)—is also unusual for the time:

"Come leave you Gothic, worn-out story,
San Giorgio and the Redemptore;
I from no building, gay or solemn,
Can spare the shapely Grecian column."

For the Spirit, the classical tradition—represented in Venice by Palladio, the architect reviled by Ruskin—displays "pure form nakedly displayed, / And all things absolutely made" and is counter to the rough and unfinished products that are often found in Gothic architecture. Clough directly criticizes Ruskin when the Spirit refers to "Ruskin's d---d pretence."

REFRESHINGLY MODERN

The poem ends with a scene that takes place after "An interval of thirty years." Dipsychus is now Lord Chief Justice, married and with a child. He is visited by a woman he once knew, whom he thought to be dead. He had an illicit "dalliance" with her when she was a prostitute. She says to him, "You called me Pleasure—my name now is—Guilt." She threatens to go away and

> *"Enjoy the minute,*
> *And the substantial blessings in it."*
>
> *Dipsychus*

die, so Dipsychus searches the newspapers to discover whether she is now "some poor corpse discovered in the Thames, / Weltering in filth or stranded on the shoals." The outcome of this search is left unknown.

Matthew Arnold called Clough "Too quick despairer" in "Thyris," but *Dipsychus* demonstrates his gift for wit and humor. Clough is a poet with a refreshingly modern voice, and his work is strongly deserving of a wider audience. BR

WHAT HAPPENED NEXT . . .

The work Clough had not published in his lifetime was gathered together by his widow Blanche in *Poems and Prose Remains* (1869). She held typically Victorian prudish views and tried to suppress works she found shocking, including *Dipsychus*. It was not until 1974 that a complete version was published in F.L. Mulhauser's edition of the *Complete Works* (Oxford University Press). Mulhauser prints an excellent account of the various drafts and manuscripts, whose richness makes it even more tantalizing that it was never finished.

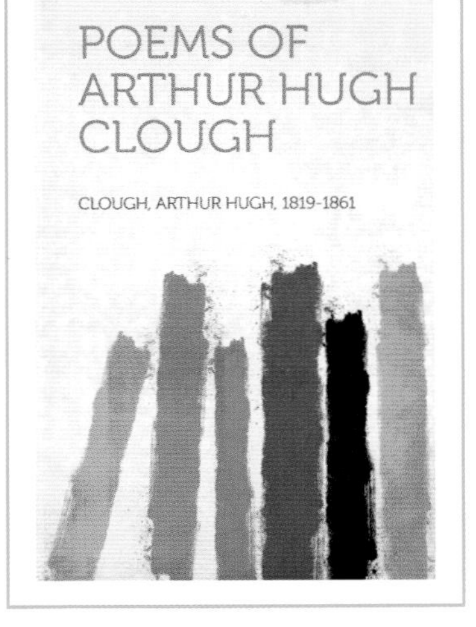

WILL IT EVER HAPPEN?

0/10

We do not know precisely where Clough was intending to take this long poem. It is hard to imagine that anyone could now manage convincingly to finish it. Clough had a curious, highly individual combination of skeptical free-thinking combined with guilt and anxiety, as well as the ability to write poetry in strict forms that also manages to sound effortless and natural. These characteristics would be very difficult for a continuator to recapture.

LA COMÉDIE HUMAINE

Author Honoré de Balzac **Year** 1851 **Country** France **Genre** Series of novels

HONORÉ DE BALZAC
Balzac's work found a vast readership and greatly influenced the development of the novel, not just in France but throughout the Western world: no one before Balzac had used this literary form to encompass so many characters and such a broad sweep of history.

Honoré de Balzac died at the relatively young age of 51, but witnessed in his lifetime an era of great change. He was born at the end of the French Revolution and lived through the Napoleonic Wars, the Restoration of the Bourbon monarchy, and the revolutions of 1830 and 1848. No wonder that his self-appointed role as "secretary of society" kept him busy. Balzac's aim with his magnum opus *La Comédie Humaine* (*The Human Comedy*) was to capture the whole of French society as he saw it, in both its splendor and its squalor. By the time of his death in 1851 the number of completed works in this sequence of novels and stories exceeded 90—and he was far from finished.

No one could accuse Balzac of doing anything by half-measures. In order to produce 90-plus works in the space of about 20 years, he spent up to 18 hours a day writing, fueled by cups of coffee. Even after delivering a script to his publisher, he would continue rewriting and reworking, making extensive, not to mention expensive, changes at page-proof stage.

Balzac's propensity toward excess spilled over into his writing style, too. His works include many lengthy descriptions, digressions, and explanations. But what he lacks in refinement, he makes up for in scale. Oscar Wilde said that "the 19th century, as we know it, is largely an invention of Balzac's." While Charles Dickens could also make some claim to this invention, Balzac was simply more ambitious. In *La Comédie Humaine*, he created more than 2,000 characters reflecting every facet of society. He pits the wealthy and privileged against thieves, moneylenders, and prostitutes, yet all of these characters are complex, often morally ambiguous. Balzac's unflinching observation of society, and his minute attention to detail, made him one of the founders of realism in European literature. The political theorist Friedrich Engels would not have shared Balzac's political views (Balzac was a reactionary and a monarchist), but commented: "I have learned more [from Balzac] than from all the professional historians, economists, and statisticians put together."

FORMING AN INTELLECTUAL CHRONICLE

Balzac believed that the French Revolution had brought about social and moral disorder, yet his own family had profited from this situation. His father had been born into a family of peasants in southwest France, but worked his

Cover: Joseph Bisat Marshall

way up from the position of clerk in a local lawyer's office to managing army supplies under the Empire and the Restoration. Balzac himself started out by studying law, but an allowance from his father when he was 20 enabled him to become a writer instead. He began his literary career by penning potboilers under various pseudonyms, and it took him almost another ten years—years in which he accrued the debts he spent the rest of his life trying to pay off—before he published his first novel under his own name, *Les Chouans* (1829), set in Brittany during the royalist counter-revolution. This eventually became the starting point for *La Comédie Humaine*.

IMPLEMENTING RECURRING CHARACTERS

Balzac wrote a Preface to the *Comédie* in 1842, by which time he had the overall structure in place. In the Preface, he claimed that the original idea had come to him "at first like a dream." This isn't true; he had not initially planned a unified work—it evolved over a number of years. The key moment came—in 1835, according to his sister—when Balzac had the idea of using recurring characters in his books. He thought that perhaps three or four thousand would be required to represent a complete society. There are, in fact, fewer characters than this in the novel cycle, but this is not to detract from Balzac's achievement, which is all the more remarkable considering that, in order to lend his work a "unity of composition," he revised his earlier books by renaming characters with names taken from later novels. There is no single, linear narrative throughout the novels; rather, the separate works form what *The New York Review of Books* calls "an interlinked chronicle."

Among the best-known novels in the *Comédie* are *Eugénie Grandet* (1833), *Père Goriot* (1835), *Illusions perdues* (*Lost Illusions*, 1837–43) and *Cousin Bette* (1846). Like many of Balzac's works, *Père Goriot* was

EUGENIE GRANDET

This illustration depicts a scene from *Eugénie Grandet* (1833), which is often considered the *Comédie*'s strongest novel. It tells the story of how everything changes in the provincial household of Grandet, an ageing miser, with the arrival of his nephew Charles from Paris. Burdened by debts, Charles's father (Grandet's brother) has taken his life and placed both his son and his debts in Grandet's care. Charles falls in love with Grandet's daughter, Eugénie, and her eventual defiance of Grandet results in tragedy. The relationship between father and daughter has some echoes of *King Lear*, and the central themes of the book—finding one's place in the world, and the role that money plays in dictating relationships—are typically Balzacian.

published first in serial form before being released as a novel. It also marked the first serious use by the author of characters who had appeared in previous books. Eugène de Rastignac, who had appeared as an old man in the philosophical novel *La Peau de chagrin* (*The Magic Skin*, 1831), features here as a naive law student, and Balzac tracks his social advancement in further novels. Among the other characters who appear in several novels are the master criminal Vautrin, the moneylender Gobseck and the lawyer Derville. Balzac's major themes include social success and the role of money in shaping social relations. He viewed human will as a source of energy that could be squandered by or stored inside an individual, and many of his characters exhaust this vital life force through self-destructive behavior. *La Comédie Humaine* is full of illicit love affairs, crime, and madness.

Similar to zoologists in the 19th century who were developing taxonomies that ordered and explained the natural world, Balzac developed his own social taxonomy by arranging his novels into three general categories:

> *"The 19th century, as we know it, is largely an invention of Balzac's."*
>
> Oscar Wilde

"Analytic Studies," which concern the principles that govern society; "Philosophical Studies," which examine the causes of human behavior; and "Studies of Manners," which show the effects of these causes. This last category was divided into six "scenes" dealing with private, provincial, Parisian, political, military, and country life. Balzac explained this structure in his Preface to the first collected edition in 1842, which was also the first time that he applied the general title to his novels. *La Comédie Humaine* is generally thought to be an allusion to *The Divine Comedy* (c. 1308–21), but whereas Dante is concerned with the afterlife, Balzac focuses on life here and now, and suggests that being virtuous doesn't always make one successful.

In 1845 Balzac compiled a catalog of his intended collection, but he was unable complete the cycle. He suffered from poor health throughout his life, which was no doubt compounded by his furious work schedule. He kept writing to fend off the bailiffs. His debts were eventually settled by his long-term lover, Eveline Hanska, when they married in 1850; Balzac died only months later. Freed from the necessity to write, would he have wanted to put down his pen? It is doubtful that he ever could have considered his work finished. **CC**

WILL IT EVER HAPPEN?

3/10 Given that Balzac was famed for rewriting his books, it is unlikely that he himself would ever have finished *La Comédie Humaine*. So if he couldn't, it's unlikely anyone else could. But one author tried: Charles Rabou cashed in on the popularity of the criminal character Vautrin by giving him prominence in the ending he applied to *The Deputy of Arcis* (1854).

WHAT HAPPENED NEXT . . .

The first collected edition of *La Comédie Humaine* appeared between 1842 and 1848. The most popular volume in the series soon became, and today remains, *Lost Illusions*. The main character of this work, Lucien de Rubempré, reappears in the subsequent volume, *The Splendors and Miseries of Courtesans*, an illustration from which is reproduced below.

DEAD SOULS

Author Nikolai Gogol **Year** 1852 **Country** Russia **Genre** Epic poem in prose

NIKOLAI GOGOL
An ardent Slavophile who believed that the tsars had been chosen by God to lead the Russian people, Gogol was dismayed when his work was widely interpreted as a veiled criticism of Nicholas I.

Russian novelist, dramatist, and short story writer Nikolai Gogol's "epic poem in prose" *Dead Souls* was first published in 1842, in its unfinished form. Despite supposedly later completing the proposed trilogy's second part, Gogol destroyed it twice, once shortly before his death, and the planned third book was never written.

EARLY LITERARY TALENT

Gogol was born and brought up in the countryside of what is now Ukraine. In 1828 at the age of 19 he went to St. Petersburg, hoping to enter the civil service or become an actor, but when neither job materialized he decided to publish at his own expense a poem he had written at school. It was a critical disaster, and he bought up and burned all the copies.

He worked in government and wrote occasionally for periodicals before catching the attention of poets Aleksandr Pushkin and Vasily Zhukovsky, autobiographer Sergey Aksakov, and critic Vissarion Belinsky with his stories based on Ukrainian folklore, intermingled with realistic contemporary incidents, published in two volumes in 1831–32 as *Evenings on a Farm near Dikanka*. Alongside work in another government post, then at a girls' boarding school and finally at St. Petersburg University, Gogol published works that juxtaposed romance with realism, humor with bitterness, and idyll with satire.

In 1836 Gogol published the short stories "The Coach" and "The Nose" in Pushkin's literary magazine *Sovremennik* (*The Contemporary*). The outrage following the first performance of his satirical comedy *The Government Inspector* on April 19, 1836 led Gogol into self-imposed exile in Rome, where he remained for six years.

After Pushkin's death in 1837, Gogol was looked to by many as the logical heir of the so-called founder of Russian literature. Indeed, Gogol wrote that Pushkin had left him the idea for the plot of *Dead Souls*. Meanwhile Gogol had become convinced that God had given him a great literary talent not only to highlight and ridicule social injustice through satire but also to instruct Russia in righteousness. It was in Rome that the author began to develop this interest in religion, which had a strong influence on his work in *Dead Souls*. As he grew more religious, he continually revised the book to nudge his hero, Pavel Ivanovich Chichikov, toward an Orthodox Christian redemption.

Cover: John Round

THE MYSTERIOUS DWARF
Gogol was an eccentric character in Russian literary history. Nicknamed the "mysterious dwarf" at school, he was known to complain that his stomach had grown in upside down. He also supposedly often went through long periods of lethargy, which led him to develop a fear that he would be mistaken for dead and buried alive. He was said to have stipulated that his coffin should have an air hole and a rope tied to a bell at ground level so that he could ring for help if he woke up in a grave. When Moscow's Danilovsky Monastery, where he was buried, was due to be demolished, Gogol's grave was dug up so that he could be moved to nearby Novodevichy Cemetery. Rumors abounded that his body was found face down, with scratch marks on the inside of the coffin lid. Whatever the truth of these stories, his gravestone is now usually found covered in candles and flowers, testament to his enduring popularity in Russia.

Gogol returned to Russia temporarily to supervise the printing of Part I of the book in 1842, published under the title *The Adventures of Chichikov* after the censor raised objections to the concept of a mortal soul.

A NEGATIVE BEGINNING

Part I of *Dead Souls* describes the adventures of the landless former civil servant Chichikov, who as the book begins is seeking his fortune by buying the names of dead serfs from landowners to relieve them of paying taxes on their deceased workers before a new census has removed them from the tax rolls, and to enable him to take out a loan against the names to create his own estate. He charms his way into the homes of several influential landowners, who each represent various stereotypical Russian character traits. Eventually, rumors begin to spread about Chichikov, and he leaves town in disgrace. At the end of Part I, we see him rushing out in his troika into the seemingly endless space of "Rus."

Gogol was said to be contemplating two further volumes to complete *Dead Souls*. He began work on Part II in 1843, but by 1845 was having deep misgivings about its content, and burned most of the manuscript. He did not work on it again for nearly three years, during which time he wrote three works of non-fiction: *Meditations on the Divine Liturgy* and *An Author's Confession* (published posthumously in 1852 and 1855 respectively), and *Selected Passages from Correspondence with Friends* (1847).

> *"Everything resembles the truth, everything can happen to a man."*
>
> Nikolai Gogol, *Dead Souls*

In the latter, he discusses his aims for Part II of *Dead Souls*, which was supposed to have been less negative than its predecessor and to provide not only a representation of Russia but also an explanation of it. The plan was for the completed book to be a kind of catechism that would save the Russian soul. Loosely based on Dante's *The Divine Comedy* (c. 1308–21), *Dead Souls* in its completed form was intended to show Chichikov redeemed and reborn as a good Christian. The already published book would represent the *Inferno* of Russian life, and the second and third parts would become its *Purgatory* and *Paradise*. Gogol also indicated in correspondence that the book was to document his own personal journey toward an Orthodox Christian understanding of spiritual perfection.

He worked on the second part of his novel for almost ten years, but was never fully satisfied with the results. He took this writer's block as a sign that God no longer wanted him to be a voice leading his countrymen to a more worthy existence. Gogol increased his prayers and ascetic practices, and began to move from place to place, including a pilgrimage to the Holy Land. He finally returned to Russia for the last time in 1848, settling in Moscow. There he continued to work on Part II, producing several chapters over the next three years, and further intensifying his interest in religion; meeting and spending much of his time with a priest, Father Matvei Konstantinovsky.

On the night of February 11, 1852, supposedly under Konstantinovsky's influence, he consigned the manuscript of Part II to the fire. The next day he began a self-imposed fast, and less than two weeks later he died, on February 21, 1852. Speculation about his madness, and rumors that he was buried alive, abounded.

REDEMPTION FOR CHICHIKOV

While Gogol almost certainly wanted to destroy the version of Part II he had created by 1845, it has been suggested that the 1852 version was burned by mistake. Neither attempt was entirely successful, with several hundred pages surviving. Both versions are usually printed in Russian editions, while English translations tend to use only what is left of the 1852 manuscript.

There are considerable differences between the two, and the surviving pages of both versions differ greatly from Part I. Chichikov continues his journey through the Russian countryside in Part II, but is more frequently absent, as other characters are allowed to take center stage. Part II is less like a "poem" than the first book, and more like a novel, with less stylistic diversity and little wordplay, and the main characters are more rounded and less caricatured. Where Gogol has presented a cutting satire of the problems in Russian society in Part I, Part II provides significantly more emphasis on how to solve them, particularly through education and religion.

In what remains of Part II, Chichikov continues with his plan, forging a will to gain the landed estate required to mortgage the dead souls, but he is discovered and arrested. He is pardoned after his lawyer defends him by interweaving the scandals of the province with his client's deeds, on the condition that he leaves town. Toward the end of Part I and in the remains of Part II, Gogol lines Chichikov up for redemption, as his hero begins to turn his main character traits, such as ambition and resourcefulness, from immoral and virtually criminal ends to more worthy ones. We can only imagine how this may have been completed in the proposed Part III.

What survives of the novel ends mid-sentence, with the prince who has arranged Chichikov's arrest giving a speech against corruption in Russian government. Just as we join *Dead Souls in medias res*, so we leave the characters there too. The book as it was left is thus not bound by the static conventions of a novel; Gogol himself called the work a "poem in prose." MJR

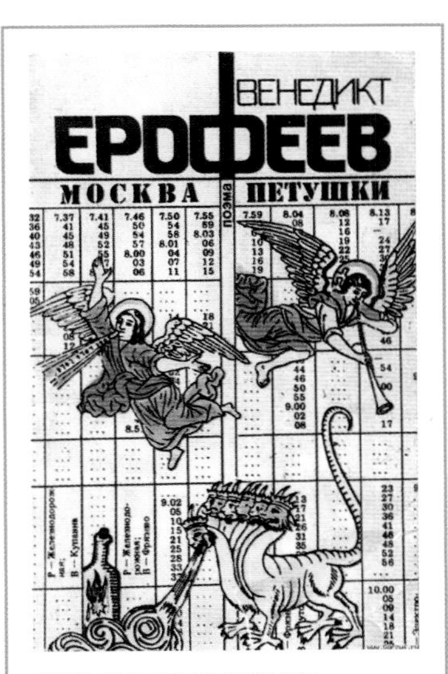

WHAT HAPPENED NEXT . . .

Fyodor Dostoevsky once famously said that all Russian realists had come "from under Gogol's overcoat." Certainly, aspects of Gogol's literary style would set trends in Russian literature long after his death. Successors to his more didactic, moralizing approach included Lev Tolstoy, Aleksandr Solzhenitsyn, and Vasily Grossman, while echoes of his irreverent, satirical, and even mocking tone are evident in the work of Mikhail Bulgakov, Daniil Kharms, and Venedikt Yerofeyev, whose 1969 novel *Moscow-Petushki* (above) was, in a direct nod to *Dead Souls*, subtitled a "poem in prose."

WILL IT EVER HAPPEN?

1/10

In her book *Designing Dead Souls* (1993), Susanne Fusso suggested that Gogol only planned to continue his novel with a second and third part if his readers enjoyed Part I, and that it was a specific strategy on his part to create demand for more by breaking off the story unexpectedly. Many critics have claimed that the book is better for ending where it does, implying that any posthumous continuation would be unnecessary.

THE ISLE OF THE CROSS

Author Herman Melville **Year** 1853 **Country** United States **Genre** Short story or novel

HERMAN MELVILLE
Melville's reputation, almost negligible in his lifetime, was revived 30 years after his death by a sympathetic biography, praise from D.H. Lawrence in *Studies in Classic American Literature* (1923), and finally by the posthumous publication of his novella *Billy Budd* (1924).

Melville's "The Isle of the Cross" is an elusive and shadowy work. It is not completely certain that it ever even existed. It was first mooted as a possible unpublished and lost work in 1990 by Melville's biographer, Hershel Parker, in *American Literature.* He suggested that the work, either a novel or a short story, was what had been known as the "story of Agatha," completed around May 22, 1853, after the commercial failures of *Moby-Dick* (1851) and *Pierre: or, The Ambiguities* (1852). If it was written, it would have represented a new direction in Melville's oeuvre because, unlike almost all his previous fiction, it would have had a female central character.

SOURCE MATERIAL

If it came about at all, it is thought by some to have done so in the following way. On a visit to Nantucket in July 1852, John H. Clifford—a New Bedford lawyer, state attorney general, and friend of Melville's father-in-law Lemuel Shaw—told Melville the story of Agatha Hatch Robertson, a local woman who had cared for a shipwrecked sailor named Robertson. They married, but Robertson later abandoned his wife and their daughter, only to return 17 years later and then abandon them once again and be exposed as a bigamist. In a subsequent letter to his friend Nathaniel Hawthorne, author of *The Scarlet Letter* (1850), Melville described "the great patience and endurance and resignedness of the women of the island in submitting so uncomplainingly to the long, long absences of their sailor husbands," and urged Hawthorne to adopt this "little idea."

Hawthorne did not take up the idea, however, although the story was close to his interests. This is probably because he had already treated something like it twice: in "Wakefield," about a Londoner who leaves his wife, but lives near her secretly for 20 years before resuming the marriage, and in "Young Goodman Brown," which is about witchcraft and mental alienation. Both these stories were published in *Twice-Told Tales* (1837).

So it is plausible that Hawthorne would not have wanted to write another work in similar vein. And it seems at least equally likely that Melville would not have wanted to go over similar ground either, although the image of Agatha Hatch Robertson could have inspired him with the idea of the redoubtable

Cover: John Round

ABSENT HUSBANDS
Stories of separation can be traced back to Homer's *Odyssey* (c.700 BCE), in which the faithful Penelope waits for the return of Odysseus (their reunion is depicted in *Odysseus and Penelope* [c.1563] by Francesco Primaticcio, near right). The absent husband seems to have been a popular and intriguing motif in the 19th century, as found in Tennyson's poem *Enoch Arden* (1864). Recent examples of the theme include the French movie *Le Retour de Martin Guerre* (*The Return of Martin Guerre*, 1982) and its US remake *Sommersby* (1993).

female as a suitable protagonist for a work of his own. Certainly, he indicated in a further letter to Hawthorne that he was interested in pursuing the idea.

Correspondence among the Melville family in 1853 makes several references to a narrative that Herman was working on called "The Isle of the Cross," which may have been his treatment of the Agatha story. In May Melville's cousin Priscilla wrote to his sister Augusta to ask "When will the 'Isle of the Cross' make its appearance? I am constantly looking in the journals and magazines that come my way, for notices of it." In June of that year Melville made a trip to New York to visit his publisher Harper's. It is not known exactly what happened to the manuscript that he took with him, but in a letter to Harper's written five months later, Melville makes reference to "the work which I took to New York last Spring, but which I was prevented from printing at that time." His use of the word "prevented" suggests that there was some sort of barrier to publication, rather than a straightforward rejection of the manuscript by the publisher. If this work was the Agatha story, it is possible that Harper's were concerned about legal action from the real-life figures who inspired the tale.

TYPEE
Melville learned all about being a castaway at first hand when he jumped ship in the Marquesas Islands. His adventures are written up in *Typee* (1846), from which this illustration is taken.

ALTERNATIVE ACCOUNT

However, a number of scholars do not accept this version of the background to the story at all. Dissenters instead argue that "The Isle of the Cross" is probably one of the now lost manifestations of "Norfolk Isle and the Chola Widow." This Melville story—about the Peruvian Hunilla, an imagined female Robinson Crusoe, who was stranded on Norfolk Island in the South Pacific Ocean until rescued—was one of the ten sketches in the novella *The Encanatadas or Enchanted Isles*, first published in *Putnam's Magazine* (1854) and later collected in *Piazza Tales* (1856).

The fantastic spirit of Edmund Spenser's "Wandering Islands" in *The Faerie Queene* (1590 and 1596; see p.24) hovers over this collection. Certainly the story of the stranded woman fits the bill of the depiction of a heroic woman, and seems a very likely possibility. Hunilla, her husband Felipe, and her brother Truxill become stranded on the island while hunting tortoises, after their ferry fails to return for them. Both men are drowned when they attempt to go fishing on a raft, and she is left living alone for years.

The description of the husband's grave strengthens the suggestion that "The Isle of the Cross" concerns this story:

> "Doubtless it was by half-unconscious, automatic motions of her hands that this heavy-hearted one performed the final office for Felipe, and planted a rude cross of withered sticks—no green ones might be had—at the head of that lonely grave, where rested now in lasting uncomplaint and quiet haven he whom the untranqil seas had overthrown."

The final image possibly underlines it too: the rescued castaway riding on a donkey whose back exhibits the shape of the cross, in honor of Christ who rode such an animal on his triumphal entry into Jerusalem in Passion Week:

> "The last seen of lone Hunilla she was passing into Payta town, riding upon a small gray ass; and before her on the ass's shoulders, she eyed the jointed workings of the beast's armorial cross."

" . . . before her on the ass's shoulders she eyed the jointed workings of the beast's armorial cross."

"Norfolk Isle and the Chola Widow"

Melville probably derived the story from the narrative of one Juana Maria, who was briefly famous as the "Female Crusoe" on San Nicolas, the most remote of California's Channel Islands. She chose voluntary abandonment on the island, her husband returning to the mainland when the island was evacuated, and took on an animal existence. It was printed in the Boston *Atlas* on January 7, 1847.

Melville, although a popular, or, at least, revered author today, was not recognized in his lifetime, during which he made his living mainly as a sailor, teacher, and customs inspector. "The Isle of the Cross" is just one more example of a work of his that never made it into the public domain—if it ever existed at all. BR

WHAT HAPPENED NEXT . . .

It is not entirely certain, *pace* Hershel Parker, that the manuscript that Melville was "prevented" from publishing was in fact "The Isle of the Cross." It is possible that the work Harper's rejected was the ghost-written *Scenes and Adventures in the Army* (the army memoir of Philip St. George Cooke), since there were copyright problems. Neither such story in manuscript has been found so speculation continues.

The novel *The Secret of Lost Things* (2007) by Sheridan Hay, features a character, Walter Geist, who is secretly purchasing the original manuscript of *The Isle of the Cross*. In this story *The Isle of the Cross* is regarded as the Agatha Hatch Robertson story.

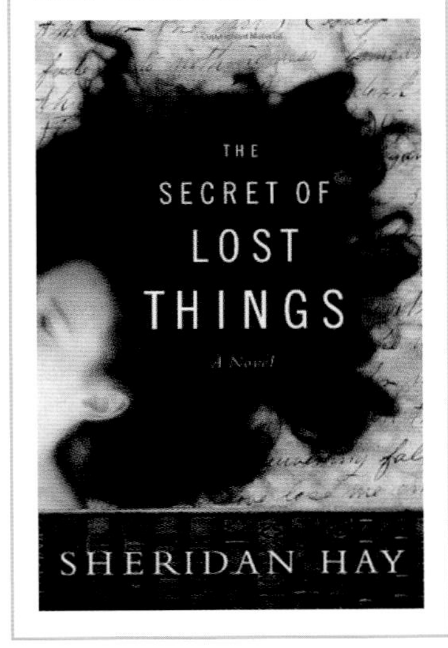

WILL IT EVER HAPPEN ?

1/10

It is very unlikely that the manuscript will turn up. If "The Isle of the Cross" was indeed directly related to "Norfolk Isle and the Chula Widow," which is highly possible, then it is not after all entirely lost, and does not need writing—it is written already. In terms of a continuation, it would be extremely difficult to imitate Melville's quirky, rhapsodic, over-the-top style. And where would be found an author who could satisfactorily get inside his mind, and harness his knowledge of English and other literatures? No one has attempted to complete, or begin even, this story or novel.

THE POOR MAN AND THE LADY

Author Thomas Hardy **Year** 1868 **Country** England **Genre** Novel

THOMAS HARDY
The author was born and raised in southwest England, an area which he memorably evoked in the finest works of his maturity. Although a great novelist, he regarded himself—and is today regarded by many critics—as primarily a poet.

Thomas Hardy's first novel, *The Poor Man and the Lady*, was composed in 1867–68. At the time of writing Hardy was engaged in architectural work with John Hicks, Arthur Blomfield, and George R. Crickmay in Weymouth, Dorset; he had entered the architectural profession as an apprentice at the age of 16. One of his projects was the restoration (or some would argue destruction) of St. Juliot's Church in Cornwall, and it was on this assignment that he met his wife Emma Gifford in 1870.

After sending the completed novel to several publishers who all rejected it, in 1869 Hardy took the manuscript to Chapman and Hall (renowned in the annals of publishing for having rejected the best seller *East Lynne* by Mrs. Henry Wood). They agreed to publish it if Hardy would guarantee £20 against any losses that it might make. However, the manuscript was subsequently read by the novelist George Meredith (*The Ordeal of Richard Feverel*, 1859; *The Egoist*, 1879), working on behalf of Chapman and Hall, who advised both parties against pursuing the project. He suggested to Hardy that he write a more shapely and less opinionated novel that would be better received by critics. The result was the densely plotted *Desperate Remedies* (1871), influenced by the contemporary sensationalist school of authors such as Mrs. Wood and Wilkie Collins in *The Woman in White* (1859).

REWORKING IN PROSE

The story of *The Poor Man and the Lady* concerned the love and marriage of a young architect and the daughter of a large local landowner. In his autobiography, *The Early Life of Thomas Hardy, 1840–91* (1928), Hardy described the novel as: "a sweeping dramatic satire of the squirearchy and nobility, London society, the vulgarity of the middle class, modern Christianity, church restoration, and political and domestic morals in general." He admits to "the tendency of the writing being socialistic and revolutionary," so it is perhaps unsurprising that Meredith thought that the novel would prove controversial to a Victorian audience.

Hardy probably recycled some of the rejected material in *Desperate Remedies* and in the novella *An Indiscretion in the Life of an Heiress* (1878). *An Indiscretion*—which records the love affair of a low-born young man, Egbert Mayne, and an aristocratic lady, Geraldine Allenville—certainly covers

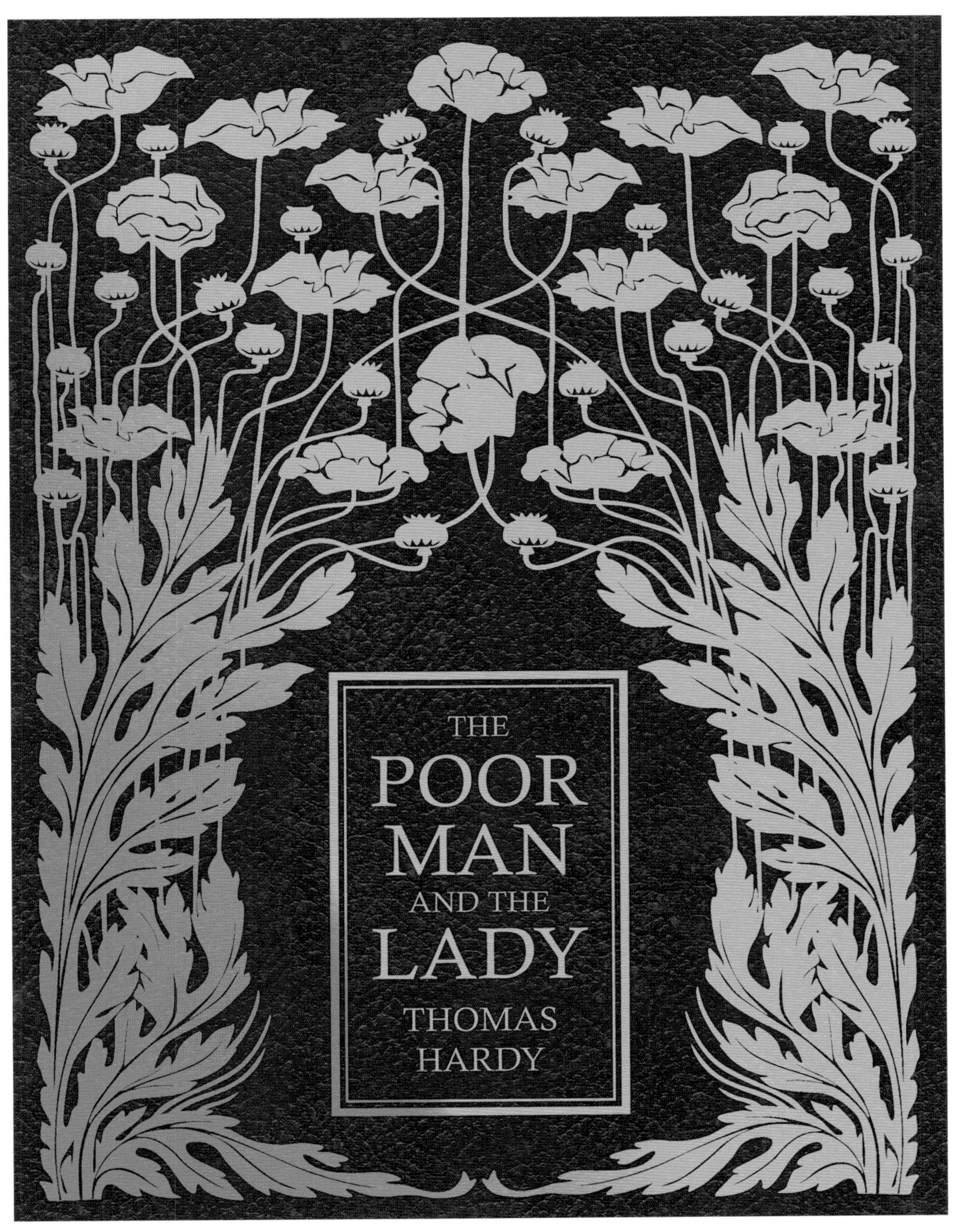

Cover: Steve Panton

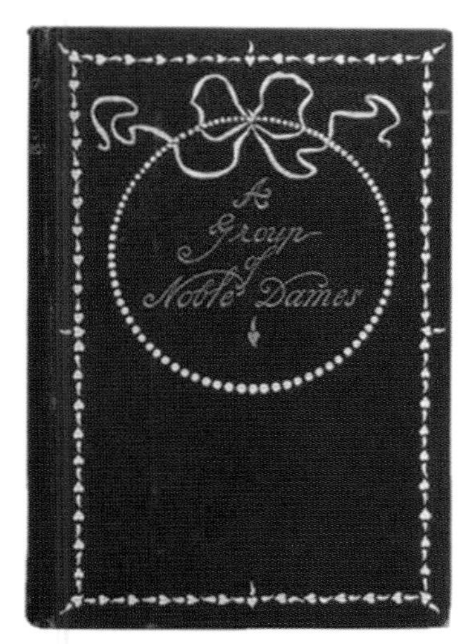

HARDY AND HIGH-BORN LADIES
Late in life Hardy tended to have crushes on high-born ladies. One such was Florence Henniker, daughter of Richard Monckton Milnes, Lord Houghton, and sister of the Lord Lieutenant of Ireland. Although Hardy wasn't poor by then, nothing would remove the fact of having been lowly born. She is probably the "one fair woman" of "Wessex Heights" (1896). Hardy's fascination with aristocratic ladies is also on display in the collection *A Group of Noble Dames* (1891).

a very similar theme, giving us glimpses of what might have been in the lost novel. The pair fall in love when young, but during a period of separation they drift apart and their class differences become accentuated.

In chapter 3, Egbert goes round to Geraldine's London house for a meeting, after they encounter each other at a performance of Handel's *Messiah*, but she does not see him, and slips a letter under the front door. The letter expresses the differences between them that have grown up over the years, and must be similar to the situation that probably existed in *The Poor Man and the Lady*:

> "It is well for you now to remember that I am not the unsophisticated girl I was when you first knew me. For better or for worse I have become complicated, exclusive and practised. A woman who can speak, or laugh, or dance, or sing before any number of men with perfect composure may be no sinner, but she is not what I was once. She is what I am now. She is not the girl you loved. That woman is not here."

In *The Poor Man and the Lady* the separation was probably final, but in *The Indiscretion in the Life of an Heiress* it is not. Egbert and Geraldine elope, and after overcoming the typical Hardyesque difficulties of getting a marriage licence, they marry. Characteristically, however, Hardy cannot allow extended happiness, and Geraldine dies after a seizure brought on by a fraught meeting with her father.

Feelings of class difference were central to life in Victorian England. Hardy, who was the son of a stonemason and jobbing builder, would have been acutely aware of them. He himself married a woman from a higher social background, and both families objected to the marriage. His wife's brother-in-

CLASS DIFFERENCES IN VICTORIAN ENGLAND
There is a very good scene in *The Indiscretion in the Life of an Heiress* in which class differences are made concretely vivid. Geraldine Allenville is laying the foundation stone of a tower on her estate and gets mortar stuck on her glove. "'Take it, take it, will you?' she impatiently whispered to Egbert." This seems to be a fictionalized version of an incident involving Queen Victoria's daughter the Crown Princess of Germany (right), wife of the Crown Prince, who later became the Emperor Frederick III (left). It happened while the princess was laying a foundation at All Saints' church in New Windsor, designed by Hardy's employer Arthur Blomfield in brutal new Gothic style: "Blomfield handed her the trowel, and during the ceremony she got her glove daubed with the mortar. In her distress she handed the trowel back to him with an impatient whisper of 'Take it, take it!'"

Another class difference is highlighted when Geraldine asks how far it is to a town. Egbert says "about two hours." She replies, "Two hours to drive 8 miles—who ever heard of such a thing!" He is thinking in terms of walking; she in terms of riding in a carriage.

law was related to Francis Henry Jeune, Lord St. Helier, son of the Bishop of Peterborough, and it can be imagined that in any marital recriminations such a humiliating fact would feature prominently.

REWRITING IN VERSE

Many years after he abandoned the novel, Hardy published a volume of poetry called *Human Shows, Far Phantasies, Songs and Trifles* (1925), which contains a work entitled "A Poor Man and a Lady." It tells the story of a working man who goes through an informal, private, and invalid marriage with a high-born lady. The lady, however, becomes properly engaged to an aristocrat. They meet in a Mayfair church and the lady speaks frankly to the poor man, casting a disillusioning light over the whole affair: "He'll be, anon, / My husband *really*. You, Dear, weren't so". And so they separate:

> "Do you recall the bell
> That tolled by chance as we said good-bye? . . .
> I saw you no more. The track of a high,
> Sweet, liberal lady you've doubtless trod.
> —All's past! No heart was burst thereby,
> And no one knew, unless it was God."

This ending is a very Hardyesque moment: the bell tolling not to celebrate a real marriage but the end of a sham one. A "satire of circumstance" he might have called it. The end of the poem is followed by a note from the author: "The foregoing was intended to preserve an episode in the story of 'The Poor Man and the Lady,' written in 1868, and, like these lines, in the first person; but never printed, and ultimately destroyed."

"I am not the unsophisticated girl I was when you first knew me."

The Indiscretion in the Life of an Heiress

Hardy subsequently spurned an opportunity to save his rejected manuscript (see right). Although readers may regret the loss, authors are commonly reluctant to expose their recycling stratagems to the unsympathetic eye of the public. Cutting and pasting one's own work is thought to be almost as bad as doing likewise with other people's. BR

WILL IT EVER HAPPEN?

It is not likely that anyone will satisfactorily be able to produce a version of this lost novel, since the plot outlined in the poem is extremely shadowy. However, Hardy does at least tell us that the lost novel was in autobiographical form, and it is possible that the sad scene in the Mayfair church was included. There have been a number of writers able to imitate Hardy's prose style, beginning with H.F. Lester's "A Rustic Zenobia" in *Ben D'Ymion* (1887), so it is feasible that an author could be found.

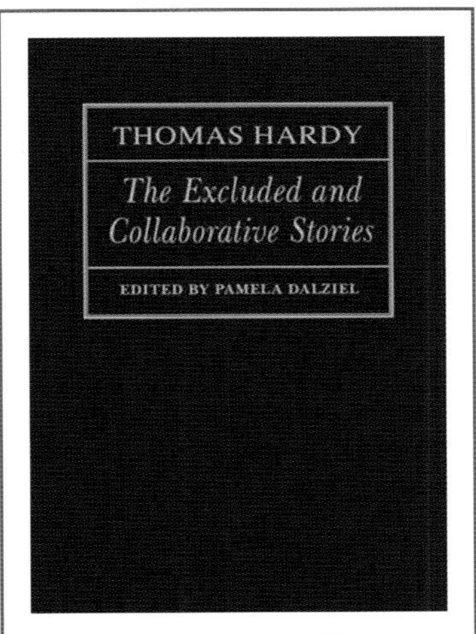

WHAT HAPPENED NEXT . . .

The abandoned manuscript of *The Poor Man and a Lady* survived, and the bibliophile and cultivated man of letters Sydney Cockerell (who became one of Hardy's literary executors) had it beautifully bound. He presented it to Hardy in 1917, but the novelist disbound it and burned it. The full story is told by Pamela Dalziel in *Thomas Hardy: The Excluded and Collaborative Stories* (1992). Hardy appears to have had similar negative feelings toward *An Indiscretion in the Life of an Heiress* (1878), which he would not allow to be reprinted in his lifetime. Even now the novella is not easy to find.

THE MYSTERY OF EDWIN DROOD

Author Charles Dickens **Year** 1870 **Country** England **Genre** Novel

CHARLES DICKENS
More popular in his own lifetime than any previous author, Dickens retains universal appeal today. His greatest strengths were his social conscience—he was among the most compassionate of writers in English—and his humor.

An unsolved crime is perhaps the most tantalizing type of story that can be found in the body of unfinished literature. Charles Dickens's *The Mystery of Edwin Drood* has been intriguing readers for almost 150 years. The obsessives who have tried to solve its puzzle have even been given their own nickname: Droodians. When Dickens died on June 9, 1870, he had published six episodes and there were six more to go. As was the case with much serial publication in the 19th century, the author was composing as the numbers came out.

Edwin Drood represents something of a change for Dickens, because there is a murder at the heart of the plot. It is possible that Dickens was rising to the challenge posed by the up-and-coming novelist Wilkie Collins, whose *The Woman in White* (1860) and *The Moonstone* (1868) inaugurated the new tradition of sensationalist crime novels.

SINISTER EVOCATIONS

The story is set in Cloisterham, which bears a heightened resemblance to Rochester in Kent, the town closest to Dickens's house at Gad's Hill. It has a vivid opening in a London opium den, written, like much of the novel, in the present tense and taking us into the nightmarish consciousness of the character:

> "An ancient English Cathedral Tower? How can the ancient English Cathedral tower be here! The well-known massive gray square tower of its old Cathedral? How can that be here! There is no spike of rusty iron in the air, between the eye and it, from any point of the real prospect.
>
> "What is the spike that intervenes, and who has set it up? Maybe it is set up by the Sultan's orders for the impaling of a horde of Turkish robbers, one by one. It is so, for cymbals clash, and the Sultan goes by to his palace in long procession. Ten thousand scimitars flash in the sunlight, and thrice ten thousand dancing-girls strew flowers. Then, follow white elephants caparisoned in countless gorgeous colors, and infinite in number and attendants. Still the Cathedral Tower rises in the background, where it cannot be, and still no writhing figure is on the grim

Cover: Joseph Bisat Marshall

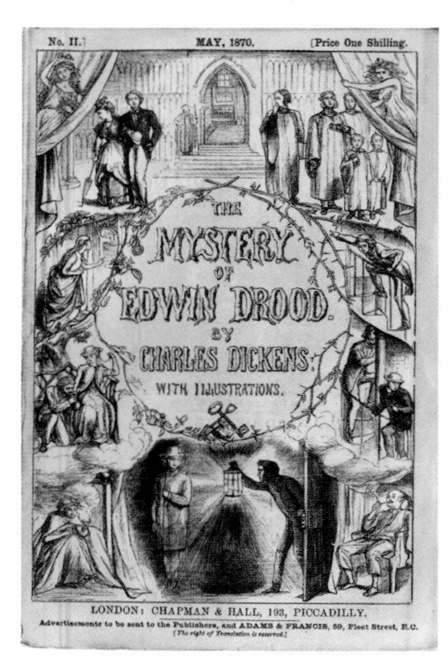

ILLUSTRATIONS

The wrapper for the serial (above) was by the Pre-Raphaelite painter Charles Allston Collins, Dickens's son-in-law and Wilkie Collins's brother. The internal illustrations (opposite) were drawn by Luke Fildes.

> spike. Stay! Is the spike so low a thing as the rusty spike on the top of a post of an old bedstead that has tumbled all awry? Some vague period of drowsy laughter must be devoted to the consideration of this possibility.
>
> "Shaking from head to foot, the man whose scattered consciousness has thus fantastically pieced itself together, at length rises, supports his trembling frame upon his arms, and looks around."

This extraordinary start makes for a striking departure from Dickens's style.

NARRATIVE IMBROGLIO

Although the novel is named after the character Edwin Drood, the story concentrates on Drood's uncle, the choirmaster John Jasper, who is in love with his pupil, Drood's fiancée Rosa Bud. Rosa has also captured the attention of Neville Landless, who is tutored by Mr. Crisparkle. He and his sister, Helena, take an instant dislike to Drood, who later disappears in mysterious circumstances. The suspicion is that John Jasper has murdered him. Jasper visits Rosa at the Nuns' House and professes his love for her. She rejects him, but he is persistent, and makes the threat that if she will give him no hope he will destroy Neville. It is then that Drood disappears.

> *"I laid aside the fancy I told you of, and have a very curious and new idea for my new story."*
>
> Charles Dickens, letter to John Forster

In fear of Jasper, Rosa goes to her guardian, the lawyer Mr. Grewgious in London. She also meets Mr. Tartar. A character called Dick Datchery descends on Cloisterham to spy on Jasper.

In the final scene, Jasper visits the London opium den again for the first time since Edwin's disappearance. When he leaves at dawn, the woman who runs it, "Princess Puffer," follows him. She vows to herself that she will not lose his trail again as she did after his last visit. This time she follows him all the way to his home in Cloisterham; outside she meets Mr. Datchery, who tells her Jasper will be singing the next morning in the cathedral service. She attends the service and shakes her fists at Jasper from behind a pillar. And there it ends.

WHO WOULD HAVE DONE IT?

There has been much controversy about where the story should go next, but there is firm evidence from Dickens himself, who outlined the plot to his friend and biographer John Forster, who reports that the novelist told him:

> "I laid aside the fancy I told you of, and have a very curious and new idea for my new story. Not a communicable idea (or the interest of the book would be gone), but a very strong one, though difficult to work."

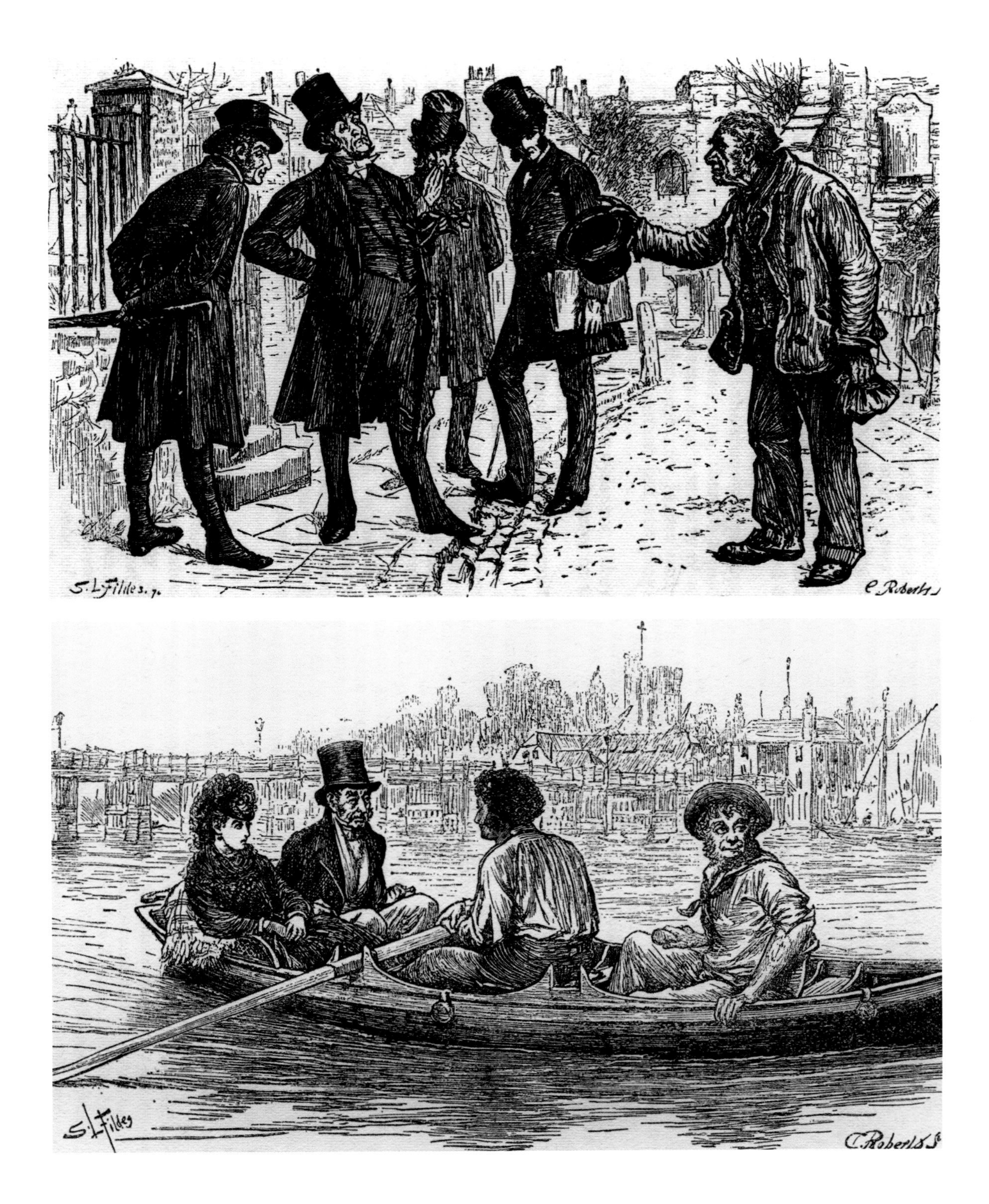
S.L. Fildes
C. Roberts
S.L. Fildes
C. Roberts

ELLEN TERNAN
Deception and evasion were haunting Dickens at the end of his life, when he was conducting a secret affair with the actress Ellen Lawless Ternan. So secret was it that after being involved in a railway accident with Ellen he did not attend the inquest in case witnesses put two and two together. It is even possible that Dickens's final collapse just before his death was not at Gad's Hill, as the official story has it, but at Ellen Ternan's lodgings in Linden Grove, Nunhead. In the more extreme versions of the myth, he died in Nunhead and his corpse was transported to Gad's Hill.

Forster continues:

> "The story, I learned immediately afterward, was to be that of the murder of a nephew by his uncle; the originality of which was to consist in the review of the murderer's career by himself at the close, when its temptations were to be dwelt upon as if, not he the culprit, but some other man, were the tempted. The last chapters were to be written in the condemned cell, to which his wickedness, all elaborately elicited from him as if told of another, had brought him. Discovery by the murderer of the utter needlessness of the murder for its object, was to follow hard upon commission of the deed; but all discovery of the murderer was to be baffled till towards the close, when, by means of a gold ring which had resisted the corrosive effects of the lime into which he had thrown the body, not only the person murdered was to be identified but the locality of the crime and the man who committed it. So much was told to me before any of the book was written; and it will be recollected that the ring, taken by Drood to be given to his betrothed only if their engagement went on, was brought away with him from their last interview. Rosa was to marry Tartar, and Crisparkle the sister of Landless, who was himself, I think, to have perished in assisting Tartar finally to unmask and seize the murderer."

"The story . . . was to be that of the murder of a nephew by his uncle."
John Forster

Dickens also told the illustrator Luke Fildes: "I must have the double necktie! It is necessary, for Jasper strangles Edwin Drood with it."

THE TRIAL OF JOHN JASPER
A curious example of literary afterlife occurred in 1914 when there was a dramatized trial in London organized by the Dickens Fellowship and G.K. Chesterton, creator of fictional priest-detective Father Brown. John Jasper (played by Frederick T. Harry) was tried for the murder of Edwin Drood. George Bernard Shaw (right) was the foreman of the jury, made up of other writers, including J. Cuming Walters, who had investigated the case in *The Complete Edwin Drood* (1905); W.W. Jacobs (author of the celebrated horror story "The Monkey's Paw," 1902); and Hilaire Belloc, of *Cautionary Tales* (1907) fame.

Shaw said that if the prosecution believed that the case relied on evidence, then he had no idea how juries function. The proceedings lasted four and a half hours, at the end of which the jury returned a verdict of manslaughter, Shaw stating that it was a compromise on the grounds that there was not enough evidence to convict Jasper but that they did not want to run the risk of being murdered in their beds. Both sides protested and demanded that the jury be discharged. Chesterton ruled that the mystery of Edwin Drood was insoluble and fined everyone, except himself, for contempt of court.

WHAT HAPPENED NEXT . . .
Playwrights and theater companies have mounted versions of *The Mystery of Edwin Drood* with varying degrees of popularity and faithfulness to the original work. An American musical (1985) with lyrics by Rupert Holmes won five Tonys and was revived in London in 2012. In literature, Matthew Pearl's *The Last Dickens* (2009) offers a fictionalized account of events after Dickens's death related to his unfinished novel. To date, there have been four film adaptations of *The Mystery of Edwin Drood*: the first two were silent pictures released in 1909 and 1914, followed by versions in 1935 and 1993 (right). A 2012 BBC television adaptation featured an original ending by Gwyneth Hughes, in which Jasper murders his father—who turns out to be Edwin Drood, Sr.

In addition to the existing text there are five pages of stray manuscript discovered by Forster called "The Sapsea Fragment," which may or may not have been intended for inclusion.

Almost immediately after Dickens's death, attempts were made to "finish" *The Mystery of Edwin Drood*, and they have continued ever since. The first three were by Americans. Robert Henry Newell's effort, published under the pen name Orpheus C. Kerr in 1870, was a burlesque rather than a continuation, transposing the story to the United States. The second, by Henry Morford, a New York journalist, was *John Jasper's Secret: Sequel to Charles Dicken's Mystery of Edwin Drood*. The third attempt, by Thomas James, claimed that it was literally "ghost-written" by Dickens's spirit. A sensation was created, with several critics, including Arthur Conan Doyle, more gullible than he should have been, actually believing in it. More recently there have been Leon Garfield's *The Mystery of Edwin Drood* (1980), Charles Forsyte's *The Decoding of Edwin Drood* (1980), and David Madden's completion (2011). BR

WILL IT EVER HAPPEN?

7/10

Doubtless many others will attempt to complete *Edwin Drood*. The continuators have to produce a plausible plot, and they also have to manage a passable imitation of Dickens's language and the curious psychological world he lived in. The problem is that, since the novel is to some extent a murder mystery, the trajectory of the plot will never be easy to determine. False clues are just one aspect of the genre. If *Great Expectations* (1861) were only half completed it would be impossible to connect up Estella and Pip's benefactor Magwitch, since most people reading it share Pip's belief that the source of his wealth is Miss Havisham. Just one of the many questions is whether Drood was in fact murdered, so that the issue is not just whodunit, but what was dun in the first place.

BOUVARD ET PÉCUCHET

Author Gustave Flaubert **Year** 1880 **Country** France **Genre** Novel

GUSTAVE FLAUBERT
Born and raised in Rouen, Flaubert then went to Paris to study law. Liking neither the city nor the subject, he returned to Normandy and devoted his life to literature.

Legend has it that Gustave Flaubert was so precise about the choice of vocabulary in his novels that he wrote only five words an hour. He was, however, prolific in his correspondence, and from his letters we know that his last novel, unfinished at his death in 1880, occupied his thoughts for at least eight years.

In 1872 Flaubert wrote to the literary salonist Edma Roger des Genettes that he was "contemplating something in which I'll vent all my anger." This was to be *Bouvard et Pécuchet*, a tale in which—according to Mark Polizzotti, the translator of a modern edition of the novel—Flaubert displays his "legendary intolerance for stupidity and the rigid bourgeois mentality." Such loathing often found expression in Flaubert's letters. Writing to Madame des Genettes in 1875, he railed: "Human stupidity is a bottomless abyss."

It was two years after first mentioning the novel that Flaubert began writing, and the process did not prove easy. He broke off part way through to write *Three Tales* (1877), seemingly disheartened both by the amount of research required for *Bouvard et Pécuchet* and by his personal circumstances. His mother, with whom he had lived for many years, had died in 1872, and he was dismayed by the political situation in France, where there were revolts following the Franco-Prussian War of 1870. He was also beset by money worries after selling his farm in Normandy in a bid to save his niece and her husband from financial ruin. All this contributed to Flaubert's somber state of mind in his final years, which in turn is reflected by the blackness that underlies this deceptively light farcical tale, originally titled "The Story of Two Nobodies."

A MEETING OF LIKE MINDS

Bouvard and Pécuchet are two middle-aged copy clerks who meet on a bench in Paris and strike up a conversation after noticing that they both write their names in their hats. They discover that they have much in common, and soon become inseparable. When Bouvard inherits wealth from his uncle, they buy a house and move to the country, where they believe they will have time to study and indulge their shared interests.

The two friends tend the garden of their new home and, pleased with the results of their labor, decide to take up farming. There begins a string of

BOUVARD
ET PÉCUCHET

GUSTAVE FLAUBERT

Cover: Steve Panton

DICTIONARY OF ACCEPTED IDEAS

In 1850 Flaubert wrote a "Dictionary of Accepted Ideas," an index of popular bourgeois opinions, with the aim that "once someone has read it he will no longer dare to open his mouth, for fear of coming out with one of the statements it contains." Flaubert's social commentary still has relevance today—for example, he says of "celebrity": "Concern yourself with the slightest detail of celebrities' private lives, then denigrate them." According to Flaubert's notes, the first ten chapters of *Bouvard et Pécuchet* were meant to form only half of the book; the second half was to comprise the Dictionary in updated form and other pastiches. Some of his notes also indicate that Bouvard and Pécuchet are copying out the Dictionary at the end of novel—a sign of possible enlightenment.

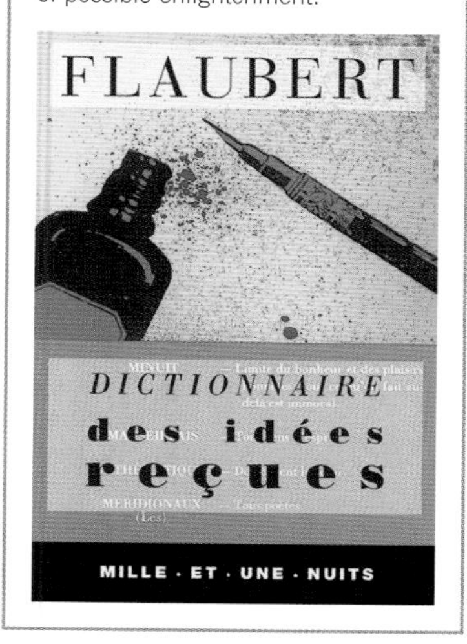

failures, and with each failure these autodidacts plunge straight into their next pursuit: they move from agriculture to the natural sciences, then archaeology, history, literature, politics, love, philosophy, religion, and finally education. But everything they attempt goes wrong. In a review of the novel in *The New York Times* in 2006, author Christopher Hitchens claims that this "undynamic duo" anticipates the lead characters of the movie *Dumb and Dumber* (1994). Having started out in a profession in which they are not paid to think, only to have good handwriting, they illustrate perfectly the famous saying that a little learning can be a dangerous thing.

In a bid to improve their minds, Flaubert's protagonists tackle each new discipline by reading books on the subject, consulting experts, conducting experiments, and undertaking expeditions. They expect to become instant masters of each subject, with definitive answers at their fingertips, and when they fail they simply move on to the next thing that takes their fancy.

> *"One would have to be insane, completely deranged to take on such a book."*
>
> Gustave Flaubert

Flaubert satirizes the acquisition of knowledge and what was, at that time, a seemingly unfailing belief in the power of science and industry. With Bouvard and Pécuchet, he suggests that any endeavor to improve the human lot is a waste of time. But he is equally merciless in his depiction of other characters, such as local officials, members of the clergy, and other villagers. As much as he detests stupidity, he abhors lazy thinking, as in the case of the priest who rejects any point of view other than that of the Church.

ASPIRING TO COMEDY

At the outset, Flaubert said he would "aspire to comedy" in the novel, but he took his research very seriously. In order for his protagonists to pursue a wide range of subjects, he devoured books on such unfamiliar disciplines as anatomy and chemistry. In August 1873 he told Madame des Genettes that since the previous September he had read and made notes on 194 books. He confided to her: "One would have to be insane, completely deranged . . . to take on such a book." By the time he finished his research, he claimed to have consulted 1,500 volumes.

Even after such thorough preparations, Flaubert lost some confidence in his writing. He told fellow novelist Émile Zola: "There are no brilliant scenes, just the same situation over and over. I'm scared it might bore people to death." On the book's posthumous publication in 1881, reviews were lukewarm. Hitchens comments that one problem is that we can see what is about to go wrong a mile off: "No sooner have our clowns embarked on a project than we see the bucket of whitewash or the banana skin." However, others have argued that such repetition intensifies the cumulative comic effect: part of the fun is in the anticipation.

WHAT HAPPENED NEXT . . .
Caroline Commanville, Flaubert's niece, became the guardian of the author's papers on his death. She was responsible for the first edition of *Bouvard et Pécuchet* (left), but has a generally poor reputation among Flaubert scholars, partly on account of her attempts to sanitize her uncle's image by censoring publication of his correspondence. However, she kept most of his manuscripts intact, and they were auctioned off only after her death in 1931. The first English language edition of *Bouvard et Pécuchet* appeared in 1896, 15 years after the publication of the original. Today it is more admired than read, and its popularity lags way behind that of Flaubert's greatest novels—*Madame Bovary* (1857) and *Sentimental Education* (1869).

While it is easy to characterize Bouvard and Pécuchet as buffoons, the novel is also a reflection on enduring friendship, and this saves it from being pure satire. This friendship survives even a failed suicide pact, and notes indicate that Flaubert intended to end the story with the two clerks back at their desks, contentedly copying out papers.

To a certain extent, Flaubert builds his novel on clichés—what the characters say, what they read in the reference works they consult. This is underlined by the fact that his protagonists are copy clerks and even when they take up different disciplines, they are still copyists, trying to put into practice what they read. He planned to extend the work with a "Dictionary of Accepted Ideas," a list of clichéd definitions that reflected bourgeois opinions.

Flaubert may have had concerns about the repetition in his novel—instead of a strong linear narrative, he adopts a structure in which the characters repeat themselves in most chapters and (had the book been completed) end up where they started—but in challenging the conventions of storytelling, and by putting two antiheroes at the center of his story, he may be said to have created the first work of modern literature, and in so doing to have influenced the work of James Joyce and Samuel Beckett. CC

WILL IT EVER HAPPEN?

7/10

The first edition, with ten chapters, was published in March 1881, based on some 4,000 manuscript pages compiled by Flaubert's niece Caroline. In places she rewrote or added to the original text. The most recent English edition (2005) contains nine complete chapters, an incomplete tenth one, two brief chapters of concluding notes, and addenda that Flaubert intended to include—the "Dictionary of Accepted Ideas" and the outline of a "Catalog of Fashionable Ideas." So in a sense it remains a work in progress.

PRAETERITA

Author John Ruskin **Year** 1889 **Country** England **Genre** Autobiography

JOHN RUSKIN
A distinguished art critic and a distinctive prose stylist, Ruskin altered Victorian aesthetic perception in his two greatest completed works—*The Seven Lamps of Architecture* (1849) and *The Stones of Venice* (1851–53). His influence is even greater today than it was during his lifetime.

John Ruskin's *Praeterita* is the major unfinished project of his life. Considered by some to be one of the most masterful autobiographies ever written, it offers a fascinating insight into the growth of Ruskin's distinctive sensibility. The chapter celebrating his undergraduate days in Oxford, "Christ Church Choir" (including a description of lizards scooting around the breakfast table of geologist William Buckland), is a memorable set piece, as is the description of his first view of Alps from the terrace at Schaffhausen. It is, however, a curious record, for it omits an account of the one event that prurient people have found more interesting than the fact that he was one of the most significant art critics of the 19th century: his marriage to Effie Gray, which was unconsummated for uncertain reasons, among them shock when faced with the facts of the female anatomy.

In other areas it is not reticent, and its frankness so alarmed his cousin Joan Severn and her husband that they tried to censor some of its embarrassing revelations. Had more of *Praeterita* been written, it would have contained details of Ruskin's relationship with the great love of his life, Rose La Touche. He met her in 1858 when she was nine and he was 39, and when she was 18 he proposed marriage to her, agreeing to wait until she was 21. However, religious differences and her mental instability meant that the wedding never took place, and she died in 1875 aged 27. Despite his secrecy over his marriage to Effie, Ruskin was prepared to be revelatory and confessional when it came to Rose La Touche.

FRAGMENTARY LAPSE

Praeterita is one of around 70 uncompleted or unbegun works of Ruskin. The vast accumulation of incomplete fragments of his work is symptomatic of his extraordinarily wide interests, which he found difficult to organize and express. He began putting *Praeterita* together in July 1885 and continued until his mind collapsed in the summer of 1889, when he was 70. During the final ten years of his life he was unable to write anything, and existed in a state of living death. At the time it was abandoned, *Praeterita* comprised two finished volumes of 12 chapters each and an unfinished third volume of four chapters.

The final published passage ends on his stay in Siena in 1870, closing with a magical description of fireflies in the evening sky:

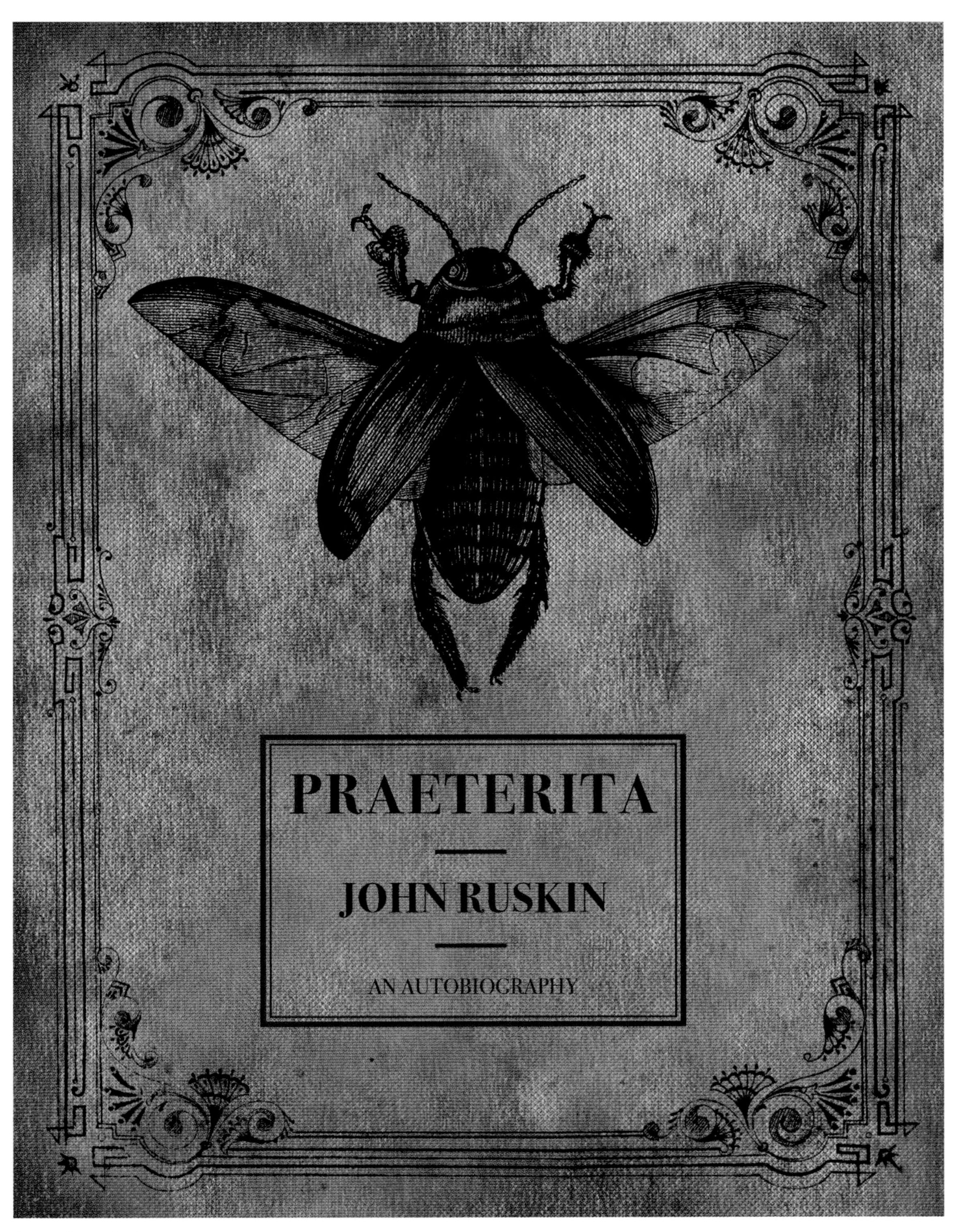

Cover: Steve Panton

ROSE LA TOUCHE
Very little was known about Rose during Ruskin's lifetime—although there was a fair amount about her (her surname withheld) in the "L'Esterelle" chapter of *Praeterita*. Ruskin's circle did not want any revelations when he died.

> "How they shone! moving like fine-broken starlight through the purple leaves. How they shone! through the sunset that faded into thunderous night . . . the fireflies everywhere in sky and cloud rising and falling, mixed with the lightning, and more intense than the stars."

There is no indication here of the mental breakdown that would occur only a few weeks later.

Praeterita does not proceed neatly and chronologically. Ruskin considers persons and places that have been important to him, and he allows memories to congregate around them. He chooses a place, such as the Campo Santo in Pisa or the Grande Chartreuse near Grenoble, and the names act like magnets that attract varied material—although in patterns that are unpredictable. There is, up to a point, a chronological sequence in *Praeterita*, but it is continually confused and distorted. He writes in Volume I chapter 7 ("Papa and Mamma"): "I think my history will, in the end, be completest if I write as its connected subjects occur to me, and not with formal chronology of plan." This is, of course, in accord with how the reflective and reminiscing mind operates: the memorizing agent wanders through chambers at will, dissolving the boundaries of time and space. It is never possible to say where the loose and chancy association of ideas will take one next.

"I think my history will, in the end, be completest if I write as its connected subjects occur to me . . . "

John Ruskin

FORS CLAVIGERA
It was in *Fors Clavigera* (1871–84) that Ruskin raised the idea of chance as an organizing principle in composition, and in a note of May 31, 1889, he promised himself that this was the principle he was going to follow in the rest of *Praeterita* and *Dilecta*, the companion volumes.

Ruskin's method meant that he never needed to refer to recent events, except in the most cursory way. Thus, although *Praeterita* was confessional, it would most likely not have been so confessional as to have included his last love: Kathleen Olander, whom he met in November 1887 and with whom he conducted a curious, stumbling affair, largely by post.

From the various plans and schemes for *Praeterita*, it is possible to put together a picture of what a more complete narrative would have been. The chapters would have been as follows:

An account of his association with Winnington School in Cheshire, which lasted from 1859 until 1868. This was a private girls' school, and some of Ruskin's happiest days were spent there. He gave lessons, which appear in disguised form in *Ethics of the Dust* (1866).

"Konigstein," covering his visit to Germany in 1859, undertaken partly to gather materials for the completion of *Modern Painters* (1843–60), including his final, memorable walk with his father.

"Boulogne Sands," about his sojourn there in 1861, when he befriended fishermen and sailed with them in the English Channel.

"The Rainbows of Giessbach," detailing a trip to Switzerland in 1866.

"Juliet's Tomb," summarizing Ruskin's involvement over the years with Verona. He had been planning to write *The Stones of Verona* as a sort of sequel to *The Stones of Venice* (1851–53).

WHAT HAPPENED NEXT . . .

Ruskin died at home at Brantwood on January 20, 1900, at the age of 81, never having fully regained his senses. Following his death, his faithful disciples E.T. Cook and Alexander Wedderburn worked to produce an enormous edition that included everything he had published and a good deal of previously unpublished material. Taking 12 years to compile, the collection of 39 volumes (1903–12) was, in its way, as impressive an act of homage as when John Hemminges and Henry Condell produced the folio edition of Shakespeare seven years after the playwright's death in 1616.

In the volume covering *Praeterita*, Cook and Wedderburn printed many cancelled passages, and also a number of the projected plans Ruskin had noted down. It offers a good idea of what further chapters of *Praeterita* would have been like. The task was made possible by the fact that Ruskin left behind a number of plans for the finished work and even fragmentary pieces. These are mainly gathered together at the end of Cook and Wedderburn's monumental Library Edition of *Praeterita*, but other plans also exist. A diary entry for February 8, 1887, lists the 12 chapters for Volume III, and another plan, also with 12 chapters, is printed in Tim Hilton's biography of Ruskin, *John Ruskin* (2002). In addition, Ruskin's letter to Mrs. John Simon dated January 16, 1887, lists the first four chapters of Volume III, and some other chapters.

Ruskin's wider cultural legacy has been far reaching, influencing a wide range of notable figures from Gandhi to Frank Lloyd Wright.

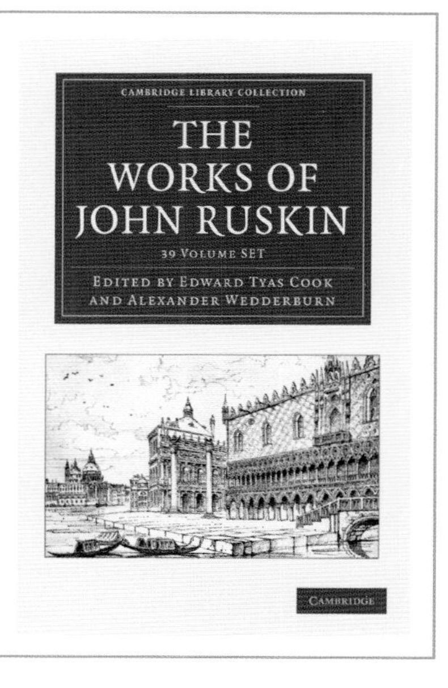

"Regina Montium," about the Righi in Switzerland.
"Matlock," one of Ruskin's favorite places, which he had known as a child. It was at Matlock that he had a mental breakdown in 1871.
"The Sacristan's Cell," concerning his stay in Assisi in 1874.
"Broadlands," regarding the Hampshire country house where the Cowper-Temple family provided Ruskin with protective asylum.
"The Vale of Thame," where Ruskin received news of Rose's death in May 1875. This chapter would probably have gone on to describe his visit to Venice when he was haunted by her ghost.
"Fairies' Hollow," about Chamouni and his last happy days there with the old Swiss guide Joseph Couttet. And Rose's last letters.
"The Vision," an account of Ruskin's severe mental attack in 1878, in which he strangled a black cat he believed to be the Devil.
"The Hunter's Rock," concerning his last visit to Lucca and Pisa in Italy in 1882.
"Calais Pier," about the importance of France throughout his life.
"Shakespeare's Cliff," the title of which refers to the cliff in Dover from which Shakespeare's Duke of Gloucester in *King Lear* (1605–06) is tempted by Edgar in disguise to commit suicide. A summing-up of Ruskin's views on England.
"The Field Under the Wood," about Brantwood, Ruskin's home in the English Lake District.

Ruskin also planned to publish a supplementary book to illustrate the narrative of *Praeterita* in greater detail, called *Dilecta*, but only one volume with three chapters was published. He wrote projected plans for this work, but they, too, were never realized. BR

WILL IT EVER HAPPEN?

5/10

A perfect conclusion is impossible, principally because Ruskin's leaps of imagination are inimitable, but also because after his death the Severns and his literary executor, the American author Charles Eliot Norton, destroyed a lot of material out of embarrassment. And a disastrous and badly organized sale of Ruskin's possessions at Brantwood meant that much of his writing was chaotically dispersed.

GASTON DE LATOUR

Author Walter Pater **Year** 1894 **Country** England **Genre** Novel

WALTER PATER
Pater's doctrine of "art for art's sake" was enthusiastically adopted during his lifetime by the aesthetic movement and, 20 years after his death in 1894, by the Metro-Goldwyn-Mayer movie company, which took "Ars Gratia Artis," the Latin version of the slogan, as its motto.

Walter Pater was a shy Oxford don who did not cultivate the high-profile poses of a John Ruskin or an Oscar Wilde, which partly explains why he is not a household name. But he is a crucial figure in the evolution of Aestheticism and Modernism, and his book *The Renaissance* (1873) is one of the most important and influential pieces of prose in Victorian literature. He also dabbled in fiction, and *Marius the Epicurean* (1885) is one of the great unread classics. Pater was a sort of forerunner to W.G. Sebald, producing novels without elaborate plot or dialogue. When he died he left behind a number of works that were published posthumously by his friend C.L. Shadwell. One of these was *Gaston de Latour*, an unfinished novel about a young man in the decadent French 16th-century Renaissance. Shadwell's edition contained seven chapters, omitting six more existing in the manuscript. Some chapters had appeared in Pater's lifetime in *Macmillan's Magazine* and *The Fortnightly Review*.

RECREATING THE RENAISSANCE

Gaston de Latour is a fascinating document, with evocative portraits of the real life figures Gaston encounters, including the writers Ronsard and Montaigne. The most arresting depiction is that of Marguerite de Valois, daughter of Henry II and Catherine de Medici, and sister of three kings of France—a dangerous and immoral woman whose reputation is comparable to that of Lucrezia Borgia. If *Gaston de Latour* were better known, Pater's depiction of her would undoubtedly be a key text in Gender Studies.

Aestheticism is traditionally supposed to bypass ethics and morality, but Pater was never quite the card-carrying aesthete, and in this novel the erotic and immoral indulgences of the period are exposed to a critical light. The narrative voice is very close to that of Pater's prose essays, and, like *Marius the Epicurean*, this novel readily modulates into speculative essay mode. Pater's understanding of the environmental atmospheres of the French 16th century is profound and brilliantly expressed, as it is in his excellent *Imaginary Portraits* (1887). His interest in *Gaston* is in the various religious tendencies, including forms of Christian aestheticism and unorthodox mysticism. It was religious intolerance that brought about the infamous St. Bartholomew's Day Massacre (1572), dealt with in chapter 6.

Cover: Gareth Butterworth

WHAT HAPPENED NEXT . . .
The bibliophile and Warden of All Souls College, Oxford, John Sparrow (famous for his minority view that D.H. Lawrence's *Lady Chatterley's Lover* deserved to be banned) acquired a copy of the manuscript of *Gaston de Latour* and presented it to Brasenose, the college of which Pater had been a fellow. In 1995 the American scholar Gerald Monsman produced an excellent scholarly edition of it, supplemented with the fragments in the Houghton Library, Harvard, and it is now possible to read the novel as far as Pater got.

Pater has the reputation of producing an impenetrably lapidary style. Max Beerbohm wrote: "I was angry that he should treat English as a dead language, bored by the sedulous ritual wherewith he laid out every sentence as a shroud." This is unjust. At his best, Pater is lively, reflective, and relaxed, witty even, and he never strays into cheapness or imprecision. BR

1/10

WILL IT EVER HAPPEN?
It's not really clear where the plot would go after Pater breaks off. No one has attempted to finish it, and it is doubtful whether anyone could. His prose has been imitated by W.H. Mallock in *The New Republic* (1877, where Pater is "Mr. Rose"), by Max Beerbohm in "Diminuendo" (1896), and by James Joyce in "The Oxen of the Sun" episode in *Ulysses* (1922). But imitation is not continuation.

WEIR OF HERMISTON

Author Robert Louis Stevenson **Year** 1894 **Country** Scotland **Genre** Novel

ROBERT LOUIS STEVENSON
In search of a warm climate that would suit his delicate lungs, Stevenson left his native Scotland and traveled the world. He eventually settled in the South Pacific. Today he is one of the most popular writers in the English language.

The end of Robert Louis Stevenson's life was rather romantic and adventurous. He set off in 1888 on a voyage round the Pacific, collecting materials for anthropological and historical work. In 1889 he arrived at Apia in the Samoan Islands, where he and his wife decided to settle and build a house. He produced work directly related to the new environment, but he also discovered that the remote self-exile stimulated his memories of his home town of Edinburgh in Scotland, and his difficult relations with his father. He set about writing a sequel to his "boys' story" *Kidnapped* (1886), called *Catriona*, which was published in 1893. He also started writing *St. Ives*, a romance set in Edinburgh during Napoleonic times, and *Weir of Hermiston*, which centered around a troubled father and son relationship. Unfortunately Stevenson was gravely ill, and died in 1894 of cerebral hemorrhage, aged only 44, leaving both novels unfinished. He was working on *Weir of Hermiston* on the morning of his death. It had four provisional titles, and drew inspiration from the controversial colonial conditions in Samoa.

FAMILY FALLOUT

Weir of Hermiston tells the story of the Weir family. Adam Weir is the Lord Justice-Clerk (the most senior judge in Scotland), a severe and gruff man who uses coarse language, likes his drink, and administers harsh justice with "gusto." His son Archie has "a shivering delicacy" and hates his father, whom he views as "the chief of sinners." He becomes a kind of Byronic hero.

One day Archie hears a mob shout at his father: "Down with the persecutor! Down with Hanging Hermiston!" Archie witnesses a trial at which his father is presiding. The accused is Duncan Jopp, a lifelong criminal. Weir is pitiless, and condemns him to death. Disgusted by his father's callousness, Archie nevertheless attends the execution. Unable to restrain his anger, he shouts: "I denounce this God-defying murder." Weir is so offended by Archie's opposition that he tells him he must give up law and leave Edinburgh. He will act as the laird at Hermiston, making the remote property a working estate again. Full of regret, Archie vows to do the best he can. Archie's solitary behavior earns him the name "the Recluse of Hermiston." The housekeeper, Kirstie, however, adores Archie, and Stevenson presents her as an enigmatic sexual presence.

Cover: Josse Pickard

COVENANTERS
Archie's mother often talks about the Covenanters. They were Presbyterians who opposed King Charles I, and they signed the National Covenant in Greyfriars Kirkyard, Edinburgh, on February 28, 1638. Later when they were persecuted many were imprisoned there.

Kirstie tells Archie about her elder half-brother, Gilbert of Cauldstaneslap, who had a daughter, Christina, and four sons: Hob, Dand, Clem, and Gib, known as the Four Black Brothers. One day, while out on business, Gilbert was attacked by thieves. He staggered home, and with his dying breath told his sons the location of his attack. The brothers rode out after the thieves, and Hob crushed one of them to death with his horse before a party of reinforcements arrived to arrest the remaining thieves. Today the brothers lead a quieter life, and Christina lives with Clem and his wife in Glasgow.

One day Archie goes to church, where he sees Christina and they fall in love. Meanwhile, Archie's former classmate, the Mephistophelean figure Frank Innes, arrives uninvited to stay. He gets his amusement from making trouble, and soon discovers that Archie loves Christina. He warns him to be careful—would Weir senior ever accept the lowlier-born Christina as a daughter-in-law? Kirstie is also worried about the burgeoning relationship. She asks him to promise that no harm will come to Christina. Archie meets Christina at the ill-fated Weaver's Stone, where John Graham of Claverhouse shot a Covenanter (see left) in the 17th century. He tells her about the warnings from Innes and Kirstie. She becomes upset and angry, but he consoles her by taking her into his arms. And there the manuscript ends.

POSTHUMOUS DEVELOPMENTS

The various manuscripts of *Weir of Hermiston* were eventually dispersed to libraries, including the Pierpont Morgan Library, New York, the Parrish Collection, Princeton University, and the F.W. Heron Collection in the Silverado Museum, California.

Two years after Stevenson's death, his British publisher, Chatto & Windus, brought out an edition that was almost exactly as the author had left it on the day he died. That no attempt was made to complete the work may well

INSPIRING IMAGE
Stevenson was influenced in his conception of the Lord Justice by Henry Raeburn's portrait of Robert MacQueen, an 18th-century judge notorious for the harsh way that he dealt with those who appeared before him. Stevenson described the artwork in his essay collection *Virginibus Puerisque* (1881):

"Another portrait which irresistibly attracted the eye was the half-length of Robert M'Queen, of Braxfield, Lord Justice-Clerk. If I know gusto in painting when I see it, this canvas was painted with rare enjoyment. The tart, rosy, humorous look of the man, his nose like a cudgel, his face resting squarely on the jowl, has been caught and perpetuated with something that looks like brotherly love. A peculiarly subtle expression haunts the lower part, sensual and incredulous, like that of a man tasting good Bordeaux with half a fancy it has been somewhat too long uncorked. From under the pendulous eyelids of old age the eyes look out with a half-youthful, half-frosty twinkle . . . He has left behind him an unrivalled reputation for rough and cruel speech; and to this day his name smacks of the gallows."

WHAT HAPPENED NEXT . . .

The unfinished novel was published with notes by Sidney Colvin. Some editions include a note from Colvin, based on Stevenson's step-daughter Isobel Osbourne Strong's projections, on how the author intended to end the novel: Archie avoids further compromising conduct with Christina, Innes courts her instead and she falls pregnant by him. Archie confronts Innes, kills him on the moor, and is arrested. Meanwhile the Four Black Brothers seek vengeance for their sister's honor (they think Archie is the father). Archie is tried before his own father and condemned to death. Kirstie learns that Innes was the father and tells the brothers, who break Archie out of prison. Archie and Christina escape to America. The ordeal of taking part in the trial of his own son is too much for Adam Weir, who dies of shock. An alternative ending was supplied by S.R. Lysaght, who visited Stevenson in 1894 and was told by him that Christina would visit her lover in prison and confess to him that she was with child by the man he had murdered.

Colvin wondered about this plot: in the legal system, would Adam Weir have tried his own son? Would an escape to happiness have been the conclusion to this dark tale, making it into too much of a romance?

In 1995 Catherine Kerrigan published a scholarly edition that added a couple of pages from an 1892 manuscript to the 1894 manuscript.

have passed without remark at the time by anyone other than those who felt cheated by the lack of a denouement. However, in the light of subsequent continuations—of Raymond Chandler's *Poodle Springs* by Robert B. Parker (see p.190), of Graham Greene's *The Empty Chair* by Michael Stanley (see p.148), of J.R.R. Tolkien's *The Silmarillion* by his son (see p.204), and of

> *"Stevenson . . . wrote in many keys. His prose was never 'far from variation and quick change.'"*
>
> Bradford Torrey, *The Atlantic Monthly*

Jane Austen's *Sanditon* by "Another Lady" (see p.46)—it is perhaps surprising that no one has tried to finish *Weir of Hermiston*. That is, unless or until one compares the idiosyncrasies of these authors with those of Robert Louis Stevenson. For all their merits, the four named above are readily (if not always convincingly) imitable; Robert Louis Stevenson is not. BR

WILL IT EVER HAPPEN?

In theory there is enough information about the various projected plots to make finishing the story possible, but the sheer genius of Stevenson's style presents a daunting prospect to a potential author. Not to mention the Scottish dialect—*Weir of Hermiston* comes with a glossary of 297 words, and that's only for the part that exists. In his book *Notes on novelists* (1914), Henry James wrote of the novel that "Among prose fragments it stands quite alone, with the particular grace and sanctity of mutilation worn by the marble morsel of masterwork in another art." Alone it seems destined to remain, untampered with by continuators.

DAS VERMÄCHTNIS KAINS

Author Leopold von Sacher-Masoch **Year** 1895 **Country** Austria **Genre** Novel

LEOPOLD VON SACHER-MASOCH
Sacher-Masoch's mother tongue was Ukrainian. He started learning German, the language in which he wrote, at the age of 12. Much of his work has been translated into French, Polish, Russian, and Ukrainian, but only his most notorious novella has been widely published in English.

Leopold von Sacher-Masoch was an Austrian journalist with utopian ideals and unconventional personal habits. He conceived *Das Vermächtnis Kains* (*The Legacy of Cain*) as a great cycle of fiction in which each volume took its title from one of the six main evils that in his view prevented human happiness. These were, in order of intended presentation, *Love*, *Property*, *The State*, *War*, *Work*, and *Death*.

The first volume was published in 1869 but the work was never completed: Sacher-Masoch tired of the project in the mid-1880s and thereafter his mental health deteriorated. But volumes one and two are extant. In "The Wanderer," the prologue to *Love*, a hunter in a forest meets a nomadic ascetic who outlines his philosophy that the troubles of the world were all caused by Cain, the Old Testament character who committed the first murder.

One of the six novellas that comprise *Love* is "Venus in Furs," which has since been published many times in several languages as a stand-alone work. Its appeal lies in its treatment of the theme of female dominance. The main character, Severin von Kusiemski, asks his lover, Wanda von Dunajew, if he can be her slave. She is reluctant at first, but gradually warms to the idea, although as her enthusiasm grows, so too does her contempt for Severin. After a series of erotic experiments, Wanda finds another lover by whom she herself wishes to be dominated; this breaks her hold over Severin, who decides that he no longer wants to be submissive to anyone. The moral of the tale, clearly set out at the conclusion, is that, in contemporary society, women have only two options: to dominate men or to submit to them. The sexes cannot be equal and enjoy each other's companionship until they have equal rights and opportunities.

PROTOFEMINISM

Such notions were a century ahead of their time, but before they could capture the hearts and minds of the Flower Power generation they brought Sacher-Masoch's name into lasting disrepute. The problem was that while it may have been acceptable to stake radical intellectual premises, the author was widely believed to practice what he preached: this was regarded as beyond the pale. At the head of the legion of his detractors was Austrian psychiatrist

Cover: Dean Martin

Richard von Krafft-Ebing, who coined the term "masochism" for the practices described in "Venus in Furs," and made the author's name a negative term for all those who are neither masochists themselves nor concerned about the socio-political ideas that underpin the text.

Although Sacher-Masoch's sexual preferences were not widely publicized during his lifetime, they were revealed on the publication in 1906 of *Meine Lebensbeichte* (titled in English as *The Confessions of Wanda von Sacher-Masoch*). In these memoirs his widow, Aurora von Rümelin, revealed that he had once entered a contract with his mistress under the terms of which he was to be her slave for six months. He later asked Aurora to act out the contents of "Venus in Furs" with him; she refused and he divorced her. **GL**

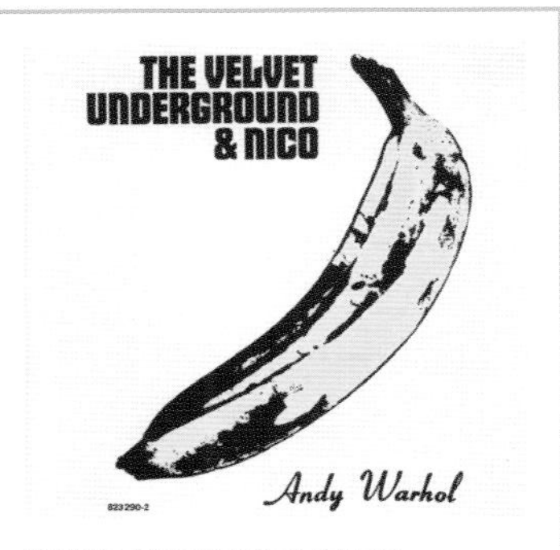

WHAT HAPPENED NEXT . . .

The Velvet Underground and Nico borrowed the title of Sacher-Masoch's novella for a track on their 1967 debut album. Their "Venus in Furs," written by band member Lou Reed, makes no reference to sexual equality, but majors in bondage and submission in lyrics such as:

> "Tongue of thongs, the belt that does await you
> Strike, dear mistress, and cure his heart."

WILL IT EVER HAPPEN?

1/10

Of Sacher-Masoch's six chosen themes, only the first and possibly the third remain contentious. No one need agree that property, work, war, and death are evil, but most people can see that they all have potential for the bad. Love was interesting because it is prima facie a good thing: the author made his best shot first. The state might be worthy of consideration, but it is hard to see an anarchist's handbook having the same popular appeal as a bondage manual.

JEAN SANTEUIL

Author Marcel Proust **Year** 1899 **Country** France **Genre** Novel

MARCEL PROUST
Proust was a sickly and self-absorbed young man whose political awakening came with the Dreyfus case (see p.124) and whose aesthetic awareness was sharpened by reading the work of Ruskin. Having thus reached maturity, he abandoned *Jean Santeuil* and began work on his masterpiece.

Marcel Proust began writing his quasi-autobiographical novel *Jean Santeuil* in 1895 when he was 24, but it was never finished and was largely abandoned by 1899. It was his first attempt at a long work; his previous forays into writing had been short stories for the magazines *Le Banquet* and *La Revue Blanche*, which in 1896 were published as the collection *Les Plaisirs et les jours* (*Pleasures and Days*).

Jean Santeuil is of importance for lovers of Proust, because it shows the author's early attempts to write a novel that concerned childhood and youth, significant places, and views on art, literature, and society—material which found its mature flowering in *À la recherche du temps perdu* (*In Search of Lost Time*, 1913–27), one of the major novels of the 20th century. Of course, by the time he came to write his great novel, Proust had matured considerably. He had translated the work of English art historian John Ruskin into French (which helped to form his artistic identity), and had experimented in literary pastiches in *Contre Sainte-Beuve* (*Against Sainte-Beuve*, published in French in 1954 and in an English translation by Sylvia Townsend Warner in 1957).

NARRATIVE FRAMEWORK

Jean Santeuil tells the story of a young man entering into the social world of Paris after an early life spent in Illiers (Proust's early home, which becomes transformed into Combray in *À la recherche*). The novel is presented in a series of "frames," when the narrator (who is more or less Proust) is staying in a small Breton farm in Beg-Meil, across the bay from Concarneau in Brittany. He meets the writer C., who is writing a novel in a nearby lighthouse.

The story opens in what would become familiar Proustian territory: the over-sensitive small boy mollycoddled by his mother. He later falls in love with Marie Kissichef in the Champs-Elysées in Paris. Also characteristically Proustian is the presented charm of provincial France. The novel flows, and is not tightly organized. Proust has the reputation of an effete aesthete, one who would soon be bored by detailed examination of anything, but *Jean Santeuil* weighs in at a hefty 828 pages in the English edition.

Jean Santeuil is called a novel, but that stretches the definition of the term somewhat, because the work contains Proust's largely unmodified views and

Cover: Gerry Fletcher

INVOLUNTARY AND UNCONSCIOUS MEMORY

Proust is best known for his presentation of involuntary and unconscious memories, in which events are associated with strong perfumes or tastes—the taste of the madeleine dipped in tea, for instance. He explores the phenomenon of associationism with the kind of philosophical rigor that ultimately has its origins in the 17th-century philosopher John Locke (right). In *Jean Santeuil* this interest can be witnessed in its early stages. One incident is especially vivid and characteristically Proustian:

"As he began to cry it was cold, and he went into his dressing room to get something to throw over his shoulders. As his hand was disordered he snatched the first coat he found. It was a black velvet, bordered with braided cords, lined with cherry satin and ermine, which bruised by the violence of the shock entered the room with a thump like a young girl seized by the hair by a fighter. Then Jean waved it, but his eyes had not yet fallen on it when he smelt the indefiniable odor of this velvet which he smelt when ten years previously he went to embrace his mother, then young, shining, happy, ready to go out . . . Confused, he looked at the cloak still fresh in its colors, yet velvety soft, like those years unrelated to to anything in life, but not faded, intact in his memory."

The use of the word "intact" shows the dawning of the idea that the past continues to exist in an almost palpable manner, waiting to be released in the receptive consciousness.

opinions, and the narrative voice is not distanced from him. Indeed, at one point in the story he forgets himself and the narrator, Jean, is referred to as Marcel. In the epigraph, Proust wrote:

> "Can I call this book a novel? This is perhaps more or less the essence of my life, assembled without mixing anything in these hours of interruption as it unrolls. This book has not been produced, it was simply harvested."

He tells his readers that "the things he wrote were rigorously true stories." He apologizes for them, saying he had "no invention and could write only what he had personally felt."

MAIN PREOCCUPATIONS

The novel is an exploration of Proust's central obsessions, to do with identifying the spiritual essences behind everyday life, so that its subject and field of research are the mind which processes reality and is opposed to materialism: "Jean secretly took pity on all those who believed in Science, who did not believe in the absolute ego or the existence of God."

These spiritual essences are "restored instantaneously by a perfume, a ray of light falling into our room, and so intoxicates us that we become indifferent to real life . . . and are momentarily freed from the tyranny of the present." However, in *Jean Santeuil* Proust has not yet quite understood how the mechanism of memory that restores lost sensations in their completeness works, but he is progressing toward it.

He thinks at this point that it is to do with the poetic imagination, a theory in line with earlier Romantic movement views. He does believe, in an almost mystic manner, that "our true nature is outside time, born to feed on the eternal," and says, "We are justified in giving first place to the imagination, because we now realize that it is the organ that serves the eternal." The main questions in *Jean Santeuil* are ones that Proust continued to reflect

CAMILLE SAINT-SAËNS

Proust is renowned for having evoked music and suggested its mysteries more effectively than any other writer, and there are premonitions of his skill in *Jean Santeuil*, when the music of Saint-Saëns is associated with his love for Françoise, and a "little phrase" from the Piano and Violin Sonata No. 1 Opus 75 encapsulates all his emotion.

on for the rest of his life: "What are the secret relationships, the necessary metamorphoses, which exist between a writer's life and his work, between reality and art, or rather, as we thought at the time, between the appearances of life and reality itself, which underlay everything and which could be released only by art?"

Proust has a reputation as a snob and a toady who chased after belle époque aristocrats, but this view is unfairly simplistic. He liked the privilege and luxury that such people offered, but he came, more and more, to see them not simply as gods but as curious specimens that an anthropologist

> *"*[Jean Santeuil] *is perhaps more or less the essence of my life."*
>
> Marcel Proust

might investigate with the same detachment as a researcher on the Trobriand Islands. This interest is on view in *Jean Santeuil*, and one episode at Réveillon is set in a château belonging in fact to Proust's friend, the society hostess Madeleine Lemaire. The house, with its long corridors, statues, lawns, and peacocks, is almost a character in its own right, similar to the locales that take on a vivid and significant existence in *À la recherche*. The château was near Esternay in Seine-et-Marne, and is also in part the inspiration for La Raspelière in *À la recherche*. Madame Lemaire is satirically portrayed as the culture vulture Madame Verdurin in *À la recherche*. It was at Réveillon that Jean met the glamorous Henri, a character modeled on

COUNTRY HOUSE
The 17th-century Chateau de Réveillon in north-central France gave Proust the model for stately homes depicted in *Jean Santeuil* and *À la recherche du temps perdu*.

MOVIE VERSIONS
Proust's introduction to a wider audience has mostly been via movie adaptations, and three so far of *À la recherche* have been excellent: Volker Schlöndorff's *Swann in Love* (1984, right, with Jeremy Irons as Swann), Raúl Ruiz's *Time Regained* (1999), and Chantal Akerman's *The Captive* (2000). Joseph Losey planned to adapt Proust in 1972, and Harold Pinter wrote a superlative screenplay, but it was never made.

the Venezuelan-French musician Reynaldo Hahn, for whom Proust felt a homosexual affection, and who is present in everything he wrote, "but like a god in disguise, invisible to mortals." Also at the château, Jean has a vivid epiphanic moment in the presence of roses, prefiguring the memorable hawthorn passages in *À la recherche*.

THE DREYFUS CASE
This cover of an 1887 edition of a French daily newspaper depicts ex-army captain Alfred Dreyfus (seated) under guard in prison on Devil's Island in French Guiana after his wrongful conviction for treason. The affair polarized French society and turned previously apolitical people such as Marcel Proust into agitators and activists.

Le Petit Journal
SUPPLÉMENT ILLUSTRÉ
Huit pages : CINQ centimes
Dreyfus à l'Ile du Diable

TOUCHING REALITY
An important distinction of *Jean Santeuil* is that it is one of only two pieces of fiction to deal contemporaneously with the Dreyfus Affair, in which a Jewish officer in the French army was wrongly accused of betraying secrets to the Germans. The other was the final two parts of Anatole France's *L'histoire contemporaine* (*A Chronicle of Our Own Times*): *L'anneau d'améthyste* (*The Amethyst Ring*, 1899) and *Monsieur Bergeret à Paris* (*Monsieur Bergeret in Paris*, 1901). (Anatole France is widely believed to be the "original" of Proust's fictional man-of-letters Bergotte.) Proust (whose mother was Jewish) became personally involved in the case, and helped to organize petitions and assist Dreyfus's lawyer Labori.

Dreyfus was found guilty and sent to Devil's Island for life in February 1895. The affair revealed a nasty streak of anti-Semitism in French society, and galvanized cultural and political life in the late 1890s in an extraordinary manner. The whole event was a complex story of fraud and dishonesty, with many of the anti-Dreyfusards believing that they were acting in the best interests of the nation, even though they accepted that Dreyfus was innocent. In *Jean Santeuil*, Dreyfus appears as Daltozzi, but his defender Colonel Georges Picquart, for whom Proust had great admiration, is there under his own name.

Also mentioned by name is Émile Zola, the novelist who was centrally involved in the defense of Dreyfus and whose famous essay on the case, "J'Accuse"—published in January 1898 on the front page of the Paris daily

WHAT HAPPENED NEXT . . .

Jean Santeuil was a preliminary limbering-up process for *À la recherche*, which Proust began in 1909. *À la recherche* manages to achieve some distance between its hero and Proust himself, whereas Proust is closer to his hero in *Jean Santeuil*.

Jean Santeuil was not, however, available to the public until 1952, when the publisher Gallimard put out an edition with a preface by André Maurois. The editor was Bernard Fallois, and it was a challenge to produce it, because the manuscript was a series of fragments in a chaotic state. In 1971 Gallimard published a new edition in the Pléiade Library, prepared by Pierre Clarac and Yves Sandre. And then in 2001 Gallimard published a new edition with a preface by the great Proust biographer Jean-Yves Tadié.

The editorial complexities concerning *Jean Santeuil* prefigure those concerning *À la recherche*, which, strictly speaking, is not finished either. Proust was working on it on his deathbed, and although earlier volumes had come out in his lifetime, the last three had to wait for posthumous publication. Since then, editors have been going back to the manuscripts, in the attempt to produce a reliable and definitive edition—a virtually impossible task. An important "intervention" occurred when *Albertine Disparue* was published in 1987, incorporating Proust's changes. This became available in an English translation (*Albertine Gone*) in 1989.

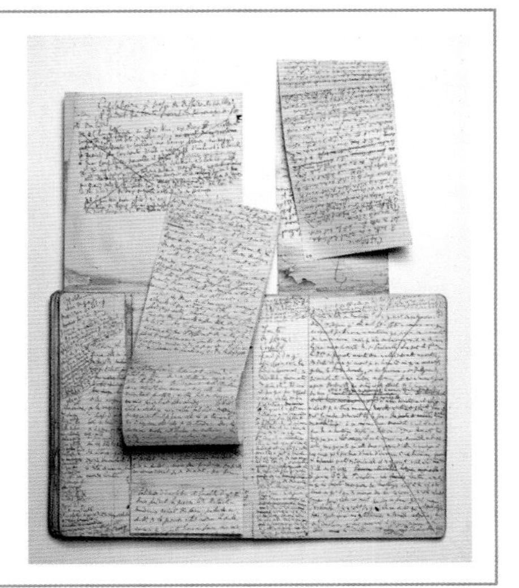

L'Aurore—led to his being put on trial for criminal libel. He was convicted but before he could be imprisoned fled to London, where he remained in exile until the French government fell. When Dreyfus was pardoned in 1899, Zola famously remarked: "The truth is on the march, and nothing shall stop it."

DEVELOPING STYLE

Jean Santeuil is an interesting work, but flawed and immature. One problem is that Proust used the novel to revenge himself on people, real and imagined: philistine parents, insensitive hostesses, self-satisfied snobs, and pretentious artists, and he emerges from the struggles with them as a charming, self-regarding, sometimes magnaminous, sometimes self-pitying young man. Snobbery is on view, as when Jean is championed by the Duc de Réveillon in a duel. Technically the novel needs much more processing, selection, and discipline, although these characteristics are becoming less demanded in modern attitudes to form. Not much *happens* in Proust's novel, but then that is true of many novels. For those who do not know *À la recherche du temps perdu*, *Jean Santeuil* is a good introduction; those familiar with the masterpiece will notice the author's early experiments with forms that he had yet to master. BR

3/10

WILL IT EVER HAPPEN?

Jean Santeuil is a fascinating document, providing insights into the mind and compositional habits of Proust. Nevertheless, Proust is, to some extent, a recherché author who is never going to reach a large readership. This fragment has now been brought into some kind of order by its various editors, and that should suffice: it would be pointless to attempt further levels of completion. Conversely, it would be rash to discount the possibility that someone will try.

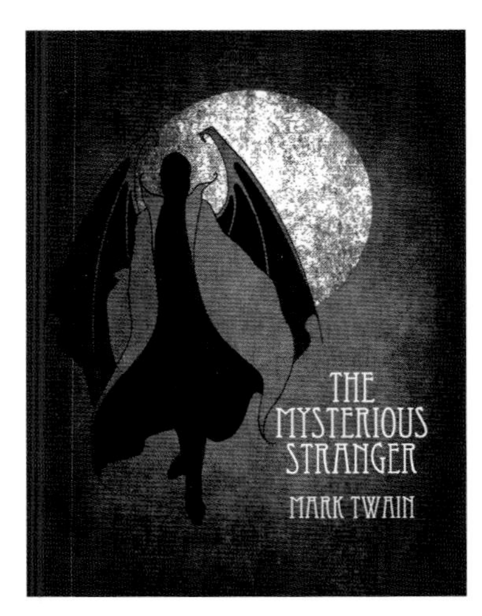
THE
MYSTERIOUS
STRANGER
MARK TWAIN

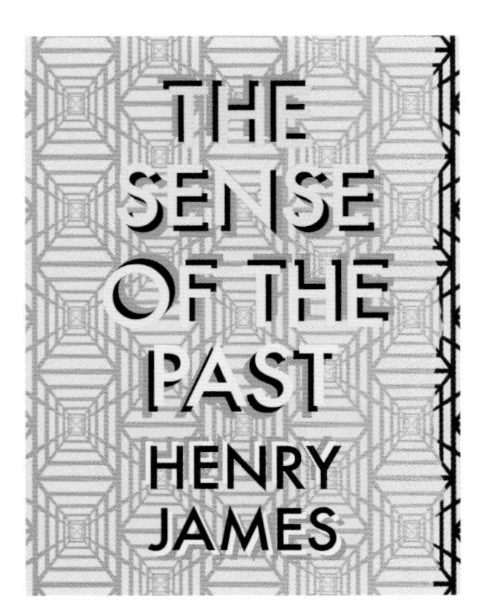
THE
SENSE
OF THE
PAST
HENRY
JAMES

NICK ADAMS
STORIES

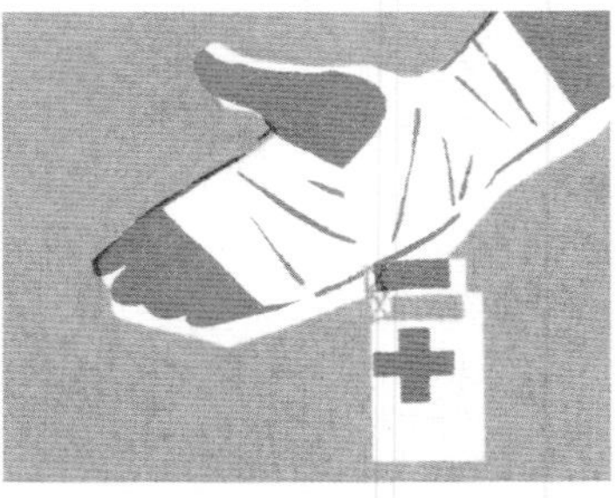
ERNEST HEMINGWAY

FRANZ KAFKA
DAS SCHLOSS

Chapter 4

THE
EMPTY
CHAIR
GRAHAM
GREENE

Il Vegliardo
Italo Svevo

ŽIVOT A
DÍLO SKLADATELE
FOLTÝNA
KAREL
ČAPEK

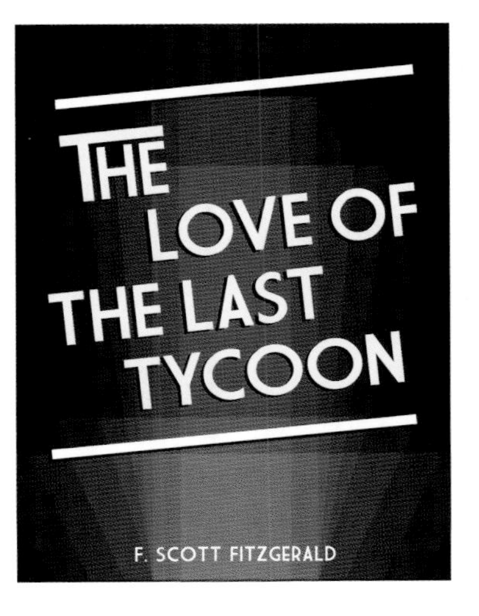
THE
LOVE OF
THE LAST
TYCOON
F. SCOTT FITZGERALD

ROBERT MUSIL
Der Mann ohne Eigenschaften

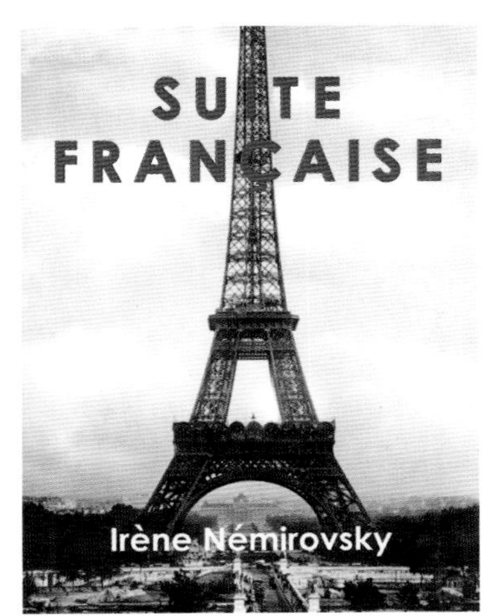
SUITE
FRANÇAISE
Irène Némirovsky

RENÉ
DAUMAL
LE MONT
ANALOGUE

Saul Bellow
The
and the

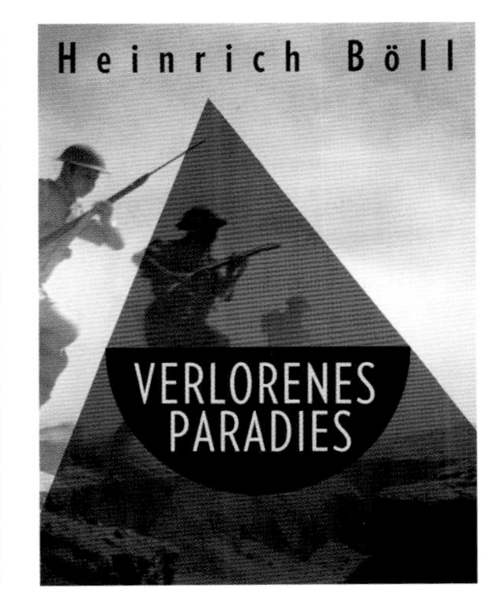
Heinrich Böll
VERLORENES
PARADIES

1900–49

IL
BIANCO
VELIERO
ITALO CALVINO

THE MYSTERIOUS STRANGER

Author Mark Twain **Year** 1908 **Country** United States **Genre** Novel

MARK TWAIN
Samuel Langhorne Clemens became world-famous as the humorist Mark Twain. But there was more to this author than wisecracks: he was also a savage moralist, in the manner of Jonathan Swift.

The Mysterious Stranger is Mark Twain's last novel. He worked on it off and on between 1897 and 1908. A Swiftian vision, it represents his attempt to deal with the Moral Sense and the "damned human race" with which he was growing increasingly disenchanted. The nephew of the biblical Satan appears as a character. It is unfinished, and survives in a number of versions. Trying to reconstruct the story is a complicated task as there are four Twain versions, not all of them in line with each other.

THE FIRST VERSION: "THE ST. PETERSBURG FRAGMENT"
Twain wrote "the St. Petersburg Fragment" in September 1897. It was set in the fictional town of St. Petersburg, a name Twain often used for Hannibal, Missouri. The date of the events was originally 1840.

THE SECOND VERSION: "THE CHRONICLE OF YOUNG SATAN"
The first sizeable version is commonly referred to as "The Chronicle of Young Satan" and relates the adventures of Satan, or Philip Traum, the nephew of Satan, in Eseldorf (which translates as "donkey village"), an Austrian hamlet in the early 18th century. Twain composed this version between November 1897 and September 1900.

THE THIRD VERSION: "SCHOOLHOUSE HILL"
"Schoolhouse Hill," the shortest of the versions, is set in the United States and involves the familiar characters Huckleberry Finn and Tom Sawyer and their adventures with Satan. Twain began writing it in November 1898 and, like the "St. Petersburg Fragment," set it in the fictional town of St. Petersburg.

THE FOURTH VERSION: "NO. 44, THE MYSTERIOUS STRANGER"
The fourth version, also known as the "Print Shop" version, sets the story in Austria in the year 1490. It tells of No. 44's mysterious appearance at the door of a print shop and his use of heavenly powers to expose the futility of humankind's existence. This version also introduces an idea Twain was toying with at the end of his life involving a concept of the divided self, composed of the "Waking Self" and the "Dream Self." It contains a conclusion, but possibly not as complete an ending as he would have intended, including a procession

THE MYSTERIOUS STRANGER

MARK TWAIN

Cover: Jayne Evans

of the skeletons of famous figures from history, and "the Missing Link." Twain wrote this version between 1902 and 1908.

THE PROPER INTENDED ENDING

Twain died in 1910. The edition posthumously published in 1916 as *The Mysterious Stranger* is composed mainly of a heavily edited "Chronicle of Young Satan," with a slightly altered version of the ending from "No. 44" tacked on. Albert Bigelow Paine, who had sole possession of Twain's unfinished works after the author's death and kept them private, searched through the manuscripts and claimed he had discovered the proper intended ending for the work. In Paine's version the date is 1590. A few boys are living

> *"Your universe and its contents were only dreams, visions, fiction!"*
>
> Satan, *The Mysterious Stranger*

happily in a remote Austrian village called Eseldorf. The story is narrated by one of the boys—Theodor, the village organist's son—in the first person. It is ironical that Theodor means "gift of God." One day, a handsome teenage boy named Satan appears in the village. He explains that he is an angel and the nephew of the fallen angel Satan. He performs several magical feats and claims to be able to foresee the future. The boys are incredulous until one of his predictions comes true. Satan describes further tragedies that will befall their friends and the boys beg Satan to change the course of events. He agrees, but operates under the technical definition of mercy. For instance, instead of a lingering life as a "paralytic log, deaf, dumb, blind, and praying

POOL OF DECEPTION
By entrusting Albert Bigelow Paine (left) with his posthumous papers, Mark Twain (right) gave hostages to fortune. Only now are scholars beginning to disentangle the great author's original material from his executor's interpolations.

night and day for the blessed relief of death," Satan simply causes one of Theodor's friends, Nikolaus, to die immediately. He also does the same for Lisa, who by dying is saved "from 19 years' pollution, shame, depravity, crime, ending with death at the hands of an executioner." Another character is granted a long life, but in a state of unaware idiocy. In carrying out these actions Satan alters "the chain of life," which in theory could lead to the butterfly effect (see p.135), but Satan (and Twain) do not stop to consider that these adjustments to individual lives actually change the whole course of the universe. The previously happy village goes through a series of convulsions involving witch trials, burnings, and mass hysteria. Satan vanishes with a brief explanation of the insubstantial pageant of life, saying that the whole universe is nothing more than a sequence of "dreams, visions, fiction!"

A LITERARY FRAUD

Beginning in the 1960s, critics studied the original copies of the story and found that the ending Paine chose for *The Mysterious Stranger* referred to the characters from different versions of the story (No. 44 instead of Satan, for example), and that the original names had been crossed out and written over in Paine's handwriting. It was discovered that Paine had not only tampered with and patched together three previously unfinished manuscripts, but had also added passages of his own in order to complete the novelette. The concoction was a literary fraud. The pioneering work of authentic reconstruction was begun by researcher John S. Tuckey in 1963. In addition to omitting a quarter of the original text, sometimes not to offend religious sensibilities, Paine's version invents the character of an astrologer who is made responsible for all the villainies.

The mood in the novel is one of savage negativity. Twain is famous as a humorist, but Satan is bitterly skeptical about this faculty, and says that most of the stupid human race only "see the comic side of a thousand low-grade and trivial things—broad incongruities, mainly; grotesqueries, absurdities, evokers of the horse-laugh." He argues that a much more destructive black laughter could "blow to rags and atoms" the "colossal humbug" embodied in "power, money, persuasion, supplication, persecution." This is as dark and pessimistic a vision as any writer has ever presented, and is far from the concept of humor as light and shallow entertainment. Twain here seems inclined to see human beings as a pernicious race of odious vermin. BR

WHAT HAPPENED NEXT . . .

In 1969 the University of California Press published a scholarly edition of all three unaltered manuscripts, edited by William M. Gibson and titled *Mark Twain's Mysterious Stranger Manuscripts*. The fact that this is 603 pages and the text of the 1916 version is 65 pages gives some indication of the scale of the problem. In 1982 the University of California Press published *No. 44, The Mysterious Stranger*, claiming it was as close as possible to Twain's final intentions. What can be seen here is the same process of disintegration and deconstruction that happens whenever scholars are let loose on texts. Shakespeare is the classic example. The public resists it, but it is better to be less deceived. Readers should never lose sight of the admonition *caveat emptor* (let the buyer beware).

WILL IT EVER HAPPEN?

7/10

It seems unlikely that the last of this story has been heard. Twain is still a popular author, so it seems probable that the story will continue to garner attention from both writers and readers. As with other works by the author, *The Mysterious Stranger* has had a vivid afterlife in film adaptations (1982), musicals, operas, and even claymation (1985). As the character of Satan in the novel is described as making a tiny squirrel and birds out of clay and bringing them to life, perhaps claymation is the most fitting format for a continuation.

THE SENSE OF THE PAST

Author Henry James **Year** 1916 **Country** United States **Genre** Novel

HENRY JAMES
An American who became a naturalized British citizen, James was preoccupied throughout his life with what he saw as the dichotomy between New World innocence and Old World cynicism.

Henry James left behind two unfinished works when he died in 1916: *The Ivory Tower* and *The Sense of the Past*. *The Ivory Tower* was intended to be James's take on early 20th-century American capitalism in the "Gilded Age," in which New York skyscrapers would have represented the operations of corrupt high capitalism as a kind of malign equivalent of the mysteries of traditional art: "The most piercing notes in that concert of the expensively provisional," as James described them in his book of travel writing *The American Scene* (1907). *The Sense of the Past* was an attempt at a time-travel story, and offered an intriguing take on the theme. It was arguably more ambitious in its concepts than *The Ivory Tower*, and dealt with more durable and traditional interests.

WINGS OF IMAGINATION

James, known principally as a realist novelist, did on occasion venture into areas of fantasy, of which the most famous example is his ghost story *The Turn of the Screw* (1898). But even in this genre he preferred to keep his stories grounded in reality. In his preface to his short story "The Jolly Corner" (1909), he described his aim as capturing a note of "the strange and sinister embroidered on the very type of the normal and easy."

James began writing *The Sense of the Past* in 1900, shortly after acquiring Lamb House, his 18th-century home in Rye, Sussex, England. The hero, American Ralph Pendrel, wants to experience the palpable details of the past:

> "What he wanted himself was the very smell of that simpler mixture of things that had so long served; he wanted the very tick of the old stopped clocks. He wanted the hour or the day at which this and that had happened and the temperature and the weather and the sound, and yet more the stillness, from the street, and the exact look-out, with the corresponding look-in, through the window and the slant on the walls of the light of afternoons that had been . . . He wanted evidence of a sort for which there had never been documents enough."

Ralph's interest leads him to write "An Essay in Aid of the Reading of History," which catches the attention of a relative who leaves his early 18th-century house in London to him in his will. Ralph goes to London, as if

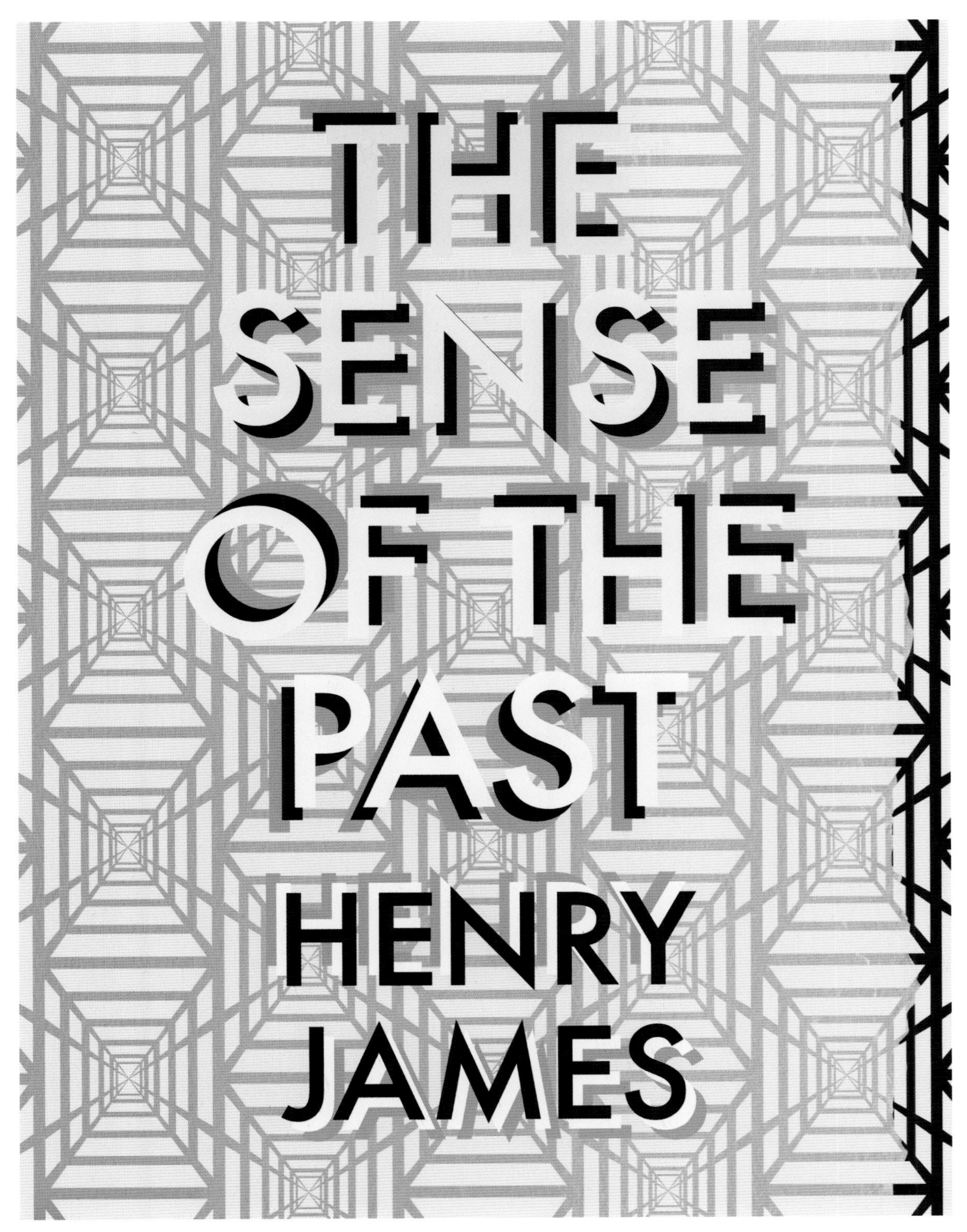

Cover: Rebecca Richardson

TIME TRAVEL

Time travel to the past has been a longstanding popular theme for novelists, first capturing the public imagination in early science fiction works such as H.G. Wells's *The Time Machine* (1895) and Mark Twain's *A Connecticut Yankee in King Arthur's Court* (1889). Traveling into the future has been equally popular as a subject, with early examples including Edward Bellamy's *Looking Backward* (1888) and William Morris's *News from Nowhere* (1890). Novels that travel forward often shade into post-apocalyptic fiction, as seen in Richard Jefferies's *After London* (1885).

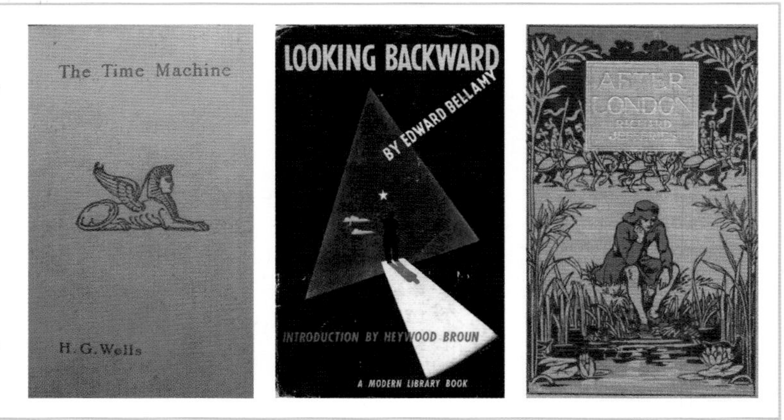

embarking on some romantic adventure requiring courage, leaving behind in the United States Aurora Coyne. Aurora wants to marry a man of action who has "been through something," and Ralph, who is a mere intellectual, does not fit the bill.

A MUSEUM OF HELD REVERBERATIONS

Ralph discovers the house in Mansfield Square to be entirely in accord with his sense of the past, "a museum of held reverberations." His first reaction is "It's Jacobean"—by which he means it's from the time of James II. Henry James is making a self-referential joke here; actually it dates from 1710, from the time of Queen Anne. There is an evocative description of the wrought-iron staircase with a wooden handrail that is tempting to slide down, and of the floor in the hall, "paved in alternate squares of white marble and black, each so old that the white was worn nearly to yellow and the black nearly to blue." There is a tradition that supernatural stories take place in the kinds of moldering Gothic buildings so loved by Hammer Films, but this setting is more civilized—the house has sash-windows with little square panes rather than magic casements. Even so, Ralph feels, on entering the house and being marooned from the present, that he is slipping into what Shakespeare in *The Tempest* (1611) calls "the dark backward and abysm of time."

Ralph sees a portrait of an ancestor, also named Ralph Pendrel. The portrait is a back view, but when Ralph holds up a candle the man in the picture turns round, comes alive, and the two men meet: "The face—miracle of miracles, yes—confounded him as his own." A strong foreshadowing of this scene can be found in James's novel *The Portrait of a Lady* (1881), in an episode where one of the characters—also called Ralph—returns home at night and enters his dining room by candlelight:

> "His own steps, in the empty place, seemed loud and sonorous . . . and whenever he moved he roused a melancholy echo . . . There was a ghostly presence as of dinners long digested; of table-talk that had lost its actuality."

TRADING PLACES

Shaken, Ralph goes to the U.S. Ambassador in London to tell him of these strange occurrences, in a distinctly convoluted conversation. There then follows an "exchange" whereby the 20th-century Ralph goes back in time, and the figure from the 1820s, "the Predecessor," comes forward. James has not actually taken Ralph back that far in time; he has in fact traveled to a similar period represented in James's novella *The Aspern Papers* (1888), in which an old woman from the Romantic movement puts the hero in touch with a period in history just out of reach. James knew a number of old ladies, including the actress Fanny Kemble and Anne Benson Procter, widow of the poet "Barry Cornwall," who gave him an almost direct access to the early decades of the 19th century.

James abandoned the novel at this point, but resumed work in 1914 with scenes of Ralph meeting his ancestor's relatives. Ralph discovers when he enters the past that he is affianced to one of them, Molly Midmore. At first with her he feels that he is "seated at the harpsichord and following out a score while the girl beside him stirred the air to his very cheek and she guided him leaf by leaf," but as time goes on he realizes that he wants to venture into variations and improvisations, and is more attracted to her sister Nan, who has for him the great virtue of being "modern." She has a high forehead and resembles a Jan van Eyck or Hans Memling painting—an unconventional style of feminine beauty for 1820. He also meets Molly's mother, her unpleasant brother Perry—"like a frightened horse who sniffs in the air the nearness of some creature of a sort he has never seen"—and Nan's suitor, Sir Cantopher Bland. Ralph finds his encounter with the past that he thought he loved unnerving.

At this point the novel comes to an abrupt halt. It is evident that James is not straying far from his lifelong interest in the International Theme, exploring the cultural contrast between Americans and Europeans. As an American Ralph is already strange and exotic, quite apart from the fact that he hails from another century. James planned that Nan would become aware that Ralph is a time-traveler, and would sacrifice her happiness to help him return to his own time and to Aurora Coyne, who would now accept him and take part in his rescue. Aurora has had, before the novel begins, a disconcerting but unspecified encounter in Europe. There is "a dark blue jar" in the novel that would probably have taken on some of the significance invested in the golden bowl in James's 1904 novel of that name.

DESIGN FLAWS

Why did James abandon the novel in 1900? To begin with there was his view that one could not really re-enter the past with conviction, a skepticism expressed in a letter to Sarah Orne-Jewett of October 5, 1901:

> "You may multiply the little facts that can be got from pictures and documents, relics and prints, as much as you like—the real thing is almost impossible to do, and in its essence the whole effect is as nought: I mean the invention, the representation of the old

THE BUTTERFLY EFFECT

The philosophical problem of going back in time is well outlined in Ray Bradbury's short story "A Sound of Thunder," first published in *Weird Science-Fantasy* in 1952. In the story big-game hunters go into pre-history to hunt dinosaurs, with the instruction not to stray from a special path. One hunter leaves the path, and on returning to the present finds it changed, because when leaving the path he trod on a butterfly. As slight as the incident was, it changed the whole course of history. This has since become known as "the butterfly effect."

> CONSCIOUSNESS, the soul, the sense, the horizon, the vision of individuals . . . You have to think with your modern apparatus a man, a woman—or rather fifty—whose own thinking was intensely otherwise conditioned, you have to simplify back by an amazing tour de force—and even then it's all humbug."

But there were deeper problems, which kept surfacing every time James came back to *The Sense of the Past*: if one visits the past how much of one's modern present does one remember? Is the past one visits the actual past, or a ghostly simulacrum? If it is the actual past, isn't it pre-scripted, leaving one with no room for one's own initiative or maneuver? If one does exercise one's initiative, doesn't this alter events in such a way that it will have an impact on the future (as per the butterfly effect)? If the past is a complete entity, how will there be room for the intrusion of an extra element? James thought he was partly solving the problem by arranging an interchange: the modern Ralph Pendrel goes back, the earlier Ralph Pendrel comes forward. He was more conscientious than some authors who take up the time-travel theme, and he agonized over the problems, feeling that he was in danger of becoming bogged down in the mechanisms and philosophical intricacies of the situation. He spent time in his notes worrying over the mysterious circumstances of the portrait. It was this and other problems that left him unable to continue, although he had been hoping when he took up composition again in 1914 to find the story a distraction from the tragedy of the First World War.

James stopped work on *The Sense of the Past* in 1915, so that he could get on with editing Rupert Brooke's *Letters from America*, and then illness and death intervened. Despite the difficulties, it is possible that, given time, James could have finished the novel, and dealt with the complex anomalies. What exists is 281 pages of text and a further 66 pages of detailed notes. The quality of writing is very high, although some readers may find the

BERKELEY SQUARE

No one has so far attempted to finish *The Sense of the Past*. However, John L. Balderston and J.C. Squire wrote a stage version, *Berkeley Square* (1926), which was put on in two London theaters: St Martin's in 1926 and the Lyric in 1929. This was, perhaps inevitably, somewhat cruder than James and the names of the characters were changed. The authors pushed the date back into the 18th century, to 1784. The work includes the hero's accidental reference to Joshua Reynolds's *The Tragic Muse* when it had not yet been painted: this is not the sort of facetious humor that James would have allowed himself. Two movie versions of the play have been made: the first was *Berkeley Square* (1933), starring Leslie Howard (left, with Heather Angel), who had also starred in the stage production. The second version, starring Tyrone Power and Ann Blyth, was titled *The House in the Square* (1951) for British release and *I'll Never Forget You* for United States release. Both movies developed the plot roughly in the direction James intended.

dialogue teetering on the edge of absurdity. T.S. Eliot said in 1918 that Henry James "had a mind so fine that no idea could violate it." In fact, James had highly subtle ideas on which his major fiction floated; the ideas behind *The Sense of the Past* were subtle too, but sank it.

A PASSION FOR THE PAST

The main themes of *The Sense of the Past* were not a radical departure from James's long-standing interests. He had always possessed a passion for the past, and there is the germ of a related idea of the American besotted with English culture in James's novella *A Passionate Pilgrim* (1871). He depicted a similar situation in his short story "The Birthplace" (1903), when the curator of Shakespeare's house in Stratford-upon-Avon wanders about the house at night, trying somehow to penetrate its history: "He . . . more than once rose in the small hours to move about, up and down, with his lamp, sitting, listening, wondering, in the stillness, as if positively to recover some echo, to surprise some secret, of the *genius loci*." He is drawn by an impulse to get "nearer to the enshrined Presence." Another work in which James explored the past and the uncanny margins of life was "The Jolly Corner." This short story is atmospherically similar to *The Sense of the Past* and also contains midnight hauntings, but this time the setting is a house in New York. The tale concerns Spencer Brydon, who has returned to the United States after several decades abroad. He encounters the alter ego ghost of the man he would have been had he stayed and become a ruthless business tycoon.

> *"The girl beside him stirred the air to his very cheek."*
>
> *The Sense of the Past*

James shared Ralph Pendrel's fascination with a venerable London, and planned to write a book about the city. He made copious notes but the project was never realized, although he signed a contract for it with Macmillan in June 1903. By 1914 he had revisited the United States and been appalled, especially in New York, by the way the past of his childhood had been mercilessly and crassly swept away. It is likely, therefore, that in the later stages of composition the theme of the past had accrued a greater urgency for James. BR

WHAT HAPPENED NEXT . . .

James's two unfinished novels were posthumously published in 1917, edited by his literary executor Percy Lubbock, and *The Sense of the Past* came complete with working notes. In 1947 F.O. Matthiessen and Kenneth Murdock edited the *Notebooks*, which contained extensive notes for the novel, and a further edition of the *Notebooks*, edited by Leon Edel and Lyall H. Powers, was published in 1987.

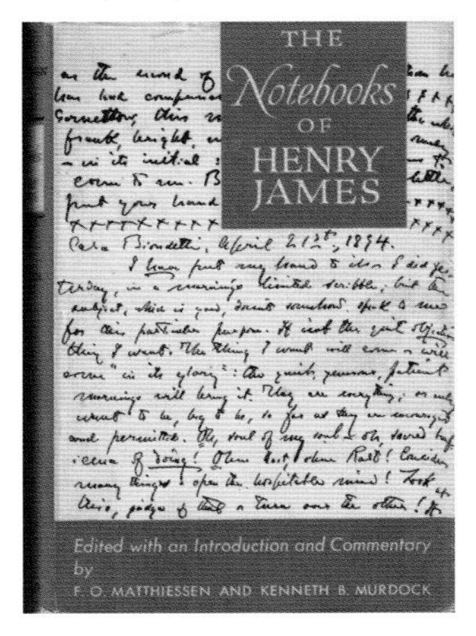

WILL IT EVER HAPPEN?

5/10

It is always possible that someone will try to finish *The Sense of the Past*, and there is sufficient information concerning the plot to make this a plausible project. However, no one will be able adequately to imitate James's style. The best parody imitation of this style is Max Beerbohm's "The Mote in the Middle Distance" in *A Christmas Garland* (1912) and "The Guerdon" (1925), but where are the Beerbohms now?

NICK ADAMS STORIES

Author Ernest Hemingway **Year** 1922 **Country** United States **Genre** Short stories

ERNEST HEMINGWAY
Born and raised in Oak Park, Illinois, Hemingway worked first on *The Kansas City Star* before becoming a roving reporter. He later turned his hand to fiction, producing seven novels and six collections of short stories, as well as two works of non-fiction.

The story of Ernest Hemingway's lost manuscripts is the stuff of literary legend. In 1922, a suitcase containing all of his fiction works was stolen in Paris. It is not known what became of the suitcase and the papers were never recovered. Among the lost works were early drafts of some short stories set in Michigan featuring Nick Adams, a character who would eventually appear in around 20 of Hemingway's shorter works.

STOWED ON A TRAIN

In November 1922, Hemingway, who was at the time making his living as a newspaper reporter, was sent by the *Toronto Star* to cover the peace conference in Lausanne, Switzerland, at which the leaders of Turkey and their British, French, and Italian counterparts (including Benito Mussolini) discussed future relations with each other in the light of the break-up of the Ottoman Empire. While there he met the editor Lincoln Steffens, who expressed an interest in his work.

Hemingway's wife, Hadley, had not traveled with him to Lausanne because she had a cold, choosing to stay behind in their flat in Paris, France. A month later she set out to join him, and packed the fiction on which Ernest (or "Tatie," as she called him whenever she wasn't calling him "Ernestoic") had been working before leaving on assignment: not just the top copies but the carbons, too. When she arrived at the Gare de Lyon she stowed her bags on her train and went to buy a bottle of water. Upon her return, the suitcase containing the manuscripts was gone. Hemingway was understandably furious. In a letter to Ezra Pound in January 1923 he wrote:

> "I suppose you heard about the loss of my Juvenalia [*sic*]? I went up to Paris last week to see what was left and found that Hadley had made the job complete by including all carbons, duplicates, etc. All that remains of my complete works are three pencil drafts of a bum poem which was later scrapped, some correspondence between John McClure and me, and some journalistic carbons. You, naturally, would say, 'Good' etc. But don't say it to me. I ain't yet reached that mood."

Just two of his early short stories were left: "My Old Man," which was with a magazine editor, and "Up in Michigan," which had been in a separate drawer.

NICK ADAMS STORIES

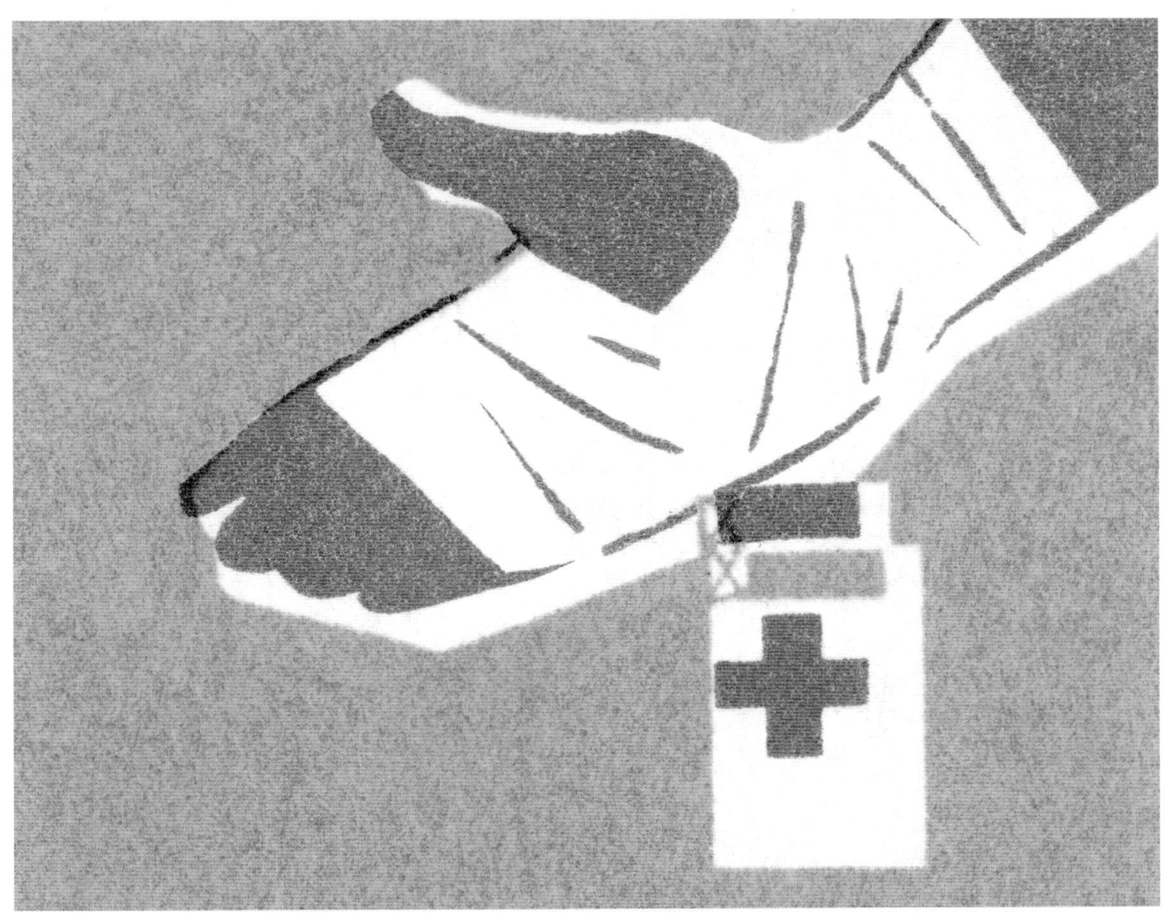

ERNEST HEMINGWAY

Cover: Hortense Franc

STYLE CHECKER
Hemingway wrote in a self-consciously economical style (right). This style has been much emulated and today there is an app available from www.hemingwayapp.com that enables writers to check how well their work compares for clarity with that of Hemingway. The program identifies highfalutin words, adverbs, the passive voice, and sentences that it deems hard to read, and highlights each of these vices of style in a different color. According to the creators, American brothers Adam and Ben Long, the best writing is that which is readily understood by schoolchildren in Year 10. However, the problem with the software it is that it low-rates many passages written by the master himself.

LOSS ASSESSMENT

There has since been much speculation about what happened to the lost papers, as well as how good they might have been or become if Hemingway had had the chance to hone them.

Most people agree that Hemingway stripped a lot of dead weight from the novel in English and demonstrated that a writer could say all that needed saying in a single volume rather than the previously conventional three volumes. His fans further insist that he was more economical with his descriptions than had been the Victorian norm (the author himself later recalled that he learned from Ezra Pound the need to "distrust adjectives"). Devotees—who often refer to Hemingway as "Papa"—credit him with originating the "hard-boiled" style, and thus laud him as the progenitor of Dashiell Hammett, Raymond Chandler, James M. Cain, and numerous other writers. A prominent example of this style of prose can be found in the opening of *A Farewell To Arms* (1929):

> "In the late summer of that year we lived in a house in a village that looked across the river and the plain to the mountains. In the bed of the river there were pebbles and boulders, dry and white in the sun, and the water was clear and swiftly moving and blue in the channels. Troops went by the house and down the road and the dust they raised powdered the leaves of the trees."

The consultant editor for the committee that awarded Hemingway the 1954 Nobel Prize in Literature expressed a widely held view when he described this as:

> ". . . lapidary writing [which] approaches the highest style of poetry, vibrant with meaning and emotion, while the pace is maintained by the exclusion of any descriptive redundancy, of obtrusive punctuation, and of superfluous or narrowing emotive signs."

MINOR NOVELIST
Hemingway's mode of expression can never be overlooked; it is close to the antithesis of the dictum *ars est celare artem* (art is to conceal art). In *Genius: A Mosaic of One Hundred Exemplary Creative Minds* (2003), Yale professor Harold Bloom described him as a "minor novelist with a major style."

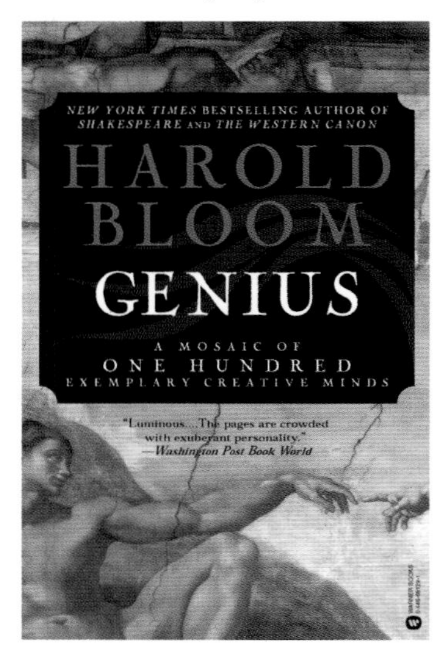

AFFECTED PROSE STYLE

However, some critics have regarded Hemingway's prose as affected. They have also commented unfavorably on his use of repetition. In the passage from *A Farewell to Arms*, for example, the author uses "and" eight times in an extract of only 76 words. This conjunction was no doubt intended as an imitation of natural (if breathless) speech, but cumulatively it may be exhausting. This is not an isolated incident, and "and" is not the only word that Hemingway overworks. In *A Moveable Feast* (1964), for example, we get "the hotel where Verlaine had died, where I had a room on the top floor where I worked."

There is also the matter of Hemingway's machismo and his lifelong love of killing animals. This self-conscious virility inspired some striking passages, such as this one from *The Sun Also Rises* (1926):

> "Afterward, all that was faked turned bad and gave an unpleasant feeling. Romero's bull-fighting gave real emotion, because he kept the absolute purity of line in his movements and always quietly and calmly let the horns pass him close each time."

"All you have to do is write one true sentence. Write the truest sentence that you know."

Ernest Hemingway, *A Moveable Feast*

But in many other places his preoccupation with what becomes a man, and doing all of it all the time, comes across as protesting too much. That was certainly how it struck theater critic James Agate, who made "the startling suggestion that 'Ernest Hemingway' is the nom-de-plume of a maiden lady of the most rigid respectability . . . [His] prose . . . lays so much stress on the author's masculinity that one suspects femininity's cloak."

THE TRUE SENTENCE

Hemingway once described his purpose in life as the search for "the true sentence." This holy grail may have shown up in the manuscripts stolen at the Gare de Lyon, but it seems unlikely. If Hemingway's prentice hand was anything like most other prentice hands, it was probably less assured than it was destined to become. Hemingway-lovers are lucky in the respect that they have an extensive body of work to savor. Perhaps there is no need to rue the loss of the portrait of the artist as a young man. **GL**

WHAT HAPPENED NEXT . . .

No one knows who stole Hadley's valise or what happened to her husband's stories. The thief was probably a Frenchman with little or no English; even if he read them and judged them masterpieces, they had no commercial value at the time so he probably ditched them or destroyed them. But for some people the wish is father to the hope that they may yet turn up. Hemingway's first full-length novel, *The Sun Also Rises*, was published in 1926.

WILL IT EVER HAPPEN?

Many people are already credited with—or accused of—writing like Hemingway. More than half a century after the author's death, English prose has moved on—or at least away—from the style with which his name remains synonymous; if it survives at all it is only in the form of parody. And in the case of these manuscripts, we have nothing to go on; there are not even fragments.

DAS SCHLOSS

Author Franz Kafka **Year** 1924 **Country** Czechoslovakia **Genre** Novel

FRANZ KAFKA
Kafka was a Czech who communicated in German because that was the local language of commerce (his father was a kosher butcher). Thus throughout his life he was regarded as an outsider by three different groups of people: Czechs, Germans, and Jews.

By the time his short life was ended by tuberculosis in 1924, Franz Kafka had gained some local celebrity in his native Prague for short works of prose fiction, including *Die Verwandlung* (*Metamorphosis*, 1915) and *In der Strafkolonie* (*In the Penal Colony*, 1919). In common with most authors, Kafka did not want to publish anything before it was finished to his complete satisfaction, so when death became imminent he wrote in a letter to his friend Max Brod that "everything I leave behind me . . . is to be burned unread and to the last page."

However, Brod ignored this instruction because he felt that as a literary executor he owed more to posterity than to the deceased. Less than two months after Kafka's funeral, Brod entered an agreement with a publisher to complete and edit three unfinished novels—*Der Prozess* (The Trial), *Das Schloss* (The Castle), and *Amerika*—which then appeared in print in 1925, 1926, and 1927, respectively.

These works have since become great monuments of world literature, partly because they seem to capture the spirit of paranoia and the worst frustrations of bureaucracy, and partly because they are oddly enigmatic and open to numerous interpretations. *Merriam-Webster's Dictionary* defines the adjective "Kafkaesque" as "having a nightmarishly complex, bizarre, or illogical quality." This mysteriousness prompted Nobel laureate Elias Canetti to call Kafka "the only essentially Chinese writer to be found in the West." According to critic George Steiner, *Der Prozess* was "an overwhelming feat of metaphysical–religious imagining and inquiry"; others have hailed Kafka as one of the first harbingers of Existentialism.

CHAMPIONED BY BROD

But whatever the novels may be, it is certain that they are not wholly the work of Kafka: they are Kafka through the filter of Max Brod. Brod, though a writer himself—best known in Kafka's lifetime for the historical novel *The Redemption of Tycho Brahe*—was predominantly a talent-spotter and, as subsequent events demonstrated, something of an entrepreneur. He was partly responsible for bringing the novelist Jaroslav Hašek (author of *The Good Soldier Švejk*, 1923, another unfinished work) and the classical composer Leoš Janácek to international attention.

Cover: Heath Killen

ATTRACTION OF OPPOSITES

Max Brod was born in Prague in 1884. By the time he entered the city's Charles University he was already something of a literary sensation, and in 1902 his celebrity emboldened him to deliver a lecture on Schopenhauer. At the end of his address, Franz Kafka—another law student in the year above—went to the front of the auditorium and objected to Brod's description of Nietzsche as a fraud. Their discussion moved on to other matters, and they found much in common, especially in their literary tastes. They soon became firm friends.

The two young men were chalk and cheese. Brod was small and physically unprepossessing, with pronounced curvature of the spine; but he was an extrovert who had a stream of attractive blondes in tow. Kafka was tall and handsome, but shy and withdrawn and constantly worried about dandruff and constipation.

For years Brod had no idea that Kafka was also a writer, but as soon as he realized he encouraged his efforts and championed his early work with colleagues on *Prager Tagblatt*, the newspaper on which Brod worked as a drama and music critic after graduation. Kafka meanwhile went to work as a clerk in an insurance company, where he remained almost until his death.

Brod died in Tel Aviv in 1968 and is buried next to Kafka in the New Jewish Cemetery in Prague.

In 1907 Brod listed in a Berlin weekly paper the contemporary authors who maintained what he termed the "exalted standards" of German literature. To already well-known novelists such as Heinrich Mann and Frank Wedekind, Brod added the name of Franz Kafka, who had thus far published nothing and would appear in print for the first time only in the following year.

When Brod—like Kafka, a Jew—fled Prague in 1939 on the last train out before Hitler closed the Czech border, he took with him a suitcase full of Kafka papers. He settled in Palestine, which in 1948 became the state of Israel. He became a drama advisor to the Habima drama company, the forerunner of the national theater of Israel, and wrote several more novels. By the time he died, aged 84, he had written 83 books.

Most of the Kafka material Brod saved from the clutches of the Nazis ended up in the Bodleian Library in Oxford, England, but around one third of it—comprising mainly drawings, diaries, letters, and drafts—remained in Brod's possession until his death, whereupon it passed to his long-time secretary, Esther Hoffe.

SCATTERING THE LEGACY

In 1988, Esther Hoffe auctioned the manuscript of *Der Prozess* for nearly $2 million; it ended up in the German Literature Archive in Marbach. She also sold some of Kafka's letters: these went to private individuals, also in Germany. Among those who disapproved of these sales was Philip Roth, American author of *Portnoy's Complaint* (1969), who pointed out the ironies that Kafka was Czech, not German, and that his three sisters had perished in concentration camps during the Second World War.

Hoffe died in 2007 and bequeathed Kafka's remaining papers to her two daughters. But the National Library of Israel contested her will and there followed years of litigation which continues to this day. The state wanted the material to form part of its collection of the works and memorabilia of great Jewish authors. Mark H. Gelber, professor of comparative literature at Ben-Gurion University, asserted: "It belongs in Jerusalem . . . Kafka was a totally engaged Jewish personality and writer." Hoffe's children, however, wanted to sell at least some of it to Germany, where it could take its place alongside Kafka's greatest novel.

The question of whether the manuscripts should be in the country of the survivors of the Holocaust or in that of the descendants of those who perpetrated it is vexed and heavy with symbolism. But Reiner Stach, Kafka's latest biographer, believes that Kafka's own views of Zionism and Judaism

> *"Has anyone ever seen that letter?*
> *What if this is all some big idea Brod had?"*
>
> Avi Steinberg

are irrelevant: "The fact that specifically Jewish experiences are reflected in his works does not, as Brod believed, make him the protagonist of a 'Jewish' literature. Kafka's oeuvre stands in the context of European literary modernity, and his texts are among the foundational documents of this modernity."

In the view of many, Max Brod not only used Kafka's work to enrich himself (and, as it turns out, his heirs) but also co-opted it into the promotion of ideals that the author himself may not have espoused. Among them was Zionism. Brod was a passionate lifelong believer in the need for a Jewish homeland, and claimed that "only sickness and sudden death" prevented

THE SMALLEST SCRAP

Kafka left only a small corpus of published work. To this Max Brod added the three unfinished novels and everything that his friend had ever sent him: "I never once threw away the smallest scrap of paper that came from him, no, not even a postcard," he subsequently claimed.

Brod later tried to create an image of Kafka as a Zionist, asserting that only his terminal illness had prevented him from emigrating to Palestine. He also promoted the author as visionary: "If humanity would only better understand what has been presented to it in the person and work of Kafka, it would undoubtedly be in a quite different position . . . Kafka is more than any other modern writer—he is the 20th-century Job." Such claims may sound hyperbolic, but that does not necessarily make them false.

AMERIKA AND DER PROZESS

Regardless of whether these books were written by Kafka, they are undeniably Kafkaesque. *Amerika* concerns the travails of Karl Rossmann, a 16-year-old who flees from Europe in pursuit of happiness but finds the United States a land of opportunity only for others, including a pair of drifters who seem to befriend him but then steal his food and clothes.

Widely acknowledged as the chef d'oeuvre, *Der Prozess* is a study of paranoia. The protagonist, Josef K, is arrested on his 30th birthday by a shadowy pair of secret agents and charged with an unspecified crime. He is later released pending the hearing, but he is not told where or when that will be held. In the meantime, other aspects of his life take on similarly nightmarish qualities: everyone he encounters knows that he's in serious trouble. On his 31st birthday, two men take him out and stab him, "like a dog." He dies without ever discovering what he'd done wrong.

LAST LOVE

In 1923, Kafka fell in love with Dora Diamant, who had run away from her conservative Hasidic family. The couple lived together in a rented room in Berlin until Kafka's health began to fail and they moved to a sanitorium in Kierling, Austria. There he succumbed to his disease in his girlfriend's arms. Diamant also kept some of Kafka's papers after his death, but they were confiscated by the Nazis in 1933.

Kafka from joining him on the shores of the Mediterranean. But there is abundant conflicting evidence to suggest that Kafka harbored serious misgivings about the project, and he has been quoted as saying that he both admired it and was nauseated by it. (Indeed, he was notably ambivalent about almost everything, and one of the aims of modern Kafka studies is to determine what he "really" thought.)

Brod's reputation has been in steady decline for many years. The falling off became noticeable in 1937, when he published the first major biography of Kafka, in which he claimed that its subject, though not "a perfect saint," was "on the road to becoming one." Such assertions—and the work as a whole—were widely scorned, not least by the critic Walter Benjamin, who wrote that it showed a "lack of any deep understanding of Kafka's life."

Brod made matters worse when his editions of Kafka's diaries (1948–49) and letters (1954 and 1958) removed all salacious references, including accounts of visits to brothels, and thereby aroused further suspicions about his reliability as keeper of the literary flame. In 2010, Avi Steinberg, author of *Running the Books: The Adventures of an Accidental Prison Librarian* (2010), went so far as to doubt the authenticity of the original dying wish: "The thing is," he told *The New York Times*, "we only have Brod's word for any of this. What if Kafka never even told him to burn his stuff? Has anyone ever seen that letter? What if this is all some big idea Brod had?"

In the light of such misgivings, what is to be made of the following note by Brod in the first edition of *Das Schloss*?

> "Kafka never wrote the concluding chapter. But he told me about it once when I asked him how the novel was to end. The ostensible Land Surveyor was to find partial satisfaction at least. He was not to relax in his struggle, but was to die worn out by it. Round his death-bed the villagers were to assemble, and from the Castle itself

the word was to come through that K's legal claim to live in the village was not valid, yet, taking certain auxiliary circumstances into account, he was permitted to live and work there."

Of course this is interesting if true, but the doubts about Brod's veracity have led to questions about which bits of the published works are authentic Kafka and which are interpolations.

Brod acknowledges—or claims to have made—a contribution to the ending of *Das Schloss*, but what else might he have altered or added? Does it matter, given that we know that the greater part of the work is genuine? (Or at least we think we do: one academic has suggested—only semi-frivolously—that the entire posthumous oeuvre might be the work of Brod, who attributed it to his strange deceased friend in order to make it more saleable.)

ABIDING QUESTION

Ultimately readers must make up their own minds. But there remains a core dilemma: the question of whether authorship is important. If a work is good, that is all it needs to be, regardless of the identity of its creator. It makes no difference to *Hamlet* if the play was written by William Shakespeare or (as some believe) by Francis Bacon or Christopher Marlowe.

In the case of Kafka/Brod, perhaps the problem stems not so much from the desire for certainty about authorship as from the wish that all works should be complete. People want loose ends tied up. Yet many writers, having produced effective beginnings and middles, fall at the final hurdle. E.M. Forster asserted that "nearly all novels are feeble at the end." This is often particularly true of thrillers, murder mysteries that succeed artistically only for as long as the suspense is maintained; the resolutions of such tales tend to be contrived, perfunctory failures.

Perhaps the elegant solution here would be to apply stylometric analysis to *Der Prozess*, *Das Schloss*, and *Amerika* and thus determine who wrote what and then bring out revised editions that feature only the undisputed work of Kafka. His imperfections, if there are any, can be pieced out, and there will be no need to worry about the input of Max Brod. Unless or until this research is carried out, we may never know which of the two men wrote these unfinished novels. However, we can be certain that at least one of them did. **GL**

WHAT HAPPENED NEXT . . .

The term "Kafkaesque" has been widely adopted in many languages to mean the isolation of people in a dehumanized world. Kafka studies became one of the most productive academic industries: it has been estimated that a new work in the field is currently published every two weeks. A few of these contributions tackle the question of authorship, but most attempt to divine the "true meaning" in a way that assumes such an objective is ever achievable.

WILL IT EVER HAPPEN?

8/10

One day the litigation will be concluded. That seems inevitable. It may be that thereafter all the papers will finally enter the public domain, in Germany, Israel, or perhaps the Czech Republic, and scholars will finally be able to determine the exact extent of Max Brod's involvement in and influence on the work of Franz Kafka. In the meantime, however, readers have to make do with the extant texts of the novels which, though not universally accepted as definitive, are still of sufficient quality to stand on their own, regardless of whether Brod turns out to have been the editor or the sole author. This is one mystery that will not have a disappointing dénouement.

THE EMPTY CHAIR

Author Graham Greene **Year** 1926 **Country** UK **Genre** Mystery novel

GRAHAM GREENE
Although the author did not start *The Empty Chair* with the intention of not finishing it, in *The End of the Affair* (1951) he notes that "A story has no beginning or end: arbitrarily one chooses that moment from which to look back or from which to look ahead."

In 1926, Graham Greene came down from Oxford and, after working briefly in Nottingham, began his first proper job on *The Times* in London. During his probationary period as a sub-editor on the newspaper, he prepared to convert from the Anglican faith in which he had been raised, and started work on a novel. His adopted Roman Catholicism remained with him for the rest of his life, but his first book proved less durable: it was abandoned at approximately 22,000 words, part of the way (probably) into chapter 5. The manuscript then disappeared from view. Greene died in 1991. Eighteen years later, François Gallix, a French academic researching "Graham Greene New Perspectives," came upon *The Empty Chair* in the Greene archive at the Harry Ransom Center at the University of Texas in Austin.

A LOCKED-ROOM MURDER MYSTERY

Greene's lost work was—or was on the way to becoming—a locked-room murder mystery. The setting is a country house party hosted by Alice Lady Perriham, an actress who married into the aristocracy and who is described as being "exquisitely conscious of looking no older than 35." The guests find on the premises the body of Richard Groves, "a dark, surly, underhand brute," with a knife sticking out of his chest. Greene was probably inspired to have a try at this classic genre by the success of Agatha Christie's *The Mysterious Affair at Styles*, published in 1920.

The discovery of the unfinished *The Empty Chair* did not create literary shockwaves, however. Although most artists' reputations decline in the years immediately following their demise, Greene's took a particular beating. Some of his lifelong themes, such as religion, had become unfashionable, and it was only after Greene's death that people began to question the veracity of one of the great stories on which his persona had been based. In *A Sort of Life* (1971), a memoir, he wrote that he had attempted suicide by playing Russian roulette alone as a child. But now that he was dead—regardless of whether the story was a confession or a claim—the truth was unverifiable and those who doubted the tale began to express their opinion openly.

Nevertheless, it was still an interesting find. It was then just a matter of deciding what best to do with it. The executors of Greene's estate agreed that the manuscript was too slim to be published as a stand-alone volume, so *The*

Cover: Isabel Eeles

SELF-CENSORSHIP

After *The Man Within* (1929), Greene was displeased with his second and third novels. In his autobiography, *Ways of Escape* (1980), he wrote that "*The Name of Action* and *Rumour at Nightfall* can now be found only in secondhand bookshops at an exaggerated price, since some years after their publication I suppressed them."

By "suppressed," Greene meant that he bought up as many copies as he could find and destroyed them. But a few escaped his net, and by the end of his life they were changing hands for around £500 ($800) each. However, after his death, the bottom fell out of the market: copies can currently be picked up online for less than half that amount.

Empty Chair did not appear in book form, but instead was serialized over five editions of *The Strand Magazine*, beginning in 2009. The periodical, founded in Britain by George Newnes, had published fact and fiction monthly over more than 700 editions since 1891. It made its name with Arthur Conan Doyle's *The Hound of the Baskervilles*, which also appeared in serial form, and later featured work by authors as varied and distinguished as Rudyard Kipling, Dorothy L. Sayers, Edgar Wallace, H.G. Wells, and Graham Greene himself. After the Second World War, circulation declined, and the magazine ceased publication in 1950. In 1998, it was revived in the United States as a quarterly, going on to publish newly unearthed stories by Mark Twain and P.G. Wodehouse.

Frank Simon, associate publisher of *The Strand Magazine*, batted away any suggestion that the author of *The Empty* Chair had not yet served enough

THE THIRD MAN

Plenty of Greene's novels were turned into films, but *The Third Man* (1949) was a film script that the author only subsequently turned into a book. The best-known bit of dialogue, however—the line about the only thing the Swiss ever produced being the cuckoo clock—was not the work of the writer but a contribution by the star, Orson Welles.

time in limbo. "Despite being dead for almost 20 years," he said, "Greene is very much alive in the conscious [*sic*] of the reading public." The magazine's managing editor, Andrew Gulli, extolled the fragment, asserting confidently that "in the case of *The Empty Chair*, Greene manages to combine many of the great characteristics of his work—seamless prose, tight dialogue—and we have characters speaking about some of the themes that Greene was famous for, such as discussions about good and evil. Although he wrote it when he was 22, it's clearly a work by Greene, the work of a mature writer."

The first part of *The Empty Chair* appeared in the June–September 2009 edition of *The Strand Magazine*. At the suggestion of Greene's son, Francis, the magazine ran a competition inviting readers to finish the novel. The $500 prize was won by Michael Stanley, the joint *nom de plume* of Michael Sears and Stanley Trollip, South African authors of the Detective Kubu mysteries.

> *"Although he wrote it when he was 22, it's clearly a work by Greene, the work of a mature writer."*
>
> Andrew Gulli

The completed work is referenced on the Michael Stanley website, where the ending is summarized thus: "At first it seems straightforward, but the case becomes more and more complicated. Inspector Maybury—an intriguing stamp-collecting detective—follows the trail. But it's the aging actor—Sir John Collis—who unravels the mystery."

A LINGERING PUZZLE

Yet Stanley's completed version is not for sale either as a printed book or in electronic form. *The Strand Magazine* retains the rights to the work, and at face value it seems puzzling that it has not capitalized on it. But there may be a clue to the reason in Gulli's insistence that "whatever happens, we want to make sure the estate of Graham Greene is happy." Perhaps the keepers of the original author's flame are unwilling to permit publication. Alternatively, it may be that they feared there would be insufficient demand. Whatever the explanation, it is certain—in view of the ease with which e-books can be generated and the large number of Detective Kubu titles that are available on Kindle and kindred readers, as well as from HarperCollins—that Stanley would have produced some sort of edition if "he" was at liberty to do so.

The Empty Chair is a mystery that has still not given up all its secrets. **GL**

WHAT HAPPENED NEXT . . .

After *The Empty Chair* returned to the light of day, Greene's former employer *The Times* printed an extract from the first chapter in a literary quiz that required readers to guess the identity of the author. Only three entrants got it right; most of them thought it was Agatha Christie (below).

This is not the first time that readers have failed to recognize Greene's work. In 1949, the *New Statesman* ran a competition for a parody of Graham Greene, who was by then well established as a novelist. Greene himself entered, under a pseudonym, and didn't win.

WILL IT EVER HAPPEN?

5/10

In a way, it already has happened: it is available from *The Strand Magazine* as a box set of the relevant back issues. But as a book? That depends on the wishes of the Greene estate, the willingness of the magazine, and the involvement of a publisher: tripartite agreements are not impossible, but they are seldom the work of a moment.

IL VEGLIARDO

Author Italo Svevo **Year** 1928 **Country** Italy **Genre** Novel

ITALO SVEVO
The son of an Italian mother and a German Jewish father, Ettore Schmitz took his pen name in reference to his own heritage: "Italo" is self-explanatory; "Svevo" means "from Swabia," a historical region of southwest Germany.

Italian author Italo Svevo—or Ettore Schmitz to give him his real name—came to fame late in life. It was not until he was in his sixties that he published *La coscienza di Zeno* (*The Confessions of Zeno*, 1923), the novel that would propel him onto the international stage. As he remarked in 1924, the year after the book was released: "Until last year, I was . . . the least ambitious old man in the world. Now I am overcome by ambition. I have become eager for praise. I now live only to manage my own glory."

Keen to capitalize on the success of his comic masterpiece, Svevo soon embarked on a sequel, *Il vegliardo* (translated in English as "Further Confessions of Zeno" or "The Old Old Man"). However, it was left tantalizingly unfinished when the author died in a car accident on September 13, 1928.

Finally fêted in literary circles in the last years of his life, Svevo made up for the decades of rejection that he had suffered as a young writer. His first two novels, *Una vita* (*A Life*, 1892) and *Senilità* (*As A Man Grows Older*, 1898), were published while he was in his twenties to an indifferent response from critics. Deeply wounded by this reception to his writing, he renounced his literary ambitions and devoted himself to commerce. It was only when he met the young Irish author James Joyce in 1907 that he was brought back into the literary fold. Joyce encouraged Svevo to take up writing again and, when Svevo produced *La coscienza di Zeno*, sent the novel to two influential French critics, Valéry Larbaud and Benjamin Crémieux, who brought it to public attention.

LATE BLOSSOM

Two years before his death, Svevo started work on drafts of his fourth novel. In August 1928 he wrote to Crémieux's wife, translator Marie-Anne Comnène: "I want to write another novel, *Il vegliardo*, a continuation of Zeno. I've written several chapters but they'll have to be done again. A certain false note has crept into them. Can it be an old man's incapacity?"

In spite of—or perhaps because of—his advancing age and failing health, Svevo threw himself into writing what would be his final novel. *Il vegliardo* sees a return to Svevo's favorite themes: moral weakness, existential alienation, and obsession with death. In the surviving fragments that are considered to be part of the novel, the author revisits many of the characters

Cover: Steve Panton

SVEVO AND JOYCE

Svevo's life changed in 1907 when he began English lessons with a young Irishman named James Joyce (below). Despite the differences in age and nationality, the two men soon realized that they had much in common and became firm friends. Joyce was instrumental in reigniting Svevo's ambitions as an author. He read and admired the older writer's first two novels, *Una vita* and *Senilità*, praising them widely to his friends. Joyce's enthusiasm was, according to Svevo's wife Livia, the "spark" that was needed to take Svevo out of his literary "half-sleep." The Italian author was not the only one to benefit creatively from the friendship: it has often been said that Svevo was the inspiration for Leopold Bloom, the protagonist of Joyce's *Ulysses* (1922).

of *La coscienza di Zeno*, including the protagonist Zeno Cosini, the neurotic, philandering antihero who is now, like his creator, entering the last years of his life. Through Zeno, Svevo explores old age and its highs and lows.

Critics are divided as to what actually would have been included by Svevo in the final version of the book: the five chapters that are commonly grouped together under the title *Il vegliardo* are remarkably diverse, although united by common themes. In one of the fragments, "Le confessioni del vegliardo" (An Old Man's Confessions), the protagonist is even given a different name, Giovanni Respiro, although the similarities with Zeno are evident. Both men are in psychoanalysis, ridden with insecurities, and dislocated from the world around them. As with Zeno's narrative, the Giovanni Respiro story is framed in the form of an autobiographical letter to his psychoanalyst. However, Bruno Maier, who edited a new version of Svevo's fourth novel that was published in 1989, is convinced that "this fragment has nothing to do with the novel *Il vegliardo*. At the very most, Svevo must have been thinking about writing a new novel altogether or, perhaps, an autobiography in narrative form under the name of Giovanni Respiro." For, as Maier points out, we learn that Respiro is born on December 19, 1861, which was Svevo's actual date of birth.

> *"If it had been completed, the novel might have been his major work."*
>
> Silvio Benco

Opinion is divided on the literary merit of *Il vegliardo*. Critic Elio Gioanola saw Svevo's text as a "substantial repetition" of *La coscienza di Zeno*, although he conceded that there was some development in the character of Zeno. Elsewhere the unfinished novel received a much warmer reception. Silvio Benco, a renowned Italian man of letters, went so far as to say that "the pages of *Il vegliardo* which have been found . . . could easily be the beginning of a masterpiece . . . If it had been completed, the novel might have been his major work."

Like his most famous fictional character, Svevo was a chain-smoker who was always having his "last cigarette." In the fall of 1928, he was sent off by his doctor for a cure in the Italian Alps, with strict instructions to stop smoking. While there, he continued work on his novel. In her memoir of their life together, his wife Livia describes him writing away furiously in his room: "Until the end he worked fervently on the novel *Il vegliardo*. That morning he was actually writing when I called to tell him everything was ready for departure. He abruptly interrupted his writing."

For some time, Svevo had been convinced that he was going to die. The morning before they set off to return to their home in Trieste, this heavy foreboding seems to have hit him with particular force. The final page on which he was working when Livia interrupted him was from the fragment "La morte" (Death), which narrates the story of an elderly couple, Roberto

SIBLING DEVOTION
This portrait of Italo Svevo and his sister Ortensia was painted by his friend, the Italian artist Umberto Veruda. Veruda, a dedicated bohemian known for his flamboyant clothing, was an important influence on Svevo. Their fellow Triestine Silvio Benco remarked that the painter gave the writer the gift of learning to laugh at life instead of dying under it.

and Teresa (again, it is controversial as to whether this would have been part of the final novel). Roberto is a firm atheist, whereas his wife is a devout Catholic who is forever trying to convert him, mirroring Svevo's own experience with Livia. Roberto suddenly falls ill and dies; Svevo was writing the death scene when he was called to leave:

> "His death was exactly the one he had not wanted: terror . . . and for a long time Teresa considered, hesitantly, the horror of that death. He had admitted to a sin: what fault? His irreligion. And she thought that at the last minute he had been converted. All that was left of Roberto on earth, that is to say in Teresa's heart, was converted. A silent conversation took place, only the fai . . ."

There the writing stops suddenly.

Svevo and his wife set off in the car back to Trieste, driven by their nephew. Pouring rain made conditions difficult; a couple of hours into their journey, they came off the road and hit a tree. The author's injuries were not immediately thought to be serious: his femur was fractured, but he seemed otherwise unharmed. However, he had a smoking-related heart condition which, when combined with the shock of the accident, proved fatal. He died just 24 hours after being admitted to hospital. JL

WILL IT EVER HAPPEN?

1/10

Svevo left behind a collection of texts that squabbling critics have been unable to piece together in a satisfactory way. Perhaps someone will uncover a missing chapter in an overlooked notebook which will draw the narrative into a coherent whole. However, it seems unlikely.

WHAT HAPPENED NEXT . . .
After Svevo's death, his wife Livia (below right, with Svevo and their daughter) gathered together his unpublished writings, sorting through copious material. She said of this task: "I found everything in great disorder, letters jumbled with unpublished work, notes for the last novel mixed with thoughts and plays. These papers reflected the absorbed, absent-minded man he had always been." The resulting volume was released in April 1929.

ŽIVOT A DÍLO SKLADATELE FOLTÝNA

Author Karel Čapek **Year** 1938 **Country** Czechoslovakia **Genre** Novel

KAREL ČAPEK
Čapek's reputation was immense in his lifetime but today he is unjustly neglected. In this respect he is the opposite of his fellow countryman, Franz Kafka, whose acclaim has almost all been posthumous. This may be because Kafka wrote in German while Čapek wrote in Czech.

Karel Čapek is a Czech author credited with coining a term that has been adopted in many languages around the world. In his 1920 play *RUR*, he took his native word for "forced labor," adapted it, and applied it to humanoid machines that performed menial tasks: hence "robot" (from the Czech *robota*) displaced "automaton" as the most widely used name for such creations.

MAN OF PARTS

It is unfortunate that Čapek should be so strongly associated with a single word when he wrote so much of great and abiding interest. His works—short stories and novels, as well as plays—are all about ideas: not only their exposition, but also their ramifications and possibilities. To that extent, he may put Anglophones in mind of his contemporary, George Bernard Shaw.

The Irish playwright tended to grade and compartmentalize his published thought into Prefaces that examined the issues and Plays that presented it in diluted popular form. By contrast, in Čapek, we get it all in a single package. *RUR* (initials that stand for "Rossum's Universal Robots") keeps the audience thinking throughout. The play opens in the factory that makes the machines. We learn first of the manufacturer's utopian wish to free humans from "the degradation of work"—straight off, Čapek launches an attack on the concept of the dignity of labor. Then he introduces questions of gender stereotyping. A visitor asks: "Why do you make male and female robots when sex means nothing to them?" The factory manager replies: "There's a demand: servants, saleswomen, stenographers. People are used to it."

The audience may at this point begin to suspect that *RUR* is agitprop, but they are mistaken: there is much more to it than that. Almost immediately Čapek turns his attention to matters of philosophy and theology. The humans who wanted godlike powers (and godlike leisure) are dismayed by the responsibilities that lack of responsibility brings. They start to long for the very thing they once disdained—"Pray for deliverance: aid mankind to return to work." When the robots (no doubt inevitably) become rebellious and demand equal status, the humans protest: "Someone must give the orders." To this they receive a dusty answer: "I don't want any master. I know everything for myself." At the end of the play, the last surviving human—now a kind of

Cover: Isabel Eeles

ARTISTIC FRATERNITY

Karel Čapek always credited the coinage of the word "robot" to his elder brother, Josef (right in the photograph, with Karel). Josef Čapek began his working life as a cartoonist on *Lidove Noviny*, a Prague daily newspaper. He then wrote and illustrated children's books, most famously *Pejsek a Kočička* (*Doggie and Pussycat*, 1929), a Czech classic that has been widely translated.

When Germany annexed Bohemia and Moravia in 1938, Josef publicly expressed his hostility to Nazism and the Western powers that connived at Hitler's expansionism. When the remainder of Czechoslovakia was invaded in the following year, Josef was arrested and sent to Bergen-Belsen, where he wrote *Básněz koncentračního tabora* (*Poems from a Concentration Camp*, 1946) before he died there just weeks before the liberation.

deity—waves farewell to the first two robots capable of procreation—the new Adam and Eve—as they go off to start their life together. It may appear that the play has gone from the world of Shaw to that of John Milton in *Paradise Lost* (1667), but it would be more accurate to say that Čapek has put a girdle round them both in fewer than 100 pages.

Čapek's other works are similarly ambitious thematically. *Trapné povídky* (*Money and Other Stories,* 1921) concerns humanity's attempts to break free from its destiny, and the ways in which its efforts invariably misfire, backfire, and are otherwise subverted. Several of his novels examine how scientific advances can be mixed blessings; he wrote a celebrated play on the same theme, *Válka s mloky* (*The War with the Newts*, 1936).

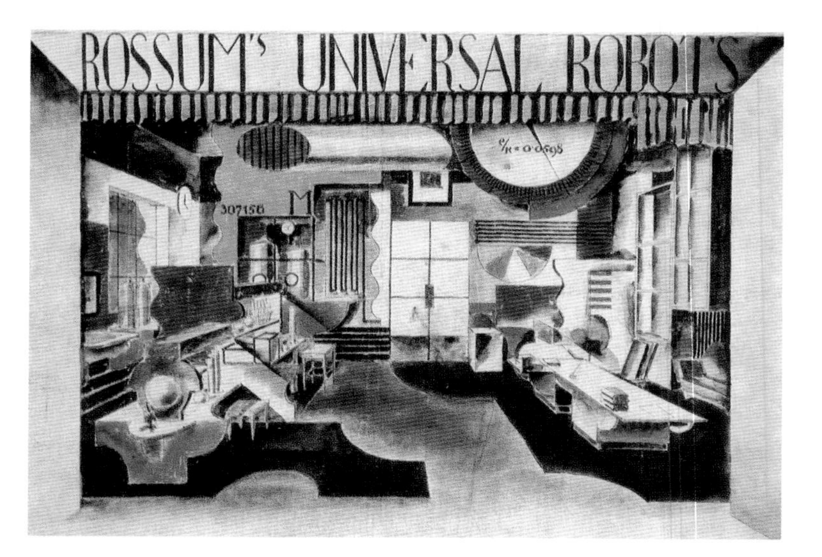

RUR

A sketch by Bedrich Feuerstein of the set design for the first performance of *RUR* in Prague in 1921. The play was a critical and popular success, and by 1923 had been translated into 30 languages.

Čapek did high seriousness, but he was not constrained by it. He also demonstrated a mastery of comedy, notably in *Ze života hmyzu* (*The Insect Play*, 1921)—co-written with his brother Josef—a satire of greed in the manner of Molière and Ben Jonson. Anyone in need of a paradigm of an intellectual need look no further than Karel Čapek.

This makes it all the more disappointing that the novel that he was working on when he died remains unfinished. The extant fragment of *Život a dílo skladatele Foltýna* (*The Life and Work of the Composer Foltýn*) takes on subjects even bigger than those Čapek had previously tackled. Here he examines the nature of perception and reality. The central character is a musician who has carved a reputation as a serious composer but still harbors doubts about his own ability. This uncertainty feeds off his failed attempts to write an opera. He has the work in his mind, and he believes it will go down in history as his chef d'oeuvre if only he can get it out of his head and onto the staff. But he cannot.

A lesser writer might have used a single narrator, omniscient or otherwise, but Čapek reveals Foltýn through the eyes of ten characters who know the composer or his work: his wife, friends, rivals, critics. Their relationship with Foltýn is symbiotic: he makes impressions on them, and their judgments of his character influence his self-image: he is buoyed by some of their

> *"Pray for deliverance: aid mankind to return to work."*
>
> *RUR*

praise, but rejects other compliments because, he thinks, the givers don't really understand him. By the same token, he dismisses some criticism, both favorable and hostile, as unworthy of his attention, but other reviews—particularly those that suggest he is a plagiarist—wound him deeply.

Multiple narratives are seldom used because they are so demanding; among the most notable authors to have adopted the format is Robert Browning, whose *The Ring and the Book* (1869) tells the story of a murder from several different points of view. This verse novel of 21,000 lines was a best seller on publication, but is seldom read today.

Which of the commentators is right about Foltýn? We never discover. That may be because the work is unfinished, but it is more likely because there is no answer. Čapek is making a more subtle point: through his prism we witness an extended meditation on the nature of truth and the tensions between appearance and reality.

In the 1930s the rise of Nazism in neighboring Germany prompted Čapek to produce works that were less cerebral and more overt calls to his compatriots for action against the enemy at the door. He lived to see the dismemberment of his country under the Munich Agreement between Hitler and British prime minister Neville Chamberlain, but died of pneumonia on Christmas Day 1938. His brother (see panel, above left) was not so fortunate. **GL**

WHAT HAPPENED NEXT . . .

Not a great deal. *Život a dílo skladatele Foltýna* remains a refined taste that may be sampled only by readers of Czech: it is unavailable in translation. This is emblematic of a continuing disconnect between the Czechs and the rest of Europe—in some ways they remain as Neville Chamberlain notoriously described them in 1938, "people of whom we know nothing." It is our loss as much as theirs.

WILL IT EVER HAPPEN?

The fragment we have seems to tell us all we need to know. Completion by another hand would be little more than a recapitulation of what Čapek has already made clear. It may be that the original author would have taken the work in an unexpected direction, but that would have been his privilege; for a continuator to do so would be a violation. However, even in fragmentary form, it deserves a wider audience than it can reach for as long as it is available only in the original Czech: this is a publishing opportunity.

THE LOVE OF THE LAST TYCOON

Author F. Scott Fitzgerald **Year** 1940 **Country** United States **Genre** Novel

F. SCOTT FITZGERALD
The key chronicler of the United States between the end of the First World War in 1918 and the 1929 Wall Street crash—the Jazz Age—Fitzgerald's output was both inspired and inhibited by his alcoholism and his unhappy marriage.

When F. Scott Fitzgerald died in December 1940 he was working on a novel about Hollywood. He was writing to the very last, to the day before he died, aged only 44. It was posthumously edited and published by the American scholar and critic Edmund Wilson as *The Last Tycoon*. Thirty-one chapters were planned, but only 17 were written. There were, however, copious notes, some of which Wilson published to accompany the fragment. Fitzgerald saw Hollywood at close hand in his later years, when, desperate to earn a living, he accepted employment as a scriptwriter, and collided with hacks with "a vocabulary of about a hundred words." It was, on the whole, a depressing and unsatisfactory experience.

The hero of the novel is the movie tycoon Monroe Stahr, based on Irving Thalberg, the mogul who died in 1936 aged 37. Stahr has conflicts with Pat Brady, based on producer Louis B. Mayer. The story is partly told through Brady's daughter Cecilia, who is in love with Stahr, who has an affair with the Englishwoman Kathleen Moore, based on the divorcée and gossip-columnist Sheilah Graham (who was also English and had an affair with Fitzgerald; her memories of him are in *Beloved Infidel*, 1958). When Stahr meets Kathleen he feels "glad that there was beauty in the world that would not be weighed in the scales of the casting department."

GREATER THAN GATSBY?

It is possible that had this novel been finished it would have been Fitzgerald's best work, and potentially the best novel written about Hollywood. Fitzgerald is a great novelist, but it has always been possible even for his admirers to find faults and have reservations; even with *The Great Gatsby* (1925) and *Tender is the Night* (1934). Fitzgerald had recovered from the nadir of addiction so movingly expressed in his autobiographical essay "The Crack-Up" (1936), and there is an assured objectivity about *The Love of the Last Tycoon*.

The novel is an extended gasp of protest as literature sees itself mortally threatened by the film industry, which is now the acknowledged legislator of morals, styles of behavior, and modes of internal thought. People behave according the diktats that have been issued from the dream factory. When Stahr and Kathleen are by the Pacific, with thousands of bathers shackled to the apparatus of leisure, the narrator tells us: "It was Stahr's sea if he wanted

Čapek did high seriousness, but he was not constrained by it. He also demonstrated a mastery of comedy, notably in *Ze života hmyzu* (*The Insect Play*, 1921)—co-written with his brother Josef—a satire of greed in the manner of Molière and Ben Jonson. Anyone in need of a paradigm of an intellectual need look no further than Karel Čapek.

This makes it all the more disappointing that the novel that he was working on when he died remains unfinished. The extant fragment of *Život a dílo skladatele Foltýna* (*The Life and Work of the Composer Foltýn*) takes on subjects even bigger than those Čapek had previously tackled. Here he examines the nature of perception and reality. The central character is a musician who has carved a reputation as a serious composer but still harbors doubts about his own ability. This uncertainty feeds off his failed attempts to write an opera. He has the work in his mind, and he believes it will go down in history as his chef d'oeuvre if only he can get it out of his head and onto the staff. But he cannot.

A lesser writer might have used a single narrator, omniscient or otherwise, but Čapek reveals Foltýn through the eyes of ten characters who know the composer or his work: his wife, friends, rivals, critics. Their relationship with Foltýn is symbiotic: he makes impressions on them, and their judgments of his character influence his self-image: he is buoyed by some of their praise, but rejects other compliments because, he thinks, the givers don't really understand him. By the same token, he dismisses some criticism, both favorable and hostile, as unworthy of his attention, but other reviews—particularly those that suggest he is a plagiarist—wound him deeply.

> *"Pray for deliverance: aid mankind to return to work."*
>
> *RUR*

Multiple narratives are seldom used because they are so demanding; among the most notable authors to have adopted the format is Robert Browning, whose *The Ring and the Book* (1869) tells the story of a murder from several different points of view. This verse novel of 21,000 lines was a best seller on publication, but is seldom read today.

Which of the commentators is right about Foltýn? We never discover. That may be because the work is unfinished, but it is more likely because there is no answer. Čapek is making a more subtle point: through his prism we witness an extended meditation on the nature of truth and the tensions between appearance and reality.

In the 1930s the rise of Nazism in neighboring Germany prompted Čapek to produce works that were less cerebral and more overt calls to his compatriots for action against the enemy at the door. He lived to see the dismemberment of his country under the Munich Agreement between Hitler and British prime minister Neville Chamberlain, but died of pneumonia on Christmas Day 1938. His brother (see panel, above left) was not so fortunate. **GL**

WHAT HAPPENED NEXT . . .

Not a great deal. *Život a dílo skladatele Foltýna* remains a refined taste that may be sampled only by readers of Czech: it is unavailable in translation. This is emblematic of a continuing disconnect between the Czechs and the rest of Europe—in some ways they remain as Neville Chamberlain notoriously described them in 1938, "people of whom we know nothing." It is our loss as much as theirs.

WILL IT EVER HAPPEN?

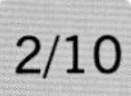

The fragment we have seems to tell us all we need to know. Completion by another hand would be little more than a recapitulation of what Čapek has already made clear. It may be that the original author would have taken the work in an unexpected direction, but that would have been his privilege; for a continuator to do so would be a violation. However, even in fragmentary form, it deserves a wider audience than it can reach for as long as it is available only in the original Czech: this is a publishing opportunity.

THE LOVE OF THE LAST TYCOON

Author F. Scott Fitzgerald **Year** 1940 **Country** United States **Genre** Novel

F. SCOTT FITZGERALD
The key chronicler of the United States between the end of the First World War in 1918 and the 1929 Wall Street crash—the Jazz Age—Fitzgerald's output was both inspired and inhibited by his alcoholism and his unhappy marriage.

When F. Scott Fitzgerald died in December 1940 he was working on a novel about Hollywood. He was writing to the very last, to the day before he died, aged only 44. It was posthumously edited and published by the American scholar and critic Edmund Wilson as *The Last Tycoon*. Thirty-one chapters were planned, but only 17 were written. There were, however, copious notes, some of which Wilson published to accompany the fragment. Fitzgerald saw Hollywood at close hand in his later years, when, desperate to earn a living, he accepted employment as a scriptwriter, and collided with hacks with "a vocabulary of about a hundred words." It was, on the whole, a depressing and unsatisfactory experience.

The hero of the novel is the movie tycoon Monroe Stahr, based on Irving Thalberg, the mogul who died in 1936 aged 37. Stahr has conflicts with Pat Brady, based on producer Louis B. Mayer. The story is partly told through Brady's daughter Cecilia, who is in love with Stahr, who has an affair with the Englishwoman Kathleen Moore, based on the divorcée and gossip-columnist Sheilah Graham (who was also English and had an affair with Fitzgerald; her memories of him are in *Beloved Infidel*, 1958). When Stahr meets Kathleen he feels "glad that there was beauty in the world that would not be weighed in the scales of the casting department."

GREATER THAN GATSBY?

It is possible that had this novel been finished it would have been Fitzgerald's best work, and potentially the best novel written about Hollywood. Fitzgerald is a great novelist, but it has always been possible even for his admirers to find faults and have reservations; even with *The Great Gatsby* (1925) and *Tender is the Night* (1934). Fitzgerald had recovered from the nadir of addiction so movingly expressed in his autobiographical essay "The Crack-Up" (1936), and there is an assured objectivity about *The Love of the Last Tycoon*.

The novel is an extended gasp of protest as literature sees itself mortally threatened by the film industry, which is now the acknowledged legislator of morals, styles of behavior, and modes of internal thought. People behave according the diktats that have been issued from the dream factory. When Stahr and Kathleen are by the Pacific, with thousands of bathers shackled to the apparatus of leisure, the narrator tells us: "It was Stahr's sea if he wanted

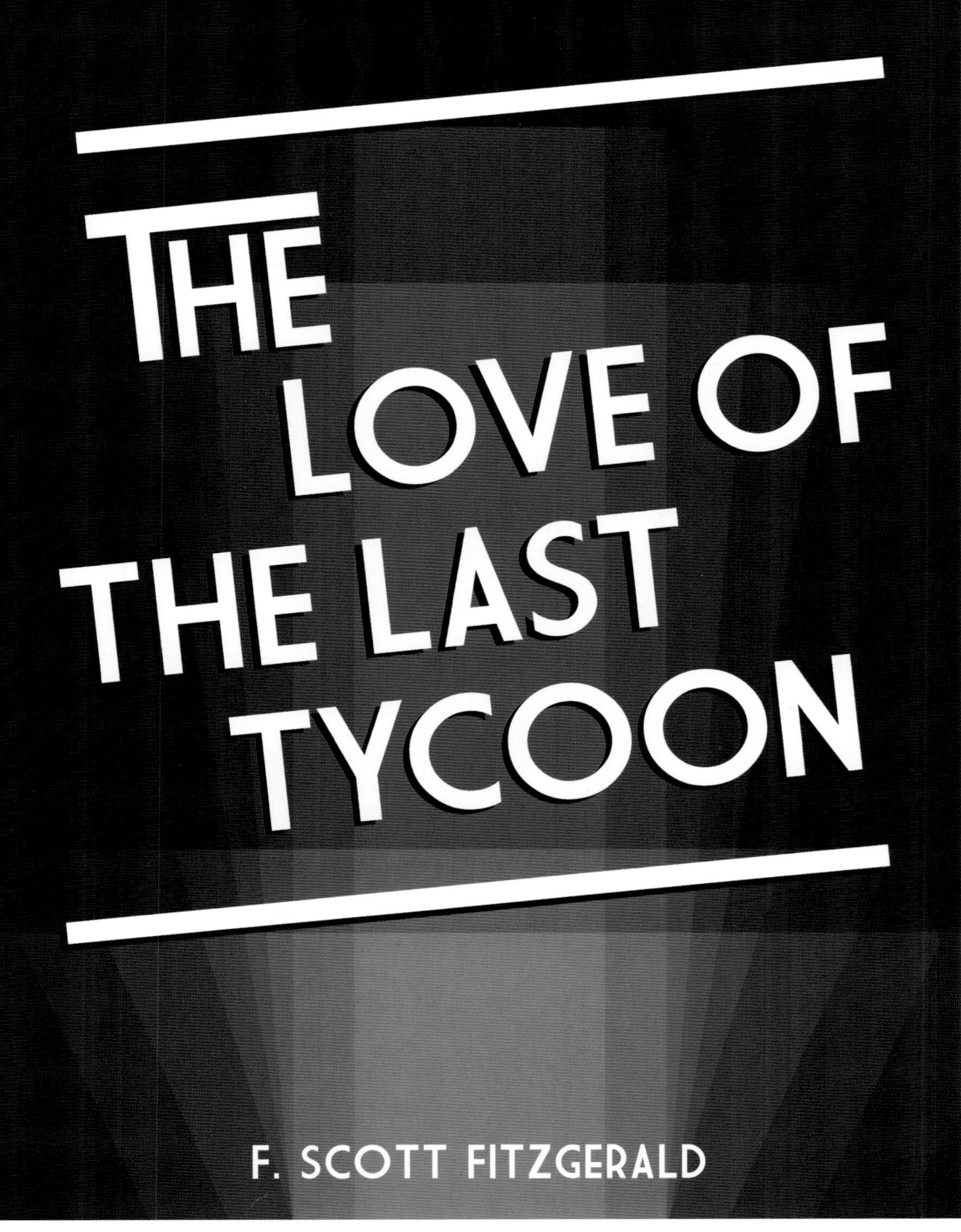

Cover: Sarah Holland

POP MUSIC

Despite his misgivings about the film industry, Fitzgerald was fascinated by it, as he was fascinated by the popular music that is the backing soundtrack for our unfolding lives. Cecilia drives up Laurel Canyon with Harold Spina and Johnny Burke's "The Thundering Beat o' my Heart" and other pieces on the radio.

it, or knew what to do with it—only by sufferance did these others wet their feet and fingers in the wild cool reservoirs of man's world." The movie industry is where the Abbé Prévost's *Manon Lescaut* (1731) is given a happy ending, even though, as Stahr protests: "it had been making money without a happy ending for a century and a half." Although literature has always been affected by the demands of the market-place and the crass tastes of the majority of readers, it has nevertheless, over the centuries, been able to strive for uncompromising aesthetic standards in a certain number of cases. The complex equations of the film industry have made this almost impossible, except for marginal "art films." Stahr does at least see the possibility that a

> *"It was Stahr's sea if he wanted it, or knew what to do with it . . . "*
>
> *The Love of the Last Tycoon*

film could be made that had an aesthetic conscience at its heart, even if it lost money. In the "nickel scene" with the English novelist he demonstrates his clear grasp of the cinematic medium, explaining how storytelling works in movies compared to novels. He is becoming victim, though, to what would now be called "suits."

The most vivid scene—Stahr's first view of Kathleen floating on a statue of Shiva, the Hindu destroyer-god, in a flood caused by an earthquake at the studio—is faithful to the spirit of authentic Hollywood kitsch. It's a surreal world, this Hollywood world, where "the naked cry" of a soprano sings Stanislaus Stange's "Come, come, I love you only" into the night as a man in rubber boots washes a car in a white fountain of light; where a bevy of actors in Regency costumes drifts by on an electric truck; and where Abe Lincoln jams "a triangle of pie" into his mouth.

NOTES TOWARD A CONCLUSION

It's not certain in detail how the novel would have continued. Accustomed to getting his way, Stahr begins an affair with the now-married Kathleen, while his rival at the studio convinces Kathleen's jealous husband, W. Bronson Smith, to murder Stahr. And Stahr might have planned to kill Brady. Fitzgerald had a conception of the ending—in a letter of September 29, 1939, he wrote to his editor, Kenneth Littauer:

> "Now occurs the final episode which should give the novel its quality—and its unusualness. Do you remember about 1933 when a transport plane was wrecked on a mountain-side in the Southwest, and a Senator was killed? The thing that struck me about it was that the country people rifled the bodies of the dead. That is just what happens to this plane which is bearing Stahr from Hollywood. The angle is that of three children who, on a Sunday picnic, are the first to discover the wreckage. Among those killed in the accident besides Stahr are two other characters we

WHAT HAPPENED NEXT . . .

In 1993, as part of *The Cambridge Edition of the Works of F. Scott Fitzgerald*, edited by Matthew J. Bruccoli, the work appeared as *The Love of the Last Tycoon: A Western Story*, the title Fitzgerald himself used. The extant 17 of the 31 planned chapters were reassembled by Bruccoli according to the author's notes, and there are significant differences between this and Edmund Wilson's edition, which was aimed at a popular audience. Bruccoli is justifiably brusque about Wilson's overweening confidence—"often indistinguishable from arrogance"—in his abilities: "He felt superior to Fitzgerald, whom he had patronized for more than 20 years. This attitude made Wilson less than the perfect editor for *The Last Tycoon*."

In 1976 an excellent film version of the novel was released, scripted by Harold Pinter, directed by Elia Kazan (his last film), and produced by Sam Spiegel. *The Last Tycoon* starred Robert De Niro as Monroe Stahr, Theresa Russell as Cecilia Brady, Ingrid Boulting as Kathleen, and featured appearances by Robert Mitchum, Jack Nicholson, and Jeanne Moreau. This film does not end as Fitzgerald imagined with a plane crash. In 2013 a television adaptation was reported to be in development by HBO, scripted and directed by Billy Ray, the screenwriter of *The Hunger Games* (2012) and *Captain Phillips* (2013).

> have met. (I have not been able to go into the minor characters in this short summary.) Of the three children, two boys and a girl, who find the bodies, one boy rifled Stahr's possessions; another, the body of a ruined ex-producer; and the girl, those of a moving picture actress. The possessions which the children find, symbolically determine their attitude toward their act of theft. The possessions of the moving picture actress tend the young girl to a selfish possessiveness; those of the unsuccessful producer sway one of the boys toward an irresolute attitude; while the boy who finds Stahr's briefcase is the one who, after a week, saves and redeems all three by going to a local judge and making a full confession."

But he hadn't got that far when he died on December 21, 1940.

OUTSTANDING DIFFICULTY

There is a technical problem in *The Love of the Last Tycoon*: that it begins as Cecilia Brady's memoir, but then slips into omniscient narration. Perhaps once Fitzgerald worked on it that would have been ironed out. BR

WILL IT EVER HAPPEN?

Fitzgerald left copious notes for the direction of the plot so it is possible for a writer to produce a plausible completion, but they may find it a struggle to replicate his sharp ear for dialogue and alert responsiveness to local color. In a sense, continuations have been attempted when the novel has been filmed and dramatized.

DER MANN OHNE EIGENSCHAFTEN

Author Robert Musil **Year** 1942 **Country** Austria **Genre** Novel

ROBERT MUSIL
Born in 1880 in Klagenfurt, Austria, Musil first studied engineering but changed course to psychology and philosophy at the University of Berlin. His first novel, *Die Verwirrungen des Zöglings Törleß* (*The Confusions of Young Törless*), was published in 1906. After the Anschluss in 1938, he fled to Switzerland, where he died.

Begun in 1921, *Der Mann ohne Eigenschaften* (*The Man Without Qualities*) is an unfinished novel by Robert Musil, who was still writing when he died in 1942. It is set in the time of the Austro-Hungarian monarchy's last days, just before the outbreak of the First World War, and attempts an ambitious assessment of a wide range of subjects and emotions.

AMBITIOUS STRUCTURE

Conceived as a three-volume work, only the first two books were completed. In the first book, "A Sort of Introduction," we are introduced to the main character, a 32-year-old mathematician called Ulrich who is engaged in an unsuccessful search for the meaning of life. His detachment and extreme passivity have brought him to the state of being "a man without qualities." A murderer and rapist, Moosbrugger, appears on the scene; he is condemned for his murder of a prostitute. Other characters include Ulrich's nymphomaniac mistress Bonadea and his friend Walter's neurotic wife Clarisse, whose refusal to submit to banal existence leads to her husband's insanity.

In the second book, "Pseudoreality Prevails," Ulrich joins the so-called "Collateral Campaign" or "Parallel Campaign," as frantic preparations are underway for a celebration in honor of 70 years of the Austrian Emperor Franz Joseph's reign. A couple of people who are part of the organization team catch the eye of Ulrich. Ermelinda Tuzzi, called Diotima, is Ulrich's cousin as well as the wife of a civil servant; she tries to become a Viennese muse of philosophy, inspiring whoever crosses her path. The nobleman in charge of the campaign, the old conservative Count Leinsdorf, has no organizational skills. General Stumm von Bordwehr of the Imperial and Royal Army is unpopular for his attempts in this generally mystical atmosphere to make things systematic, and the German Count Paul Arnheim is an admirer of Diotima's combination of beauty and spirit, without feeling the need to marry her.

While most of the participants (Diotima especially) try to associate the reign of Franz Joseph I with notions of humanity, progress, tradition, and happiness, the followers of Realpolitik see a chance to exploit the situation: Stumm von Bordwehr wishes to get the budget for the Austrian army raised

ROBERT MUSIL

Der Mann ohne Eigenschaften

Cover: Claire Köster

FASHIONISTAS ANATOMIZED
As an illustration of the power of Musil's writing, the following is an extract from "Pseudoreality Prevails," in which female fashion is analyzed:

"In those days, even a person of few prejudices, unhampered by shame in appreciating the undraped human body, would have regarded a display of nudity as a relapse into the animal state, not because of the nakedness, but because of the loss of the civilized aphrodisiac of clothing. In full dress, with frills, puffs, bell-skirts, cascading draperies, laces, and gathered pleats, they had created a surface five times the size of the original one, forming a many-petaled chalice heavy with an erotic charge, difficult of access, and hiding at its core the slim white animal that had to be searched out and that made itself terribly desirable. It was the prescribed process Nature herself uses when she bids her creatures fluff out their plumage . . ."

8½
Der Mann ohen Eigenschaften has inspired productions in other media, including Federico Fellini's classic movie *8½* (1963). The film stars Marcello Mastroianni as a successful director named Guido Anselmi who has got everything in place to make another hit but is stuck for a story to tell. Like Ulrich, Guido is struggling to find a focus. Unable to derive inspiration from his chaotic environment, he immerses himself in the distraction of childhood memories and indulgent fantasies.

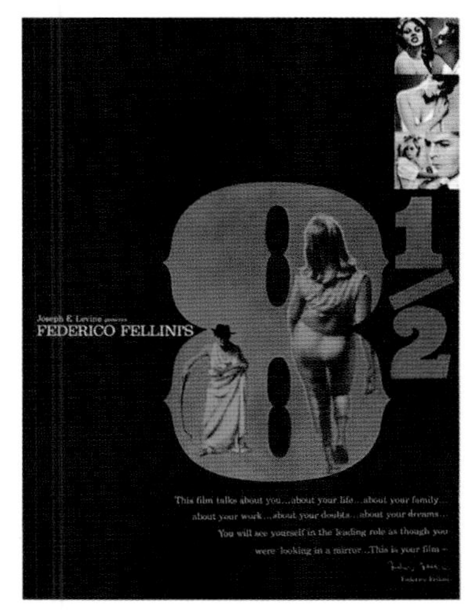

and Arnheim plans to buy oil fields in an eastern province of Austria. Musil's critique is that what was envisaged as a celebration of peace and imperial harmony turns out as a combination of war, imperial collapse, and national chauvinism. The novel provides an analysis of the political and cultural processes that contributed to the outbreak of the First World War.

The last volume, entitled "Into the Millennium (The Criminals)," is about Ulrich's sister Agathe. The two siblings experience a mystically incestuous stirring upon meeting after their father's death. Ulrich says:

> "But even I have been able to love something, and a Siamese sister who's neither me nor herself, but just as much me as herself, is clearly the only point where everything comes together for me!"

EMBARRASSMENT OF CHOICE

Ulrich is unable to focus on a central direction. For example, when faced with changing the rooms of his château, he is paralyzed by a multiplicity of choices, ranging from "the Assyrians to Cubism":

> "He was in that familiar state . . . of incoherent ideas spreading outward without a center, so characteristic of the present, and whose strange arithmetic adds up to a random proliferation of numbers without forming a unit. Finally he dreamed up only impracticable rooms, revolving rooms, kaleidoscopic rooms, adjustable scenery for the soul, and his ideas grew steadily more devoid of content."

Almost 1,000 pages into the book (of 1,130 pages in the English edition), he confesses:

> "I have never subjected myself to an idea with staying power. One never turned up. One should love an idea like a woman; be overjoyed to get back to it. And one always has it inside oneself! And always looks for it in everything outside! I never formed such ideas. My relationship to the so-called great ideas, and perhaps

> even to those that really are great, has always been man-to-man. I never felt I was born to submit to them; they always provoked me to overthrow them and put others in their place."

It's not just Ulrich who is all at sea so far as straightforward commitment is concerned. Clarisse comes to the conclusion that one is "obliged to surrender oneself to an illusion if one received the grace of having one." General Stumm decides to map out all of the great ideas of the day as if they were the plans for a military campaign, only to discover that they invariably end in contradiction. He lays out his charts and documents for Ulrich to consider, then sadly admits:

> "The whole thing is—although I can't actually believe what I'm saying—what any one of our commanding officers would be bound to call one hell of a mess!"

"I have never subjected myself to an idea with staying power."

Ulrich, *Der Mann ohne Eigenschaften*

IMPOSSIBLE TASK?

Evidently this lack of focus also afflicted the author. Even if Musil had lived longer, he might have struggled to finish *Der Mann ohne Eigenschaften*. When he died—like Robert Louis Stevenson, of a cerebral hemorrhage (see p.114)—he left a vast proliferation of drafts, notes, false starts, and projections as he tried to work out a proper ending.

Since Musil's death, *Der Mann ohne Eigenschaften* has received almost universal critical acclaim, but has never achieved the popularity it perhaps deserves. This is partly because it is unfinished, but mainly because of its disdain for conventional structure. Most people's response to the work is the same as that of Samuel Johnson to *Incognita* (1692), an early work by William Congreve: they would rather praise it than read it. This is a mistake, and many commentators, even in the English-speaking world, where German literature sometimes struggles to establish itself in translation, have averred that Musil is ripe for revaluation. Certainly, as has been seen with numerous other unfinished works, the lack of an ending is not necessarily a reason to prevent this happening. BR

WHAT HAPPENED NEXT . . .

It was left to Musil's widow Martha to assume the role of keeper of the flame. Two volumes had already been published in 1930 and 1933. There was a mass of manuscripts and drafts to deal with. In 1943 she published a 462-page collection of material from the literary remains including 20 chapters surviving as galley proofs withdrawn from Part III, as well as drafts of the final incomplete chapters and notes on the development and direction of the novel.

WILL IT EVER HAPPEN?

3/10

It is unlikely that anyone will have the energy or genius to finish this novel. It is an impressive achievement as it stands and defies imitation. One of the great novels of the 20th century, it is much admired and respected—this alone is likely to deter potential continuators, never mind its length and lack of a straightforward and accessible plot. Moreover, *Der Mann ohne Eigenschaften* is a "novel of ideas"—in some ways a continuation of the Nietzschean exploration of nihilism—and this genre has fallen out of favor in more recent times.

SUITE FRANÇAISE

Author Irène Némirovsky **Year** 1942 **Country** France **Genre** Novel

IRÈNE NÉMIROVSKY
Having fled from Russia after the Bolshevik Revolution of 1917, Némirovsky was disinclined to run again when the Nazis occupied her adoptive France in 1940. She paid for her decision to stay there with her life.

The story behind *Suite Française*—the tragic fate of its author, her ambitious plans for the work, its survival and eventual publication decades later—would make a gripping novel in itself. While Irène Némirovsky's fiction is now inevitably read in the context of her death, it is difficult to deny that she offers a powerful portrait of France under German occupation, all the more so considering that she was writing as the events were taking place.

ENDLESS FLIGHT

Némirovsky was born in Kiev in 1903 into a wealthy Jewish family; her father was one of the richest bankers in Russia. Irène learned fluent French from her governess and developed a love of writing as a teenager, filling her notebooks with not only narrative but also detailed thoughts on characters and plot. The family left their homeland during the Russian Revolution of 1917, moving first to Finland, then Sweden, and finally, in 1919, Paris. Irène's father rebuilt his banking fortune, and Irène enrolled at the Sorbonne. Aside from her studies, she enjoyed the parties and balls of high society. She married the banker Michel Epstein in 1926 and three years later published her literary debut, *David Golder*. That same year, Irène gave birth to her daughter Denise. By the time her daughter Elisabeth was born in 1937, Némirovsky was the author of nine best-selling novels.

At the outbreak of the Second World War in 1939, Irène and Michel sent their daughters to live in Issy-l'Evêque, in Burgundy, the home village of the girls' governess. Once the Germans occupied Paris the following June, the Némirovskys left the capital, and settled in the same village as their daughters. The comfortable life they knew disappeared forever. Within months, a new law was passed that conferred an inferior legal status on Jews in France; further race laws swiftly followed. The family had to wear the yellow star at all times. Michel no longer had the right to be employed as a banker, and Irène's work could not be published. Nonetheless, she continued writing, and succeeded in having some short stories published under various pseudonyms. In 1941 she began her greatest project, *Suite Française*—according to Paul Gray in *The New York Times*, perhaps the first work of fiction about the Second World War.

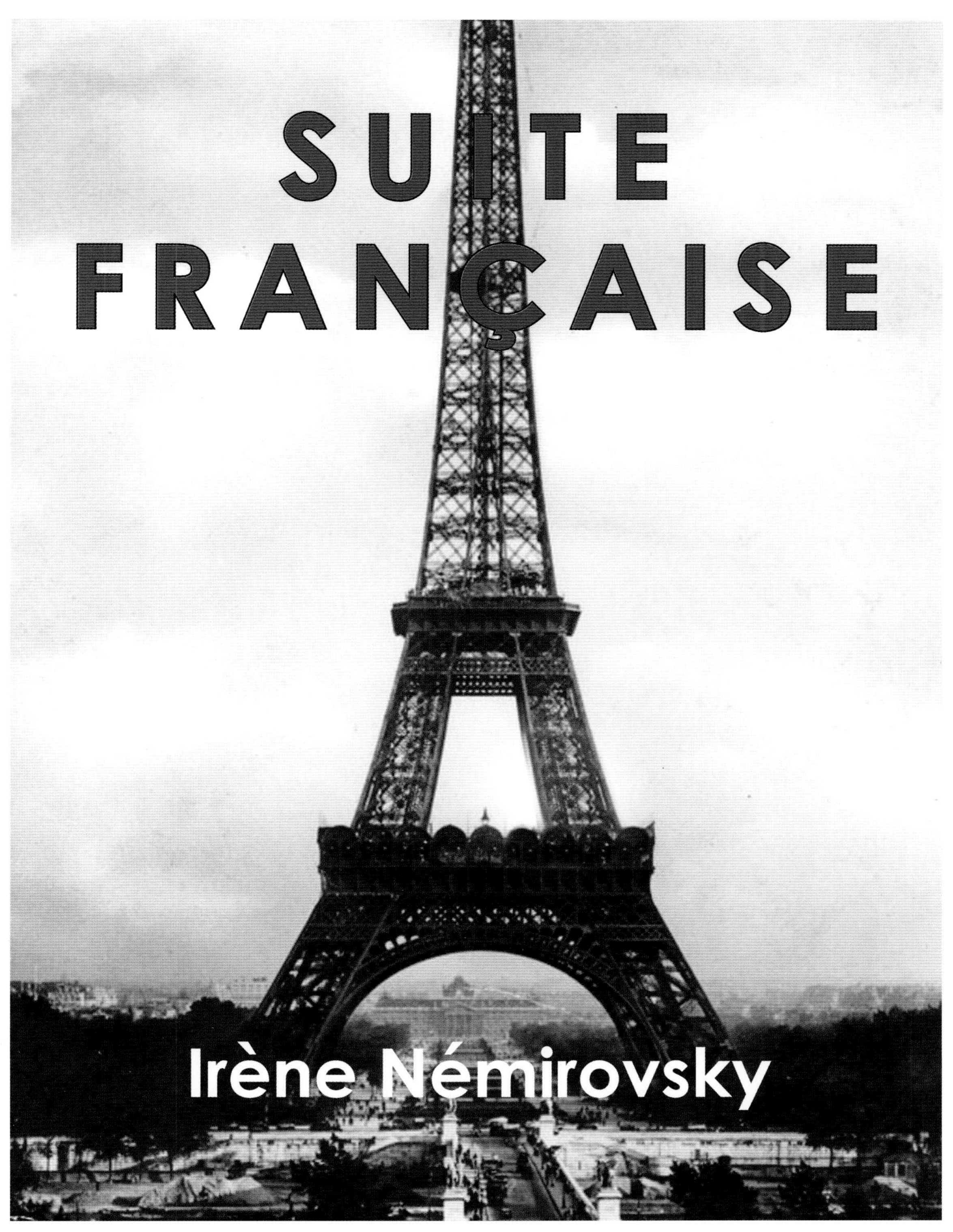

Cover: Dean Martin

ANTI-SEMITIC ACCUSATIONS

Suite Française became a literary sensation on publication, but not without controversy, as some critics suggested that Némirovsky's earlier works express anti-Semitic views and contain unflattering portraits of Jewish characters—particularly her first novel, *David Golder*, which depicts a villainous Jewish businessman who is bled of his fortune by his rapacious, unfaithful wife and his materialistic daughter. They commented that Némirovsky converted to Catholicism in 1939 and contributed to anti-Semitic magazines. Her defenders contended that her novels frequently feature unsympathetic characters; what interested her was the ignoble way that people often behave in extreme circumstances. They remarked that most of the right-wing periodicals became increasingly anti-Semitic after she had begun to write for them, and that she was desperate to support her family. Of her religious conversion, they argued that she might have been trying to protect her children from persecution. "She certainly made a lot of mistakes," said the publisher Carmen Callil, "but given her times and her circumstances, they might well be excusable."

Némirovsky started by making detailed notes on her characters and her thoughts on the situation in France. She planned a 1,000-page book constructed on a musical framework, like a symphony. Inspired by J.S. Bach's *French Suites*, she envisaged a literary composition of five sections—each with its own rhythm and tone, but with intermingling themes—chronicling the collapse of France. She wrote every day, but by June 1942 she sensed that she would not be able to finish her work. In her "Notes on the State of France" she commented: "I do not lack the courage to complete the task but the goal is far and time is short." Believing her situation to be hopeless, she wrote her will and left instructions for the disbursal of her possessions. On July 13 Némirovsky was arrested by French police on account of being a "stateless person of Jewish descent" and within days was transported to Auschwitz, where she died of typhus in the infirmary a month later. Michel Epstein was arrested in October 1942 and died in the gas chamber at Auschwitz in November.

SAVING THE WORK

The Némirovskys' governess fled Issy-l'Evêque with the two girls, and they spent the rest of the war in hiding, pursued by the French police. Denise put the manuscript of *Suite Française* in her suitcase as they left the village and carried the leather-bound notebook, crammed with her mother's tiny handwriting, from one hiding place to another. After the war, Denise refused to read the notebook, believing its contents would be too painful to look at. It was only before passing it to an archive in the late 1990s that she decided to type it out. She had thought the notebook contained a diary or just notes, but instead discovered a masterful account of France at its darkest hour. She sent the manuscript to the publisher Editions Denoël, and in 2004, 62 years after it was written, it was published for the first time.

As published, *Suite Française* comprises two novellas. "Storm in June" depicts a group of Parisians as they flee the German invasion in June 1940. Thirty short chapters follow the fortunes of a large cast of characters, and examine the behavior of the individual at a time of national crisis. The Péricands, an upper-class Catholic family, and Gabriel Corte, a self-absorbed writer, are annoyed at the inconvenience of leaving their affluent lives behind. The most sympathetic characters are the Michauds, bank clerks whose compassion contrasts sharply with the selfishness of those around them.

The second novella, "Dolce" (a musical term meaning "gently"), tells the story of a rural community under occupation a year later. Although some characters from "Storm in June" reappear, Némirovsky takes a more focused

"I do not lack the courage to complete the task but the goal is far and time is short."

Irène Némirovsky

approach. At the center of "Dolce" is the relationship between Lucile Angellier, who lives with her mother-in-law while her unfaithful soldier husband is in a German prisoner-of-war camp, and Bruno von Falk, a German officer billeted in the same house. As the reader wonders where the attraction between Lucile and Bruno will lead, Némirovsky poses wider questions: forced to coexist with German soldiers, some villagers choose collaboration, others resistance. How might we behave in a similar situation? The section ends as the German troops leave the village in July 1941 to head to the Russian front.

Suite Française became an immediate best seller on publication, and Némirovsky was awarded the prestigious Prix Renaudot, the first author to receive the honor posthumously. *Le Monde* lauded the book as "a masterpiece . . . ripped from oblivion." In an interview with the BBC in 2006, Denise Epstein said: "For me, the greatest joy is knowing that the book is being read. It is an extraordinary feeling to have brought my mother back to life. It shows that the Nazis did not truly succeed in killing her. It is not a vengeance, but it is a victory." **CC**

WILL IT EVER HAPPEN?

5/10

The appendices of *Suite Française* reproduce Némirovsky's notes on the story beyond the surviving two fragments—specifically her plans for the third part, "Captivity." There are no outlines for the fourth and fifth parts, "Battles" and "Peace." Némirovsky herself noted that the rest of the work was "really in the lap of the gods since it depends on what happens." That any part of the story ever saw publication is perhaps remarkable enough.

WHAT HAPPENED NEXT . . .

In 2007 Editions Denoël published *Chaleur du Sang* (*Fire in the Blood*), a second newly discovered novel by Némirovsky. Two pages of the manuscript were found in the suitcase that Denise Epstein rescued after her mother's arrest. Researching a biography of Némirovsky, Olivier Philipponnat and Patrick Lienhardt discovered the rest of the script amid the papers given by Irène to her editor for safekeeping in spring 1942.

LE MONT ANALOGUE

Author René Daumal **Year** 1944 **Country** France **Genre** Novel

RENÉ DAUMAL
The son of a teacher, René Daumal was an outstanding student who rejected mainstream studies in favor of wacky pseudo-sciences such as pataphysics, which is said by its exponents to lie beyond the realm of metaphysics.

If the overworked term "cult novel" is to have any real meaning, it should be applied to works like René Dumal's bizarre fragment *Le Mont Analogue* (*Mount Analogue*). Well outside the mainstream of literature, since the 1960s it has been hailed as a masterpiece by a dedicated following of readers prepared to accept the mystical and the occult as valid grounds for a root-and-branch critique of the modern Western rationalist view of the world and its denial of a spiritual dimension to human existence.

Pithily subtitled "A Novel of Symbolically Authentic Non-Euclidian Adventures in Mountain Climbing," *Le Mont Analogue* was intended to be an expression in allegorical form of the author's lifelong quest to experience a reality beyond the world of everyday consciousness. Born in the Ardennes region of eastern France in 1908, Daumal was by his own account a death-obsessed, intellectually hyperactive youth. He learned Sanskrit to access the wisdom of the East and indulged in mind-altering experiments, exploring lucid dreaming, sensory deprivation, and parapsychology. Aged 16, he by chance discovered the hallucinatory effects of the chemical carbon tetrachloride. Inhaling this substance transported him to "another world," providing what he felt to be irrefutable evidence of a higher reality waiting to be found. He repeated the experience many hundreds of times.

RISING STAR

Daumal began to write poetry, situating himself in the radical French literary tradition of Arthur Rimbaud, who in the previous century had called for a "derangement of all the senses." Astoundingly precocious, by the age of 20 he was established as an exciting new figure on the Parisian literary scene, leading a clique dubbed "the Simplists." Briefly publishing his own review, *Le Grand Jeu*, he haughtily rejected an invitation to join the Surrealist movement. His poems were much admired and he went on to publish a novel, *La Grande Beuverie (A Night of Serious Drinking*, 1938), in which his drinkers experienced elaborate baroque visions of heaven and hell.

But Daumal's preoccupations were never exclusively, or perhaps even primarily, literary. He became involved with followers of Armenian guru George Gurdjieff, preacher of the "Fourth Way" to spiritual enlightenment, and dedicated his life to what Gurdjieff called "the Work"—the arduous search

Cover: Heath Killen

THE HOLY MOUNTAIN

Le Mont Analogue was one of the major inspirations behind *The Holy Mountain* (1973), a cult movie by avant-garde Chilean-French director Alejandro Jodorowsky. An adept of "psychomagic," shamanism, and the Tarot, Jodorowsky sets his characters on a climb to the summit of a mountain where they are to find the secret of immortality. After many bizarre adventures and digressions, they encounter the mountain's nine immortal masters, but find them faceless and inert dummies. The characters are then returned to reality by turning the camera on the film crew, destroying the movie illusion. Jodorowsky's film cannot be seen as a literal attempt to represent and complete Daumal's fiction because his own preoccupations carry the action and imagery far from the original.

to escape from the "waking sleep" of ordinary life. Gurdjieff saw "intentional suffering" as part of "the Work," and Daumal certainly suffered. Indeed, his spiritual pursuit probably killed him. Abuse of carbon tetrachloride and other substances had a disastrous effect on his health. By the age of 30 he was a toothless, half-deaf tubercular wreck. Rejecting modern medicine and convinced that the destruction of his body was raising his spirit, he refused to seek treatment for his worsening condition.

It was in this deteriorating physical state that he began writing *Le Mont Analogue* in 1939. The occupation of France by the Nazis in the following year brought new austerities and dangers, especially as Daumal's wife was Jewish. By 1944 *Le Mont Analogue* was still unfinished and Daumal terminally ill. On May 21 a friend called at his apartment to suggest he write notes to allow the book to be completed posthumously by others. In the middle of a sentence, Daumal left his desk to answer the friend's knock on the door. The sentence was never completed, the author dying before he could resume writing. He was aged 36.

LEGACY

The unfinished novel that thus became Daumal's last testament tells of an expedition to the eponymous mountain, which is located somewhere in the South Pacific. By far the largest peak on Earth, it is hidden from human sight by the curvature of space—cod science playing its usual facilitating role in fantasy fiction. In a scenario bearing resemblances to the 19th-century proto-science fiction of Jules Verne, seven explorers representing various human types assemble for an expedition to seek the elusive mountain, led by the deeply wise Sogol, a professor of mountaineering. Daumal represents

Sogol's protean mind through a description of his studio, which is hung with scraps of paper on which information from the most varied realms of human knowledge—the periodic table, Chinese pictograms, mathematical formulae—are written, so the sage can wander among them making arcane links between apparently unconnected ideas.

The expedition embarks on the yacht *Impossible* and, thanks to Sogol's exceptional mathematical calculations and intuition, discovers the location of the mountain. The yacht enters Port des Singes (Port of Monkeys), which allows access to the invisible object of the quest. We are told a good deal about the customs of those humans who live around the foot of the mountain and about those who act as guides on its slopes. This gives Daumal an opportunity to express disdain for many aspects of modern industrialized society—for example, both electricity and explosives are forbidden in these communities. Especially striking is the local currency, the peradam. This is a type of spherical crystal found on the mountain slopes, in larger quantities the higher one climbs. Hidden to ordinary eyes, the crystals reveal

> *"What is above knows what is below, what is below does not know what is above."*
>
> *Le Mont Analogue*

themselves by a "sparkle, like that of dewdrops" only to those who seek them "with sincere desire and true need."

As the expedition members embark upon the arduous ascent toward the summit of the mountain, frustratingly the novel comes to its abrupt end. From fragments of text found with the manuscript, it seems that Daumal intended at least some of his characters to climb up to the highest peaks and return with fresh spiritual insights: "What is above knows what is below, what is below does not know what is above."

The attraction of Daumal's text is its presentation of a mistily symbolic, even potentially hackneyed subject—the mountain ascent as an allegory of a spiritual quest—in precisely detailed form and a clear, good-humored, paradoxical prose. The overall impression is of a peace and serenity intended to inspire readers to engage in their own spiritual quest: indeed, the book's last chapter was meant to have had the title "And You, What Do You Seek?"

Even in its unfinished form, *Le Mont Analogue* has certainly succeeded in providing such inspiration for many members of its cult readership. **RG**

WHAT HAPPENED NEXT . . .

Published posthumously in France in 1952, Daumal's *Le Mont Analogue* attracted little attention and the author was largely forgotten. After the book appeared in English translation seven years later, however, it developed a small but enthusiastic following, especially among the Beats and their hippie successors on the U.S. west coast, appearing on the shelves of "alternative" bookstores such as San Francisco's legendary City Lights.

WILL IT EVER HAPPEN?

4/10

Daumal did leave some indications of the direction in which his novel was moving. It would certainly have ended with an appeal to readers to seek their own path up the symbolic mountain. But Daumal nowhere indicates exactly what the explorers would have found if they arrived at the final summit. If the book were ever completed, it would not be Daumal's vision on the page.

THE CRAB AND THE BUTTERFLY

Author Saul Bellow **Year** 1949 **Country** United States **Genre** Novel

SAUL BELLOW
The Canadian-born child of Russian immigrants who moved from Montreal to Chicago when he was nine years old, Bellow wrote vibrant prose that derived much of its energy from the speech patterns and idioms of Yiddish, his parents' native language.

Saul Bellow's writing career began with a work called *The Very Dark Trees*. It failed to find a publisher, and Bellow destroyed the novel in 1942. However, a reader at Vanguard Press encouraged the author to try again and in 1944 the publisher released Bellow's debut novel, *Dangling Man*. His follow-up novel *The Victim* was published in 1948, prompting the rival publishing company Viking to offer him a generous $3,000 advance on his next novel. At the same time he was awarded a Guggenheim fellowship, and used the opportunity to move with his wife Anita to France. There he set about writing a new book, called *The Crab and the Butterfly*.

A BLEAK NARRATIVE

Only one chapter of *The Crab and the Butterfly* survives, and most of the literature on Bellow ignores it. According to James Atlas in his biography *Bellow* (1999), it is a bleak narrative about two men talking to each other from adjacent beds in a Chicago hospital. One of the protagonists is Weyl, a moody intellectual, not unlike the characters Joseph and Leventhal in Bellow's first two published novels. Weyl explains to the other main character, Scampi:

> "We're more and more in the open of our natures, nearer and nearer to the original personal quality in people. That's bringing the fight pretty close to the bull, it's full of risks, and if we're murdered it will be because the original nature is murderous; if not, because there's something redeeming in the original thing and a reason for all the old talk about nobility."

Atlas views this philosophizing as a form of provincial showing off, and an unfortunate legacy from all the courses Bellow took in Chicago on Great Books. In *Saul Bellow's Heart: A Memoir* (2013), his son Greg recalled that one of the men was dying and the other was clinging to life:

> "The character who dies is the part of Saul that clings to the familiar, doomed, academical fictional forms of his European 'mentors,' the survivor is the writer with the freewheeling style of writing who was about to burst forth in the pages of *The Adventures of Augie March* [1953]."

Bellow was soon having trouble with it, but he reached 100,000 words.

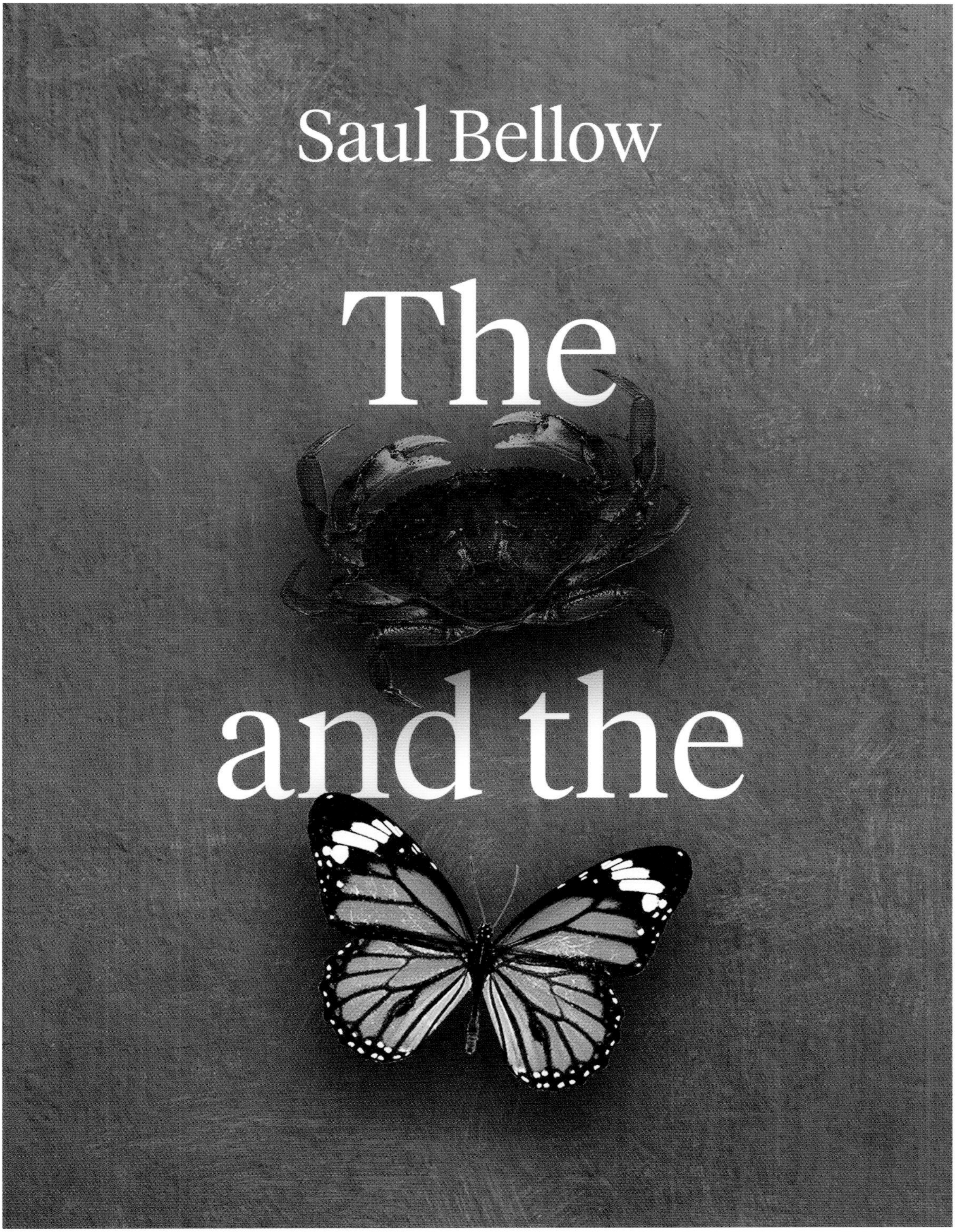

Saul Bellow

The

and the

Cover: Heath Killen

FESTINA LENTE

Other than the very bare and rudimentary outlines of the plot, what is to be surmised about *The Crab and the Butterfly*? One possibility is that Bellow was influenced by Classical and Renaissance emblems, in which the crab and the butterfly in combination gave visual form to the Latin mottos *"festina lente"* and *"propera tarde"* (make haste slowly). Such emblems appear on coins like the one below from the reign of the Roman Emperor Caesar Augustus (63 BCE–14 CE) and in a number of emblem books, such as Geffrey Whitney's *Choice of Emblems* (1586), the earliest publication of its kind.

SOURCE OF INSPIRATION

It's possible that Bellow drew on his own memories of hospital in *The Crab and the Butterfly*. When he was eight years old he developed peritonitis and pneumonia and spent six months in the Royal Victoria Hospital in Montreal. He felt that he faced death and "had gotten away with it." These hospital experiences, in which physical disease could easily flow into "emotional disorder" surface in *Herzog* (1964) and *Humbold's Gift* (1975). And they probably had their part to play in this pessimistic lost novel. A girlfriend called Shirley Teper refers to "the topography of scars" (both physical and mental): "It was his crucible, the primary life experience that defined him. It gave him an absolute standard of truth—raw truth—of values and priorities. It showed him there was no one to count on."

> *"Unexpected intrusions of beauty. That is what life is."*
>
> *Herzog*

The background to the writing was that Bellow hated Paris. The weather was gray; the French were inhospitable. He was there for two years and was never invited into a French home. "I was terribly depressed," he later said. In his foreword to a translation of Dostoevsky's *Winter Notes on Summer Impressions* (1955), Bellow wrote: "Old cultures are impenetrable; none is more so than the French."

Still, he made contacts in Paris with the French philosophers Georges Bataille, Albert Camus, and Maurice Merleau-Ponty at the home of his friend from Chicago, the psychiatrist Harold Kaplan. Other Paris friends included the writers Herbert Gold, Mary McCarthy, Lionel Abel, and William Phillips.

LITERARY HAUNTS

Paris was a haven for exiles, and among their favorite haunts in the French capital were two cafés: Les Deux Magots and the Café de Flore (right) on the corner of the Boulevard Saint-Germain and Rue St. Benoit. Both are still open today, and are places of pilgrimage for literary types.

At the time, many Americans in Paris were attempting to write "The Great American Novel." In a 1983 article for *The New York Times*, Bellow described the city's allure: "For the soul of a civilized, or even partly civilized, man Paris was one of the permanent settings, a theater, if you like where the greatest problems of existence might be represented." (It also had many extracurricular attractions, which may be not unconnected with the fact that he subsequently went on to have five wives.) He frequented the Café de Flore on the Boulevard Saint-Germain, whose clientele included the intellectuals Jean-Paul Sartre and Simone De Beauvoir, although a disgruntled compatriot once complained, "I don't see any geniuses here." Bellow recalled in the memoir *To Jerusalem and Back* (1976): "I used to go down to the Pont Royal bar to look at Sartre." Needless to say, Sartre did not look at him.

AN EPIPHANY

However, it was in Paris that Bellow experienced an epiphany. His son Greg recalled it thus:

> "Saul was walking down the street watching the merchants hose fruit and vegetables into the Seine, ridding themselves of once useful commodities that had lost their value and creating tiny rainbows of water in the gutter. At that very moment, the first lines of *The Adventures of Augie March* poured out of him, as if they been sitting there for a long time."

This image seems to suggest the flushing away of the European tradition like so much rubbish, and the manifestation of a new fictional covenant in the rainbow. As Bellow wrote in *Herzog*, "Unexpected intrusions of beauty. That is what life is." Finally, simply, the time had come. He laid *The Crab and the Butterfly* aside and started the new novel. He wrote the first half very quickly, revising little.

The Adventures of Augie March was published to great acclaim in 1953, winning the National Book Award in 1954. In a 1953 interview for *The New York Times Book Review*, Bellow told reviewer Harvey Breit: "The great pleasure of the book was that it came easily. All I had to do was be there with buckets to catch it. That's why the form is loose." He wrote to Keith Opdahl in March 1961 that the earlier novel "was too heavy, and I let it go and turned to *Augie March*." He told Edward Hoagland at a similar time that "*Augie March* was written in a jail-breaking spirit." So this is a case of a novel being abandoned because a better one came along—perhaps the loss of *The Crab and the Butterfly* is a blessing. BR

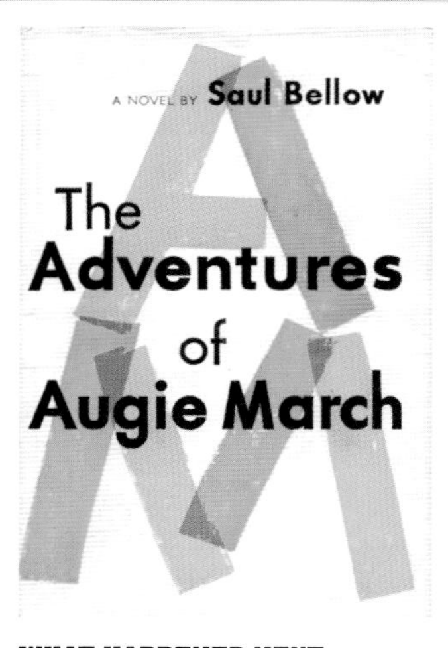

WHAT HAPPENED NEXT . . .
Bellow never returned to *The Crab and the Butterfly,* and he is supposed to have destroyed the manuscript, except for one chapter. After *The Adventures of Augie March* was published he went on to write 11 more novels, most of them very highly regarded.

0/10

WILL IT EVER HAPPEN?
We know so little about *The Crab and the Butterfly* that it would be impossible for anyone to attempt to finish it. And Bellow would not be an easy writer to imitate. The novel will simply have to remain in decent and uninvaded obscurity. For his fans, however, there is the consolation of Bellow's numerous other fiction works that are available.

VERLORENES PARADIES

Author Heinrich Böll **Year** 1949 **Country** West Germany **Genre** Novel

HEINRICH BÖLL
The Nobel committee's decision to award Böll its literature prize was influenced by his novel *Group Portrait with Lady* (1971), an affecting study of the travails of a poor German woman throughout the first half of the 20th century.

Heinrich Böll, winner of the 1972 Nobel Prize for Literature, was a Roman Catholic and a pacifist who became renowned for the power with which he depicted the suffering during the Second World War of ordinary, non-Nazi Germans—fighting battles that they hoped to lose—and the effect of the conflict on the postwar nation.

In the 1930s, Böll refused to join the Hitler Youth. During the war he fought on the Eastern front, was wounded four times, deserted, and was captured by the U.S. army and held as a P.O.W. After returning to civilian life, he joined Gruppe 47, an influential literary circle whose other members included Ingeborg Bachmann and Günter Grass, and began writing short stories. He then produced two novels, *Der Zug war pünktlich* (*The Train Was on Time*, 1949), about the despair of soldiers, and *Wo warst du Adam?* (*Adam, Where Art Thou?*, 1951), about the boredom and needless regimentation of military life. He followed these with *Billard um halb zehn* (*Billiards at Half-Past Nine*, 1959), a complex work of interwoven flashbacks and interior monologues, and *Ansichten eines Clowns* (*The Clown*, 1963), an account of a well-paid entertainer's alcohol-fueled descent into the gutter. *Die verlorene Ehre der Katharina Blum* (*The Lost Honor of Katharina Blum*), about the Red Army Faction terrorist group, was published in 1974 and in the following year turned into a movie directed by Volker Schlöndorff.

WAR GUILT

Of Böll's numerous posthumous publications, the pick is *Der Engel schwieg* (*The Silent Angel*, 1992), which draws heavily on the author's experience as a soldier returning to Cologne after the war and finding his native city devastated by bombing. This novel contains passages recycled from "Verlorenes Paradies" ("Paradise Lost"), an earlier work that he began in 1949 but abandoned after two chapters.

The fragment is an overture to what looks set to have become a restatement of Böll's abiding themes. A recently demobilized soldier reflects on the meaning of the conflict and his own role in it: "I suddenly realized that we are all guilty of everything." Although the past weighs heavily on him, he still has to contemplate the future: he visits the home of his former lover, Maria, whom he has not seen for seven years. Her house, once magnificent,

Cover: Isabel Eeles

is now badly damaged and full of displaced persons unknown to him. He learns that she still lives there but is not at home.

When he enters Maria's bedroom, their affair returns to him in cruelly distorted form: what was once a source of joy is now agonizing to recall because he knows that it has dried up and gone forever; all his other memories are of the pain he felt and inflicted during the conflict.

"Verlorenes Paradies" eventually appeared in *Der blasse Hund* (*The Mad Dog*, 1997) along with various Böll short stories. It is of considerable interest to scholars who compare and contrast it with *Der Engel schwieg*, but can it justifiably be classified as an unfinished novel? Is it rather an early, discarded draft? Certainly the subject matter of both works is the same. However, since war guilt and conscience were Böll's lifelong preoccupations, it is entirely plausible that he intended to make both excavations from the same vein. **GL**

WHAT HAPPENED NEXT . . .
"Verlorenes Paradies" is worth reading on its own and, for those unfamiliar with Böll's other work, it serves as a useful introduction to one of the greatest German novelists of the late 20th century. Its belated publication helped to restore the author's reputation after he had briefly fallen out of fashion in the period immediately following his death.

WILL IT EVER HAPPEN?
Böll made the subject of German war guilt pretty much his own, and it seems unlikely that the contributions of a continuator would ever be welcomed. Contemporary German literature has moved on to other subjects, notably the consequences of the national reunification achieved in 1990. Like Horace, Böll has built a monument more lasting than bronze; it needs no polishing.

IL BIANCO VELIERO

Author Italo Calvino **Year** 1949 **Country** Italy **Genre** Novel

ITALO CALVINO
Born in 1923 in Havana, Cuba, Calvino moved with his parents back to their native Italy in 1925. He trained to follow in his father's footsteps as a globetrotting agronomist but always yearned to become a writer. By the time of his death he was the most widely translated Italian author.

In 1947, Italo Calvino published his first novel, *Il sentiero dei nidi di ragno* (*The Path to the Nest of Spiders*). It was a runaway success, selling 5,000 copies—a substantial number in the context of Italy's fragile postwar economy. Written in just 30 days at the end of 1946, the young author's book was inspired by his experiences with the communist partisans during the Second World War. After such a swift and easy ascent to literary stardom, it was almost inevitable that his next attempt would meet with more difficulty. Toward the end of 1947 he started work on a second novel, *Il bianco veliero* (*The White Schooner*), which he would labor over for the next two years but eventually shelve. The author died in 1985 without ever publishing his early manuscript.

BASIS OF REPUTATION

Today, Calvino is best known for his postmodern works: *Le cosmicomiche* (*The Cosmicomics*, 1965), *Le citta invisibili* (*The Invisible Cities*, 1972), *Se una notte d'inverno un viaggiatore* (*If on a Winter's Night a Traveler*, 1979), and *Signor Palomar* (*Mr. Palomar*, 1983). However, there exists another Calvino, who was one of the leading lights in the neorealist movement that flourished in postwar Italy. Neorealism boasted in its ranks some of the most distinguished figures in 20th-century Italian culture, including Alberto Moravia, Cesare Pavese, and Elio Vittorini. Neorealist works were characterized by a sense of political commitment, an awareness of the social issues of the day, and a new linguistic freedom, which saw writers adopt a less literary syntax in order to get closer to the language of the people. Through working at the publishing house Einaudi, Calvino came to know many of the major neorealist authors as friends and was deeply influenced by their work. He became very close to Pavese in particular, who pushed him to write *Il sentiero dei nidi di ragno* and gave him valuable advice along the way. It was Pavese's persuasive arguments that convinced the editorial board at Einaudi that they should publish the book. *Il sentiero dei nidi di ragno* is typically neorealist in style: the story is told through the eyes of Pin, a young partisan in the resistance movement, and the language is that of everyday speech, pared of rhetorical flourishes, interspersed with the odd dialect word here and there. The influence of Ernest Hemingway is evident.

Cover: Tom Howey

THE REVOLUTIONARY
Calvino was brought up to challenge convention: in deeply conservative, Catholic Italy, his parents' decision to give him an entirely secular education was unusual. When the Germans occupied northern Italy he joined the Resistance, an experience that inspired *Il sentiero dei nidi di ragno*. After the war he joined the Italian Communist Party and worked on its newspaper, *L'Unità*, and its magazine, *Rinascita*. In 1957, disillusioned by the Soviet invasion of Hungary the previous year, he renounced his party membership.

Il bianco veliero was written in the same neorealist style. Although little is known about the plot of the book, the "white schooner" of the title appears to be a truck that drives around the countryside bearing black market goods. The protagonist is the driver, a young girl.

Shortly after Calvino embarked on the novel, he ran into difficulties. In May 1948 he wrote to fellow author Marcello Venturi: "For seven or eight months now I've been mucking about with a novel that I began in a moment of weakness and it's turning out to be very bad, causing me to waste lots of my time. But at least it'll get rid of my desire to write novels for four or five years, which is what I dream of doing, and will allow me to study kind of seriously and learn to write decently."

In spite of his reservations, Calvino persevered with the novel. When his collection of short stories, *Ultimo viene il corvo* (*The Crow Comes Last*) was published in 1949, *Il bianco veliero* was announced in the notice launching it. By this time, Calvino's publisher was obviously confident that it would soon be finished. However, the author was unhappy with his work and put it to one side. In April 1950, when thanking literary critic Dario Puccini for his review of *Ultimo viene il corvo*, Calvino wrote: "I am well aware that my 'cold and detailed approach' and 'mechanical technique' are my most serious dangers. I reached a point of no return along this route in the novel I finished a year ago [*Il bianco veliero*] and which I have not yet decided to publish. Now I will try other routes, but it is not easy."

Other letters from this period testify to the problems that Calvino was experiencing with developing a style with which he felt comfortable. In a letter to Elsa Morante in March 1950, he wrote that he felt like "a prisoner of a kind of style" and needed to escape from it. Later that same year, he noted to Natalia Ginzburg, a colleague at Einaudi and another neorealist writer: "Writing is very difficult; it really is not the joke it once seemed to me."

ELSA MORANTE
One of the critics Calvino trusted most, Morante herself became a successful novelist—her best-known work is *La Storia* (*History*, 1974)—and the wife of Alberto Moravia.

WHAT HAPPENED NEXT . . .
Having set aside *Il bianco veliero*, Calvino embarked on another neorealist novel, *I giovani del Po* (*Youth in Turin*) in 1950. He would continue to work on it for the next 18 months, but again found himself frustrated by the limitations of the neorealist style. He described experiencing a moment of epiphany in the summer of 1951:

"Instead of making myself write the book I *ought* to write . . . I conjured up the book I myself would have liked to read, the sort by an unknown writer, from another age and another country, discovered in an attic."

The result of this was *Il visconte dimezzato* (*The Cloven Viscount*). Written in 30 days, this dazzling comic novel about a knight torn in two by a cannonball marked a complete revolution in Calvino's writing, from neorealism into fantasy.

Many years later, he reflected on this difficult period in an interview for *Paris Review*: "For several years I tried to write another [novel]. But the literary climate was already being defined as neorealism, and it wasn't for me."

In 1950, Calvino sent the finished manuscript of *Il bianco veliero* to a select group of friends, inviting them to comment on it. In his March letter to Elsa Morante, he said that he wanted a "dispassionate, detailed, rigorous verdict" from her on the book. Her response contained severe criticisms. She found the construction of the book "cold," which Calvino conceded was

> *"Writing is very difficult; it really is not the joke it once seemed to me."*
>
> Italo Calvino

probably because "the heat of inspiration—too thin anyway—with which I'd started out writing it cooled along the way, and I decided to finish the book more out of the pigheadedness of not wanting to leave anything unfinished than because I was really keen on it." He concludes that "the only thing that can be salvaged from the novel is the landscape." Morante was not the only bearer of bad news: Natalia Ginzburg and Elio Vittorini, editors at Einaudi, were disappointed with what they read. Their criticisms put the final nail in the coffin for Calvino, who consigned his manuscript to a locked drawer. **JL**

WILL IT EVER HAPPEN?

8/10

Calvino may have decided not to publish *Il bianco veliero* in his lifetime, but we know that a finished manuscript exists somewhere. Although the executors of his estate have kept it under lock and key so far, it seems highly probable that the novel will eventually be released.

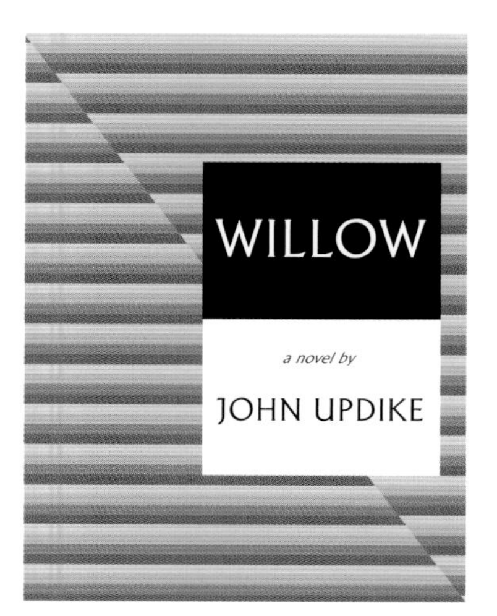
WILLOW
a novel by
JOHN UPDIKE

RAYMOND
CHANDLER
POODLE SPRINGS
"The girl gave him a look which ought to have
stuck at least four inches out of his back."

Chapter 5

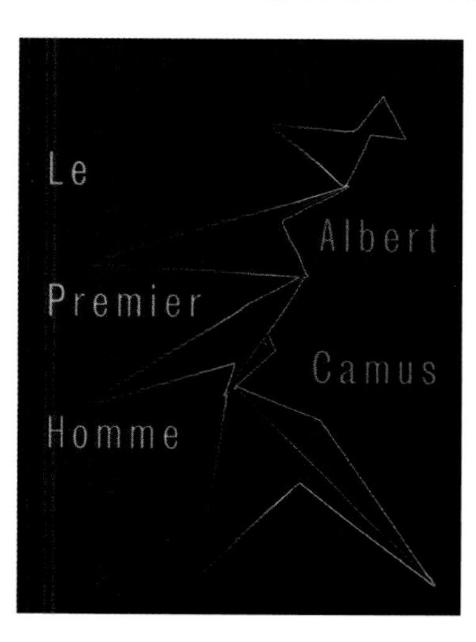
Le
Premier
Homme
Albert
Camus

PRINCE
JELLYFISH
HUNTER S.
THOMPSON

Sylvia
Plath
JOURNALS

1950–75

THE LONG GOODBYE
HARPER LEE
J.R.R.
TOLKIEN
the
Silmarillion

I N G E
B O R G
B A C H
M A N N
T O D E S
A R T E N

WILLOW

Author John Updike **Year** 1951 **Country** United States **Genre** Novel

JOHN UPDIKE
A remarkably prolific author, John Updike wrote more than 20 novels, numerous short stories, and copious poetry. He was also a regular contributor to *The New Yorker*. His abiding themes are sex and the United States.

In his book *Conversations with John Updike* (1994), James Plath discussed the author's early writings, and an unfinished novel called *Willow* came up. It was written in 1951 when Updike was at Harvard. He got two thirds of the way through, and then abandoned it. He told Plath, "I wouldn't dare look at it for fear of being intensely embarrassed." None of the text is available, but there are some clues to what it was about. It describes a town resembling Shillington, Pennsylvania, where Updike was born in 1932, and foreshadows some of his stories about the fictional town of Olinger.

Shillington is a typical example of provincial America, and it proved a great source for Updike's sharp-eyed attachment to what Henry James called "solidity of specification." He mined the particulars of his own private life for his fiction, and the precise particulars of his environments. This might seem a recipe for the worst kind of banal low-level realism, but Updike's vivid attention somehow transforms most things he touches, and imbues them with almost epiphanic status. It's worth noting that he had an artist's alertness for visual appearances—he attended the Ruskin School of Drawing in Oxford after leaving Harvard.

GREENHORN RUTTING

In 2005 Updike published his twenty-first novel: *Villages.* It surveys the career of Owen Mackenzie, who was born in Willow. The writing is classic Updike, scrupulously registering the details of humiliations and embarrassments that men feel when they are growing up, especially in the sexual territory. Could it be that *Villages* is very like *Willow*? Quite possibly, although *Villages* was created with the confidence and maturity that Updike acquired after a writing career lasting more than 50 years—it seems unlikely that the young Updike would have been capable of the crisp virtuoso summation of eight men in terms of their golf styles. Like his character, Updike is capable of reconstructing the small town "store by store, house by house, in his mind's eye 60 years afterwards." In *Villages* the town of Willow is "where sin cast its shadow, which did not slide away like most shadows, but had a sticky, pungent quality." It is more or less the America of Norman Rockwell's *Saturday Evening Post* illustrations, except that you find a used contraceptive in the road, "like a collapsed balloon."

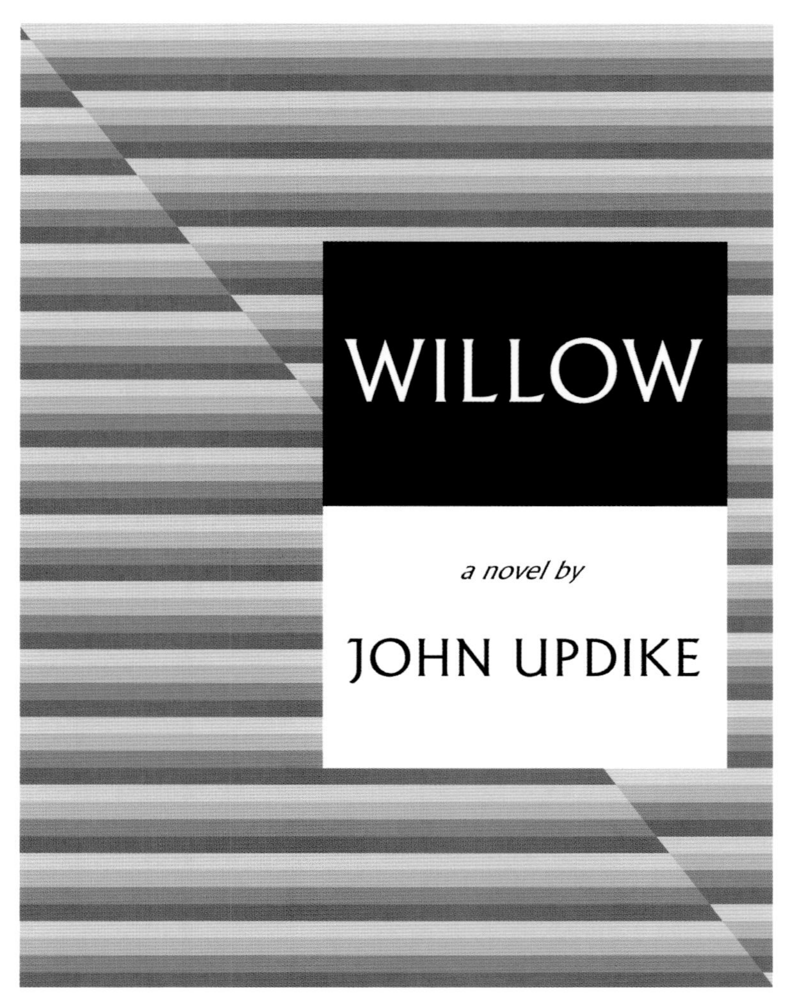

Cover: Steve Panton

WHAT HAPPENED NEXT . . .
Willow was locked away in a secure vault in the Updike archive at the Houghton Library, Harvard (below), after his death in 2009. According to the librarian Leslie Morris, it will not be available to readers until October 1, 2029, along with *House* and *Go Away*. So this is not only a novel that we shall never read in its entirety, but one that we shall have a long wait to read even in its fragmentary state. The reason perhaps why Updike did not want the public to see *Willow* is that it might reveal callow and amateurish writing, but also that it might contain material used in later works. Authors are always wary of being accused of recycling, since it seems to convict them of poverty of invention and imagination.

Willow, presumably, charted the sexual coming-of-age as youngsters indulged in "gasoline-charged roaming," although they would have less assurance than the accomplished Owen "keeping women in the air like a juggler's gaudy balls." In his dicussions with Plath, Updike admitted that its subject matter "wasn't so different" from the work of his maturity.

In 2014 former *New York Observer* books editor Adam Begley published a mammoth biography of Updike, underlining the fact that his subject habitually quarried the life close to him, sometimes riskily so, both aesthetically and ethically. Begley quotes Updike as saying that *Willow* was something like an early version of *Couples* (1968), a novel notorious when it came out for exposing extreme sexual pornographic explicitness in small-town America. BR

WILL IT EVER HAPPEN?
It's surely not worth anyone's while to fabricate an Updike-like fiction, so it seems unlikely that anyone will try. Eventually the manuscript will be exposed to the harsh light of day, but by then Updike's literary reputation will have settled down, and embarrassing revelations, both aesthetic and biographical, will do less harm.

POODLE SPRINGS

Author Raymond Chandler **Year** 1958 **Country** United States **Genre** Detective novel

RAYMOND CHANDLER
In a letter written in 1958, Chandler remarked of his story, "I don't know whether the marriage will last or whether [Marlowe] will walk out of it or get bounced. Of course I have to have a murder and some violence and some trouble with the cops."

Raymond Chandler started off believing that his most famous literary creation, private eye Philip Marlowe, hero of seven novels published between 1939 and 1958, was and always had to be a loner. He wrote: "The whole point is that the detective exists complete and entire and unchanged by anything that happens, that he is, as detective, outside the story and above it, and always will be. That is why he never gets the girl, never marries, never really has any private life, except insofar as he must eat and sleep and have a place to leave his clothes." No one knows what made Chandler change his mind about the nuptials, but by February 1958 he was working on a story in which Marlowe is married to Linda Loring, the spoiled, beautiful daughter of a rich man in his 1953 novel *The Long Goodbye*. By the time of his death just over a year later, Chandler had completed only the first four short chapters—just 31 pages—of this work, which he entitled *Poodle Springs*.

WHERE CHANDLER LEFT OFF

In 1988, the executors of Chandler's estate hired Robert B. Parker to pick up the story where Chandler left off. Parker had written his doctoral thesis on fictional private eyes, including Marlowe, and gone on to become a best-selling author of detective fiction; his greatest character was a gumshoe named Spenser.

Poodle Springs was completed and published 30 years after Chandler's death to widespread critical acclaim. Another celebrated writer of crime fiction, Ed McBain, was quoted on the cover of the paperback edition proclaiming that Parker "sounds more like Chandler than Chandler himself."

And he does. There are plenty of hard-boiled wisecracks and similes that revive the spirit of the original creator: "He rummaged the cheap Scotch out of the drawer and poured some into a couple of paper cups. I had a swallow. It tasted like something you'd take for mange."

But there are some problems with the book. One is that Marlowe doesn't easily time-travel from Chandler's nib to that of a writer who has lived through the Summer of Love. Chandler's hero—his name probably an amalgam of Philip Sidney and Christopher Marlowe—belonged in an age of chivalry: that was really the whole point of him, that he was a knight in shining armor

RAYMOND CHANDLER
POODLE SPRINGS

Cover: Josse Pickard

dumped on the sleazy backstreets of 1930s Los Angeles. Fast-forward half a century, and when Parker's Marlowe finds a vibrator in the drawer of a woman whose house he's searching, he tells us about it.

Another difficulty is the pesky marriage. Not only does it seem a strange U-turn, but when Mrs. Marlowe tells her husband "This isn't working," it's hard to suppress the thought that that's Parker's voice, not Linda's. (Maybe if Chandler had lived, his fragment would have ended up as a subplot rather than a full-blown novel.)

But Parker is good. He works it out—the couple reconcile eventually. Indeed, he does a much better job of tying up all the threads of the plot than Chandler himself managed in his best book, *The Big Sleep* (1939). *Poodle Springs* is Chandleresque, but for it to be Chandler it would have to have Chandler's shortcomings as well as his virtues. GL

WHAT HAPPENED NEXT . . .
Robert B. Parker (below) died in 2010. A year later, his widow and two sons commissioned Ace Atkins to continue the Spenser series. Parker's own unfinished novel, a Spenser fragment called *Silent Night*, was completed by his literary agent, Helen Brann, and published in 2013.

WILL IT EVER HAPPEN?

0/10

Although the book exists, it does not necessarily contain the story that Chandler intended. Such continuations—books in which one author takes up another's theme, as distinct from a sequel by the original writer—are highly popular with readers who want more of the same from novelists who have been prevented by death from supplying it.

LE PREMIER HOMME

Author Albert Camus **Year** 1960 **Country** Algeria **Genre** Novel

ALBERT CAMUS
Born in 1913 in Algiers, Camus lost his father before his first birthday, a victim of the First World War. Camus was a communist who spent much of his life writing for and working in the theater; his plays, however, are the least popular part of his oeuvre.

The manuscript of this work in progress was found in the wreckage of the automobile in which Albert Camus and his publisher, Michel Gallimard, were killed on January 4, 1960. Camus was 46 years old. The fragment continues on the main themes of his novel *L'Étranger* (*The Stranger*, 1942): a sense of dislocation that is linked with colonialism, the heat of Algeria, and existential morality. The opening sentence of that novel—"Mother died today"—exemplifies these concepts. Camus had to come to terms with French colonialism first hand and he felt it as a raw and unknown experience. He describes it thus: "This was the very country into which he felt he had been tossed, as if he were the first inhabitant."

Two years after Camus's death, Algeria achieved independence from France. The author's position on the Franco-Algerian conflict had been opposed by many, but his morality was consistently pacifist and he condemned both sides in the conflict when innocent people were killed. The foundation of his thinking about French colonialism can be seen in *Le premier homme* (*The First Man*), with descriptions of the early French settlers being landed in deserts with no housing, and a hostile native population.

Most of this autobiographical book is about growing up in poverty in a small flat in Algiers. It is "a poverty naked as death," which makes any superfluity all the more valuable: a visit to the cinema with grandma, a squeeze on the arm from his mother, the smells on the way to school.

We read again and again of Camus's love for Algeria, "this magnificent and frightening land" with a "ferocious sun" and a "sky that was gray with heat." This is combined with a childlike pleasure in play, swimming, and soccer. It is these qualities that make him an attractive writer; the experience is always fresh and expressed directly and openly, partly because of the poverty: "Poor people's memory is less nourished than the rich."

At the heart of the novel is a moving scene in which a teacher persuades the mother and grandmother of Jacques, the Camus character, to let the boy continue at school. The teacher acts as a bridge between the boy and the outside world, taking over the role of the father Jacques never knew and constantly seeks. He tells Jacques never to forget his mother. The work ends with Jacques a "muscular adolescent" who is playing soccer for the school team, has kissed a girl, and is earning money at a vacation job. Then there is

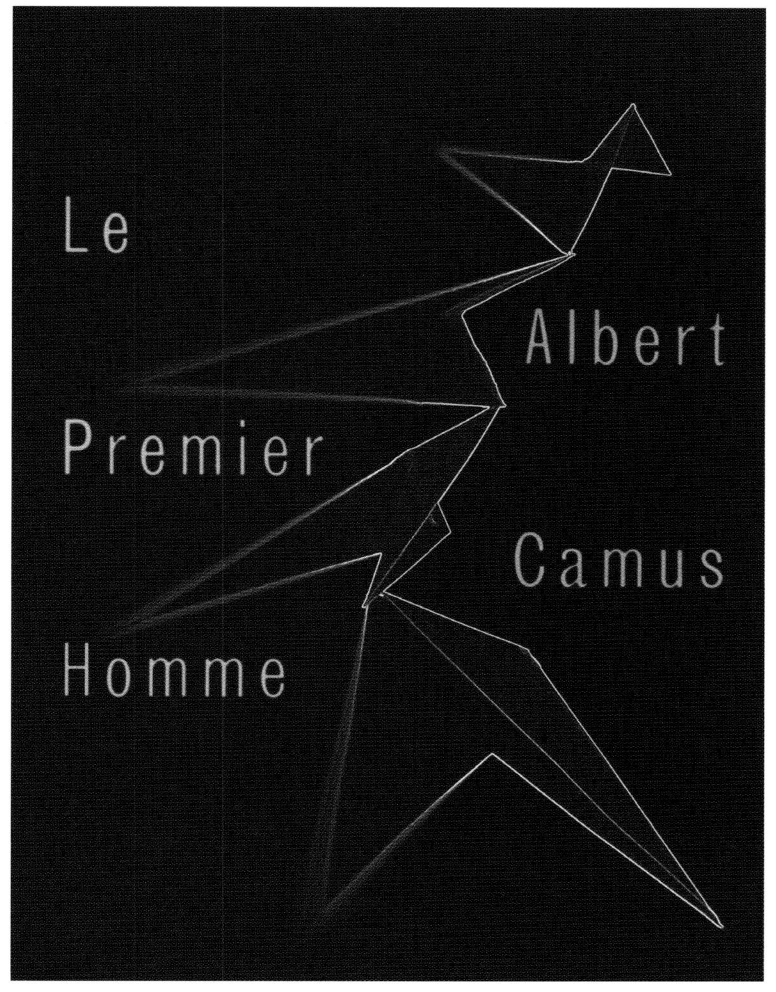

Cover: Tom Howey

WHAT HAPPENED NEXT . . .
Le premier homme was not rushed into print: the house of Gallimard published a French edition in 1994 and an English-language translation came out in the following year. Although as an unfinished work it was never as popular as *L'Étranger*, it enhanced Camus's reputation as the human face of Existentialism (in contrast to Jean-Paul Sartre). In 2011 a movie version starring Jacques Gamblin was released. The screenplay, which supplied a speculative conclusion to the story, was written by the Italian Gianni Amelio, who also directed.

a short piece reflecting on what has gone before and Jacques' passion for life. Where *Le premier homme* would have gone is anyone's guess; we can only lament that it is incomplete. BT

WILL IT EVER HAPPEN?

6/10

The Appendix contains a letter Camus wrote to his teacher expressing his gratitude, together with the reply that reads: "You have remained Camus: bravo"—a sort of postscript to the life. There are numerous biographies of Camus to take us beyond his schooldays, so we know what happens next. It is not obvious that the work is unfinished, although—rather like François Truffaut's movie *Les quatre-cent coups* (1959)—we know there must be more to come.

PRINCE JELLYFISH

Author Hunter S. Thompson **Year** 1960 **Country** United States **Genre** Novel

HUNTER S. THOMPSON
In a letter of 1959 to his friend Roger Richards, written around the time that he began work on *Prince Jellyfish*, Hunter S. Thompson declared: "As things stand now, I am going to be a writer. I'm not sure that I'm going to be a good one or even a self-supporting one, but until the dark thumb of fate presses me to the dust and says 'you are nothing,' I will be a writer."

Hunter S.Thompson is famous for what became known as "Gonzo Journalism"—a form of reportage in which the writer is more implicated in the events than the detached and objective observer is traditionally supposed to be. He became internationally notorious as the author of *Hell's Angels: The Strange and Terrible Saga of the Outlaw Motorcycle Gangs* (1967), which depicted his association with the motorcycle club. A reviewer for *The New York Times* said that his prose "crackled like a motor-cycle exhaust."

His best-known work is *Fear and Loathing in Las Vegas: A Savage Journey to the Heart of the American Dream* (1971), which charts all kinds of excesses, especially in the drug counter-culture. Its fame received an extra shot in the arm from the 1998 movie adaptation, directed by Terry Gilliam and starring Johnny Depp and Thompson's actual cigarette filter (a TarGard Permanent Filter System).

Thompson also became renowned for his implacable hatred of U.S. President Richard M. Nixon, whom he accused of representing "that dark, venal, and incurably violent side of the American character" in *Fear and Loathing on the Campaign Trail '72* (serialized in *Rolling Stone* before being released as a book in 1973). By this time the author was so well known that it was becoming increasingly difficult for him to be one of God's spies in reporting on the mysteries of the counter-culture scene.

Thompson was a verbose writer, once submitting 30,000 words on Gun Control Laws when *Esquire* demanded something short and snappy. Those influencing his stance of hard-bitten machismo include Ernest Hemingway, Norman Mailer, J.P. Donleavy, and Nelson Algren (author of *The Man with the Golden Arm*, 1949). Images of Thompson and his work are reinforced by the weird illustrations of the English cartoonist Ralph Steadman, with whom he first collaborated on the article "The Kentucky Derby is Decadent and Depraved" (1970) for *Scanlan's Monthly*.

LOOSE CANNON

Before he became famous, Thompson gained experience as a journalist in New York and in Jersey Shore, a semi-derelict industrial town in the Susquehanna Valley about 130 miles (208 km) northwest of Philadelphia in

Cover: Heath Killen

PLEASURE FROM PAIN

Fear and Loathing in Las Vegas documents the drug-addled road trip taken by Thompson (as his alter ego Raoul Duke) and his lawyer (Dr. Gonzo) as they descend on Las Vegas to chase the American Dream. The epigraph to the novel is a quotation from Dr. Samuel Johnson that partly excuses the ways of excess: "He who makes a beast of himself gets rid of the pain of being a man." The novel received a lukewarm reception from critics on publication, although Christopher Lehmann-Haupt described it in *The New York Times* as "a kind of mad, corrosive prose poetry that picks up where Norman Mailer's *An American Dream* left off and explores what Tom Wolfe left out." Terry Gilliam's movie adaptation received a similarly unenthusiastic appraisal upon its release, but has since become a cult film.

Pennsylvania. He wrote mainly factual pieces, but he dabbled in fiction too. In 1959, while living in "an illegal sub-basement at 57 Perry St" New York he started on his first novel, an autobiographical work titled *Prince Jellyfish*, and "tried like hell to finish it."

About 30 pages of *Prince Jellyfish* have been printed so far, sketching three episodes in the life of protagonist Welburn Kemp. (They appear in *Songs of the Doomed*, a collection of Thompson's essays, short stories, and articles that was published in 1990.) In the first of these the character finds himself in a Charles Street apartment in Manhattan, a place presided over by the Empire State Building, "that great phallic symbol, a monument to proud dreams of potency that is the spirit of New York." It is New Year's Eve and Kemp is on the way to a party in upmarket Morningside Drive with no date. He tries to pick up a girl on Sheridan Square and follows her back home, where her partner attacks him with a belt, producing comic-book sound-effects: "*Swaacckkk*! . . . His knees went rubbery and he screamed in terror. Over his shoulder he saw the man lash out again. *Swaacckkk!*" The girl screams, "Hit him again Jack! He's crazy."

He gets to the party and meets a girl called Ann Farabee. He tells her about the encounter, describing a somewhat different version of the events: "'Well, he won't be beating people for a while,' Kemp said quietly. 'When I left him he could hardly breathe.'" He constructs an alternative scenario in his mind:

> "Kemp saw himself standing off a whole pack of lunatics with whips, cutting them down like weeds with the back of his hand . . . nimble and quick, silent and deadly . . . 'Attack *me*, will you!' . . . whap! . . . slash! . . . screams of pain . . . now standing above a ring of prostrate bodies, wiping the blood off the back of his hand with a handkerchief."

The girl is impressed and "her eyes seemed (to Kemp) like dark coals of smouldering sensuality." Some kissing takes place as midnight comes, with the inevitable sound of "the clatter of ice cubes and broken glass." She ditches the poor "boob" she came with, David Bibb, and goes off into the night with Kemp.

The second episode deals with Kemp's job interview a few days later. He wants to be a reporter, and tries to impress an editor. The interview is largely humiliating. He is offered a job as a copyboy at a derisory salary, and tells the boss: "You must be out of your damned mind." He thinks when hits the windy street: "The sleazy little bastard! I should have hauled off and bashed him in the face!"

The subject of journalism is one that Thompson knows about, and provides a pretext for being close to a variety of subjects and visiting numerous places. However, unlike some authors who exploit self-referentiality when they deal with writing, he does not go in for postmodernist games. He is sufficiently skeptical to see that the image Kemp has of the profession is clichéd and over-romanticized:

> "He had a vision of himself as a reporter—trench-coated, saber-tongued, a fearless champion of truth and justice. He saw himself working late at night, lonely and feverish at a desk in the empty newsroom, pounding out stories that would rock the city at dawn . . . Day after day he had turned out his quota of tripe, waiting impatiently for that call to the battlements, that urgent summons to a higher duty, that day when he would charge into the fray as the legendary reporters of an earlier and more fortunate generation had done before him."

The next chapter is "Cherokee Park" and takes place at Kemp's home town in Kentucky the following September. Too embarrassed by a recent drunken incident to go out with friends, he borrows his parents' car and drives out to

RIDING TO FAME

The book that launched Thompson's writing career was an account of the year he spent with two California chapters of the Hell's Angels. He was upfront with them about his project, and they responded with greater candor than they had ever previously shown to an outsider. The relationship between the reporter and his subjects became so close that at one point he began to wonder whether he was writing about them or being absorbed by them. He remained friendly with some members for the rest of his life.

JOHNNY DEPP

The actor described his long friendship with Thompson (they first met in 1994) as "a major love affair." Depp has played a Thompson-based character twice on screen: first in *Fear and Loathing in Las Vegas* (1998), and after the author's death in *The Rum Diary* (2011).

RACE PREJUDICE
"The Kentucky Derby is Decadent and Depraved," an article about the deplorable behavior of the crowd at this famous annual event, was the first collaboration between Thompson and illustrator Ralph Steadman. Initially, however, the pair did not get on—Steadman later admitted that "I really didn't think we'd have anything more to do with one another. I thought he didn't particularly like me, or my work." In 2012 the article was adapted into an audio book (right), with Tim Robbins reading the role of Thompson and Ralph Steadman playing himself, accompanied by a musical soundtrack by Bill Frisell.

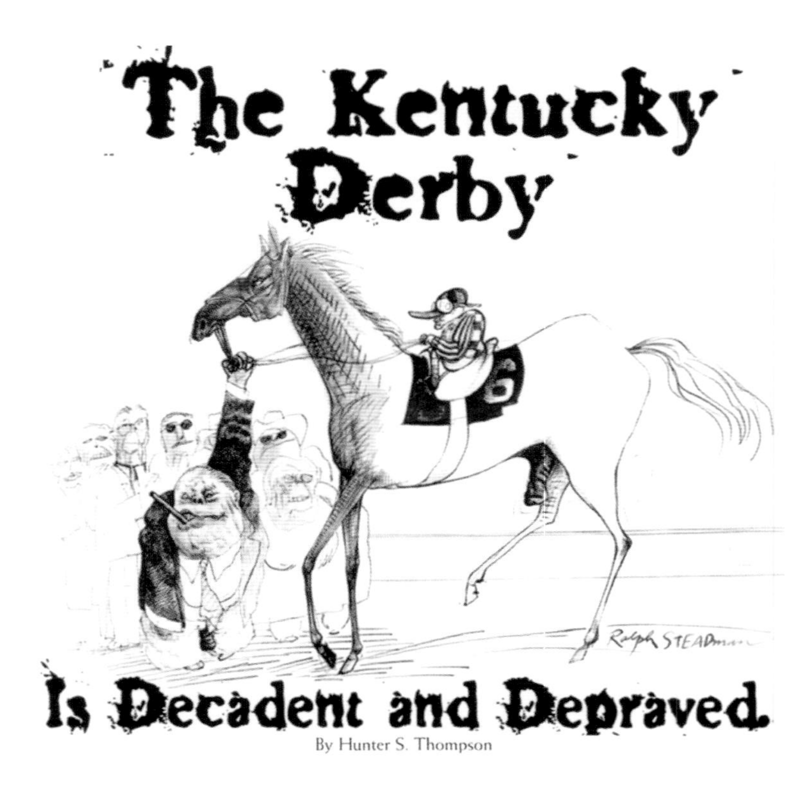

the park that contains memories of childhood sports and "trembling hours" of teenage necking. He sees an old school-friend in the Hi-Dee-Ho club, but doesn't speak to him. He drives down to an old trysting spot and almost crashes into the car of a courting couple, before returning home, his nerves "all to pieces." And there *Prince Jellyfish* ends.

THE RUM DIARY

In a letter to his editor Angus Cameron in March 1960, Thompson described some of the difficulties that he had faced while trying to complete the work:

> "Since September . . . the people who sheltered me have applied for divorce, I was beaten by hoodlums in New York, put in jail in Virginia Beach, arrested for drunken driving in Louisville; then I was taken by plane to San Juan where the man who hired me to write sports copy proved to be an insolvent liar. All this has somewhat hindered the progress of the book."

Despite overcoming these ordeals to eventually finish *Prince Jellyfish*, Thompson was unable to find a literary agent who would take it. He shelved the manuscript and in 1961 began work on a second autobiographical novel, *The Rum Diary* (which would also struggle to find a publisher), based on his experiences as a journalist in Puerto Rico. Around this time he also took a job as a security guard at Big Sur hot springs, shortly before it became the

Esalen Institute. Drawn by its reputation as a bohemian haven for artists and eccentrics, he hoped to use his time there to write what he called "The Great Puerto Rican Novel." However, his gun-toting habits and a candid article about the community for *Rogue* magazine (a rival to *Playboy*) soon led to his eviction.

THE DESTRUCTIVE ELEMENT

It would be interesting to read the whole of *Prince Jellyfish*, if only to have an explanation for the novel's title. The writing is not Thompson's best, but it is clear that he is trying to live up to the standards elicited in Conrad's preface to *The Children of the Sea* (1897), which Paul Kemp is reading in chapter 19 of *The Rum Diary* (1998): the novelist should *see* and should write not according to formulae but to the truths of artistic conscience. Thompson quoted to a friend Conrad's phrase in *Lord Jim* (1900): "In the destructive element immerse!"

> *"He had a vision of himself as a reporter . . . a fearless champion of truth and justice."*
>
> *Prince Jellyfish*

For Thompson, as for Conrad, "the destructive element" was the source of creativity. The former liked to give himself respectable literary credentials and claimed, at one time or another, that he got the phrase "fear and loathing" from Kierkegaard, Nietzsche, or Kafka (it actually came from Thomas Wolfe's *The Web and The Rock*, 1939).

Thompson had 30 years or so more of hell-rousing and merry capers. Suffering from a nexus of health problems he committed suicide with a firearm at the age of 67 at his house Owl Farm, Woody Creek, Colorado. His funeral went off with a bang, since in accordance with his wishes his ashes were fired out of a cannon in a ceremony funded by his friend, the movie star Johnny Depp. BR

WHAT HAPPENED NEXT . . .

The Rum Diary, a novel based on Thompson's experiences in Puerto Rico, involving machismo mayhem and too many doses, was eventually published in 1998. In 2011 it was released as a film starring Johnny Depp. It gives some idea of what *Prince Jellyfish* might have been like.

Prince Jellyfish has never been published in its entirety. Two other unpublished Thompson novels are *The Night Manager* (1985), about a San Francisco striptease club, and *Polo is my Life* (1990), a sex 'n' drugs odyssey.

WILL IT EVER HAPPEN?

5/10

There is a chance that the manuscript of *Prince Jellyfish* will surface, and aficionados will be able to read the real thing. There also remains the possibility that would-be Thompsons will attempt some sort of imitation. A copious diet of narcotics may leave them sufficiently fortified to produce plausible hallucinatory pyrotechnics, but they will also have to be able to write—and many critics have declared Thompson to be "inimitable." Thompson himself said that "only a person has Been There can possibly understand" his subjects. It's feasible that, if it survives, the Thompson estate will one day publish *Prince Jellyfish* in an expensive limited edition, resembling Thompson's semi-autobiographical *Fire in the Nuts*. Written in the late 1950s, this short story about an aspiring writer struggling in New York City was released in 2004 with illustrations by Ralph Steadman. Only 176 copies were printed, all of which were signed by both author and artist.

JOURNALS

Author Sylvia Plath **Year** 1963 **Country** United States **Genre** Diaries

SYLVIA PLATH
Plath was born and raised in Boston, Massachusetts. She won a Fulbright Scholarship to Cambridge University, which was where she met Ted Hughes. In her Journals she noted that "everything in life is writable about if you have the outgoing guts to do it, and the imagination to improvise."

Sylvia Plath has attracted considerable media attention over the years, although much of it has been prurient and ultimately irrelevant so far as literary valuation is concerned. Famously married to and then later separated from future Poet Laureate Ted Hughes—whom she met in Cambridge, England, and married on June 16, 1956 (the date consciously chosen for being Joyce's Bloomsday)—she committed suicide in February 1963, at the age of 30.

As her surviving husband, Hughes took responsibility for editing her poems posthumously and for supervising the estate. These actions generated controversy among votaries of Plath, who thought he had been high-handed in the selection and editing. (Although arguably any editing is bound to seem high-handed, unless an elaborate and truly complete variorum edition is produced.) Ardent fans have even been to Plath's burial place in Heptonstall, Yorkshire, and chipped the word "Hughes" off her gravestone in protest. Such followers tend to regard Plath as the major poet, and Hughes as a minor poet who fed off her, exploited her, and impeded her production, but the truth of the matter is that they influenced each other as writers, and both benefited from the close relationship.

In addition to the works published posthumously, there are two missing Journals: one which Hughes destroyed, covering the last months of her life, and another which disappeared, possibly stolen and destroyed by Plath's mother on a visit. Hughes explained why he destroyed the Journal in an interview published in the *Paris Review* in 1995: "What I actually destroyed was one Journal which covered maybe two or three months, the last months. And it was just sad. I just didn't want her children to see it, no. Particularly her last days."

Plath was a species of graphomaniac, who recorded as much as she could of her life, even detailed descriptions of nose-picking. Such attention to detail presents a very full picture of a writer struggling with images of identity and self-definition. In a sense, however, the *Journals* aren't strictly speaking literature, but a by-road of literature. Plath, had she lived, would almost certainly not have wanted to publish them, and they weren't written with publication in mind. Those journals intended eventually for publication tend to be more crafted and artistically discriminating.

Cover: Tom Howey

WHAT HAPPENED NEXT . . .
Interest in Plath continues, emphasized in 2003 by the movie *Sylvia* with Gwyneth Paltrow as the poet. Plath's daughter, Frieda, refused to collaborate in the making of the movie, or give permission for the poems to be used. In 1998 Hughes published *Birthday Letters*, a collection of poetry which tells of his relationship with Plath. It has been much castigated by some supporters of Plath, but it is a powerful commemoration.

CUTTING REMARKS

An edition of the surviving Journals was produced in 1982, edited by Frances McCullough. This was heavily censored, in part to reduce the hostility Plath displayed toward her mother. *Letters Home* (1975) contained the letters Plath wrote to her mother, although these weren't always frank and full. In 2000 a fuller edition of the *Journals* was published, edited by Karen V. Kukil, which gave readers the opportunity to see what had been suppressed in the earlier edition. It also included two Journals that had been "sealed" by Hughes until February 11, 2013 (the 50th anniversary of her death), but were "unsealed" shortly before his death in 1998 with the approval of his and Plath's children.

Perhaps the ideal solution for such situations, if editors fear the embarrassments of disclosure, is to send private papers to the British Museum with "do not open until 2100" written on the packet. By that time an author's works will have made their own way, or will have failed, without the interfering clutter of ancillary items. BR

WILL IT EVER HAPPEN?

2/10

One journal was definitely destroyed. The other is unlikely to turn up. Doubtless writers will nonetheless continue to reimagine and speculate on Plath's life, especially the last months, when she was at once depressed and highly productive.

THE LONG GOODBYE

Author Harper Lee **Year** 1964 **Country** United States **Genre** Novel

HARPER LEE
Given a year off work on full pay to write a novel, Harper Lee produced a work that was more like a collection of short stories. But an agent and a publisher helped her to recast the manuscript into her acclaimed—and only—full-length work of fiction.

Nelle Harper Lee is the American novelist famous for *To Kill a Mockingbird* (1960), an acclaimed work that is frequently found on lists of the best 100 modern novels, and in one poll came top. It has sold 30 million copies, and—unlike some other best sellers—has probably been read by most people who possess a copy. (The fact that it has been banned in parts of the United States at various times may well have helped to swell the number of readers.) Despite the runaway success of that novel, she was unable to complete any subsequent works.

ONE-HIT WONDER

The subject of *To Kill a Mockingbird* is the dominant malaise of racism in certain Southern States, a phenomenon of which Lee had first-hand experience when growing up in, Monroeville, Alabama. The story, seen through the eyes of his daughter Scout, is of Atticus Finch (memorably played by Gregory Peck in the 1962 film), a lawyer who defends Tom Robinson, a black man accused of raping a young white woman. The plot recalls an incident in Lee's own life, in which her lawyer father defended two black men accused of murdering a white storekeeper; he was unsuccessful, and they were both hanged.

After the publication of *To Kill A Mockingbird* Lee began work on a second novel, *The Long Goodbye*, but by the mid-1960s she had abandoned it. It is uncertain what caused her to cease writing, but her newfound celebrity seems to be at least partly to blame. Not only did it leave her with less time for writing, but it placed her under considerable pressure to repeat the success of her earlier novel. As she remarked to her cousin Dickie Williams, "When you're at the top, there is only one way to go."

Very little is known about the contents of *The Long Goodbye*. One possible hint is that Lee said of Maycomb, the fictional town in *To Kill a Mockingbird*, "This is small-town middle-class southern life as opposed to Gothic," suggesting it was unlike the "Southern Gothic" genre practiced by writers such as William Faulkner and Flannery O'Connor. Another clue is that she said in 1964 that she wanted "to be the Jane Austen of south Alabama," indicating a desire to be a votary of the realistic.

After putting her pen down on *The Long Goodbye*, Lee helped Truman Capote, who had been a childhood schoolfriend, with research that he was

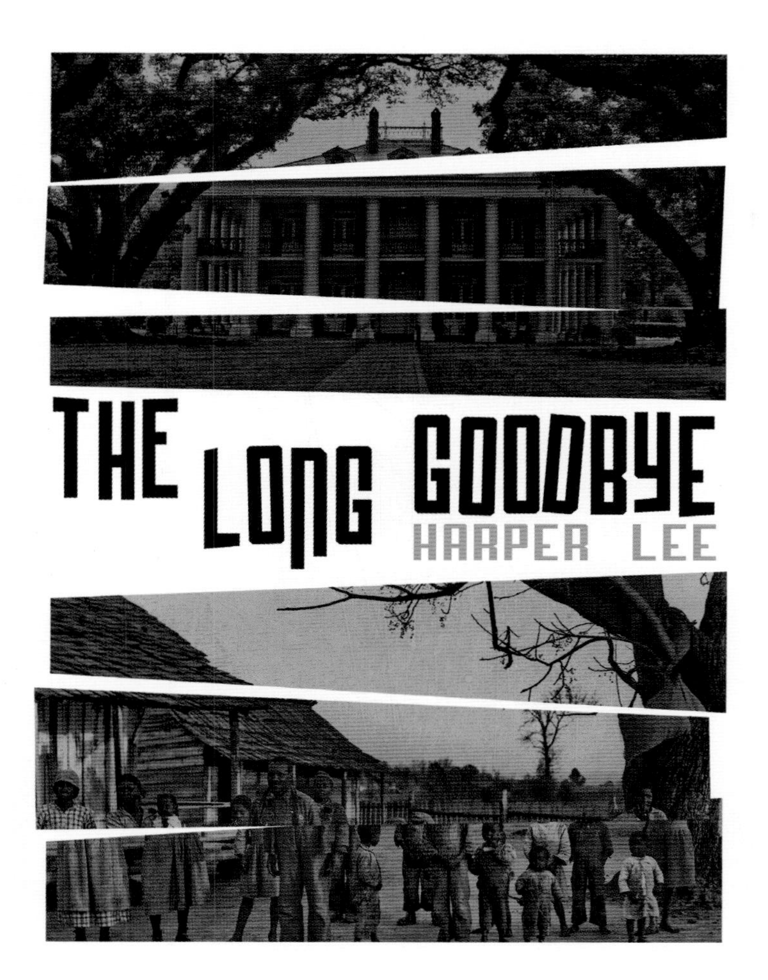

Cover: Dean Martin

undertaking for *In Cold Blood* (1966). (Some conspiracy theorists go so far as believing that it was Capote who wrote *To Kill a Mockingbird*.) In the mid-1980s she began a documentary book about an Alabama preacher suspected of being a serial killer, but again abandoned the writing. BR

WHAT HAPPENED NEXT . . .
On November 5, 2007, George W. Bush presented Lee with the Presidential Medal of Freedom (below). In 2015, Lee's second novel, *Go Set a Watchman*, featuring the adult Scout, was published. A sequel to *To Kill a Mockingbird*, the story actually predates that novel—after submitting it for publication in the mid-1950s, Lee was persuaded by an editor to write a novel from the point of view of the young Scout instead. Having believed the manuscript subsequently lost, Lee was "surprised and delighted" when it was rediscovered in 2014.

WILL IT EVER HAPPEN?
We have no idea what *The Long Goodbye* was going to be about, and Harper Lee has given no indication. She has been as reclusive as J.D. Salinger for many years, which has, of course, merely intensified the public's desire to invade her privacy. It would be impossible for an imitator to begin it, let alone finish. It would be like trying to make bricks without either clay or straw.

THE SILMARILLION

Author J.R.R. Tolkien **Year** 1973 **Country** England **Genre** Epic fantasy fiction

J.R.R. TOLKIEN
Tolkien's major academic work was a scholarly edition of the medieval English poem *Sir Gawain and the Green Knight*. He also contributed entries on many words of Germanic origin beginning with the letter "W" to the first edition of the *Oxford English Dictionary* (1928).

J.R.R. Tolkien was an Oxford professor whose immersion in Old Norse, Anglo-Saxon, and Middle English texts inspired him to turn his hand to fiction in *The Hobbit* (1937), a coming-of-age story about a fantastical human-like creature's quest for dragon's gold, and its sequel *The Lord of the Rings* (1954), a modern version of the heroic epic. Both books sold in vast quantities and garnered praise from some noted critics, including the poet W.H. Auden, who rated the former "one of the best children's stories of [the 20th] century" and wrote of the latter: "No fiction I have read in the last five years has given me more joy."

Tolkien was prevented by death from completing the third volume in the series, *The Silmarillion*, which he had extensively planned and partly written. A history of the universe within which *The Hobbit* and *The Lord of the Rings* take place, the origins of this work in fact predate the other two. Tolkien first began working on the stories that would eventually comprise his "Legendarium" during the First World War, while recovering from trench fever that he had contracted on the front line. He continued working on the tales for several years and after *The Hobbit* was released he sent some of them to his publisher George Allen and Unwin under the title *Quenta Silmarillion*. They were rejected on the grounds of not being commercially publishable, and the publisher asked him instead to write a sequel to *The Hobbit*. This Tolkien duly did, but he never abandoned *The Silmarillion*, which grew to be increasingly multilayered and complex.

COOL CRITICAL RECEPTION

Following Tolkien's death in 1973, his youngest son, Christopher, began work on editing the existing drafts of *The Silmarillion* with the help of Guy Gavriel Kay, who would later make a name for himself as an author of fantasy fiction. These two men had considerable difficulty in deciphering and filling out the work. Some parts of it were inconsistent with what had gone before; other parts were palimpsests, sometimes of the most confusing kind, in which it was unclear which was the latest or the preferred version. The marginalia were mutually contradictory.

Undaunted, however, Tolkien junior and Kay pressed on, and the result of their labors was published in 1977. Sales of the book were stronger

Cover: Isabel Eeles

than ever—Tolkien had a global army of fans who had been waiting for a generation to get their hands on the great man's next instalment and after his death had started to fear that they might never get it.

But the critical reception was much cooler than that afforded to Tolkien's earlier books. The reasons for this are readily identifiable. Firstly, the work strives to draw together all the threads of the earlier narratives. This desire to tie up all the loose ends is a not uncommon failing in multi-volume enterprises set in alternative worlds: the authors start off showing us the inner workings of their universe and are then (for whatever reason, perhaps a crisis of confidence; perhaps hubris) overcome by a perceived need to present an Olympian view, explaining parallels between the fiction and reality. *The Silmarillion* traces the history of Tolkien's invented world from its creation to the time in which the *The Hobbit* and *The Lord of the Rings* stories were set. It also attempts to create a cosmos that is like a not-entirely-happy synthesis of pre-Christian Nordic myth and Dante's *Divine Comedy* (c.1308–21). *The New York Times*' review of the book lamented that Tolkien "cares much more about the meaning and coherence of his myth than he does about . . . rich characterization, imagistic brilliance, powerfully imagined and detailed sense of place, and thrilling adventure."

The other main problem with the book is that there is a notable falling off in the quality of prose. In a review of *The Silmarillion* for the *New Statesman*, Peter Conrad commented that "Tolkien can't actually write." The author undeniably had a tendency to lapse into archaism, but this propensity was mostly kept in check in his previous novels. In *The Silmarillion*, however, it atrophies into passages such as:

THE INKLINGS

Tolkien and a group of like-minded academics met informally from time to time in The Eagle and Child pub in Oxford to discuss fantasy fiction. Of the other Inklings, the most famous was C.S. Lewis (far right). The first of Lewis's Chronicles of Narnia, *The Lion, the Witch and the Wardrobe* (1950) has numerous merits but shares with *The Silmarillion* a strain of unoriginality. The opening of the novel creates a gripping world of evil that retains its power until the appearance of Father Christmas begins a steep and rapid descent into thinly disguised Christian allegory. Not that there is anything wrong with Christian allegory; it is merely that the start of *The Lion, the Witch and the Wardrobe* comes from its author's imagination while the end comes from the minds of the authors of the New Testament.

"And thou, Melkor, shalt see that no theme may be played that hath not its uttermost source in me, nor can any alter the music in my despite. For he that attempteth this shall prove but mine instrument in the devising of things more wonderful, which he himself hath not imagined."

This perhaps is not entirely his fault—after all, Tolkien hadn't finished *The Silmarillion*, and one of the main things that writers do when they revise their work is cut. It is possible that Christopher Tolkien was inhibited, not only by the confusing manuscripts, but also by conflicting and possibly irreconcilable desires: one to make *The Silmarillion* as good as possible; the other to remain faithful to the text as his father had left it.

TRANSCENDING CRITICISM

Sales of the book nonethless soared, and therein lies another issue—some art transcends criticism. Tolkien's fiction has been deprecated by some

> *"And thou, Melkor, shalt see that no theme may be played that hath not its uttermost source in me . . ."*
>
> *The Silmarillion*

highly educated readers because it is derivative of early English and even older Scandinavian works. But in a sense all art is unoriginal: Shakespeare borrowed plots from the work of English chronicler Raphael Holinshed; Paul Simon's "American Tune" is based on a chorale from J.S. Bach's *St. Matthew Passion*; and J.K. Rowling was inspired or influenced in the Harry Potter books by countless earlier works, including *The Lord of the Rings*. To set the highest store by originality may make us overlook the merit of the finished products. Let scholars seek sources; leave the common reader to enjoy the narrative drive and the powers of expression that make some books better than the sum of their parts.

Certainly, such criticisms have done little to dent the popularity of *The Silmarillion* and Tolkien's other works—total sales of his books are estimated to be in the region of around 300 million copies. Ultimately, however, the author's literary achievement is best measured by *The Hobbit* and *The Lord of the Rings*, which he completed himself. It is unfair to compare *The Silmarillion* with these works without the benefit of Tolkien's final polish. **GL**

WHAT HAPPENED NEXT . . .

Christopher Tolkien published much more of his father's work in a 12-volume series entitled *The History of Middle-earth* (1983–96). Many fans noticed inconsistencies with the earlier material, but that did not reduce their enjoyment. The apparently insatiable public appetite for Tolkien and Tolkieniana is further attested by the popularity of Peter Jackson's movie adaptations of *The Lord of the Rings* (2001–03) and *The Hobbit* (2012–14).

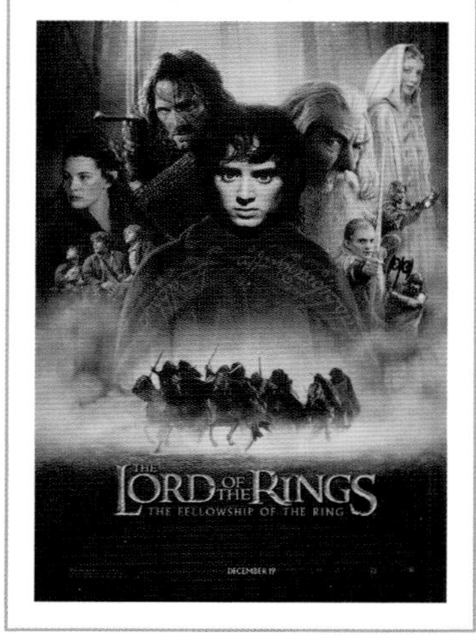

WILL IT EVER HAPPEN?

8/10

More to the point, will it ever stop happening? It is ironic that the work of Tolkien should have become the focus of a cult with religious overtones that devotes itself to constant re-examination of the canonical texts and produces a stream of works of exegesis. The author, a Roman Catholic, always maintained that his works were Christian, but he never pretended that they were anything other than children's books.

TODESARTEN

Author Ingeborg Bachmann **Year** 1973 **Country** Austria **Genre** Novel

INGEBORG BACHMANN
Although Bachmann's reputation is based on her poetry and prose fiction, her main preoccupations were philosophical. She was particularly concerned with the shortcomings of language.

Ingeborg Bachmann was born in 1926 and at the age of 12 saw Nazi troops welcomed into her home town of Klagenfurt at the time of the Anschluss (the political union of Germany and her native Austria). After the Second World War she went to university and then worked as a script editor for a radio station. She found fame as a poet (her main influence was Rainer Maria Rilke) and became a member of Gruppe 47, an influential literary circle whose other members included Günter Grass and Heinrich Böll. She abandoned verse in the 1960s to concentrate on writing novels.

In 1953 Bachmann moved from Austria to Italy, where she lived with the German composer Hans Werner Henze, who set several of her works to music. She later had an affair with Swiss playwright Max Frisch.

In 1971, she published *Malina*, the first part of a planned series of novels entitled *Todesarten* (*Ways of Dying*). In September 1973, she failed to stub out a cigarette properly and died a month later from the burns she had suffered in the resulting apartment blaze.

EXTANT FRAGMENT

Todesarten is set in Vienna and the time is "today." There are three main characters: the first-person female narrator, a famous writer whose name is never revealed; Malina, with whom she lives; and Ivan, a Hungarian whom she loves. The latter is thought to have been at least partly modeled on the poet Paul Celan, with whom Bachmann had a long love affair in her youth.

The narrator of the novel is writing a fairy tale called "The Mysteries of the Princess of Kagran." In this story-within-a-story, the heroine encounters a stranger who keeps his face hidden from view. She is fascinated by his air of mystery and falls in love with him, but as soon as she does so he disappears.

Bachmann's account of the protagonist's progress with the fairy tale is intercut with descriptions of mundane events. The latter often overwhelm the former: this is not just another book about a writer writing, it is also about the ways in which life both inspires and inhibits creativity. And what goes for life in general goes particularly when love intrudes—the narrator spends more of her time running around after her White Rabbit-like boyfriend than

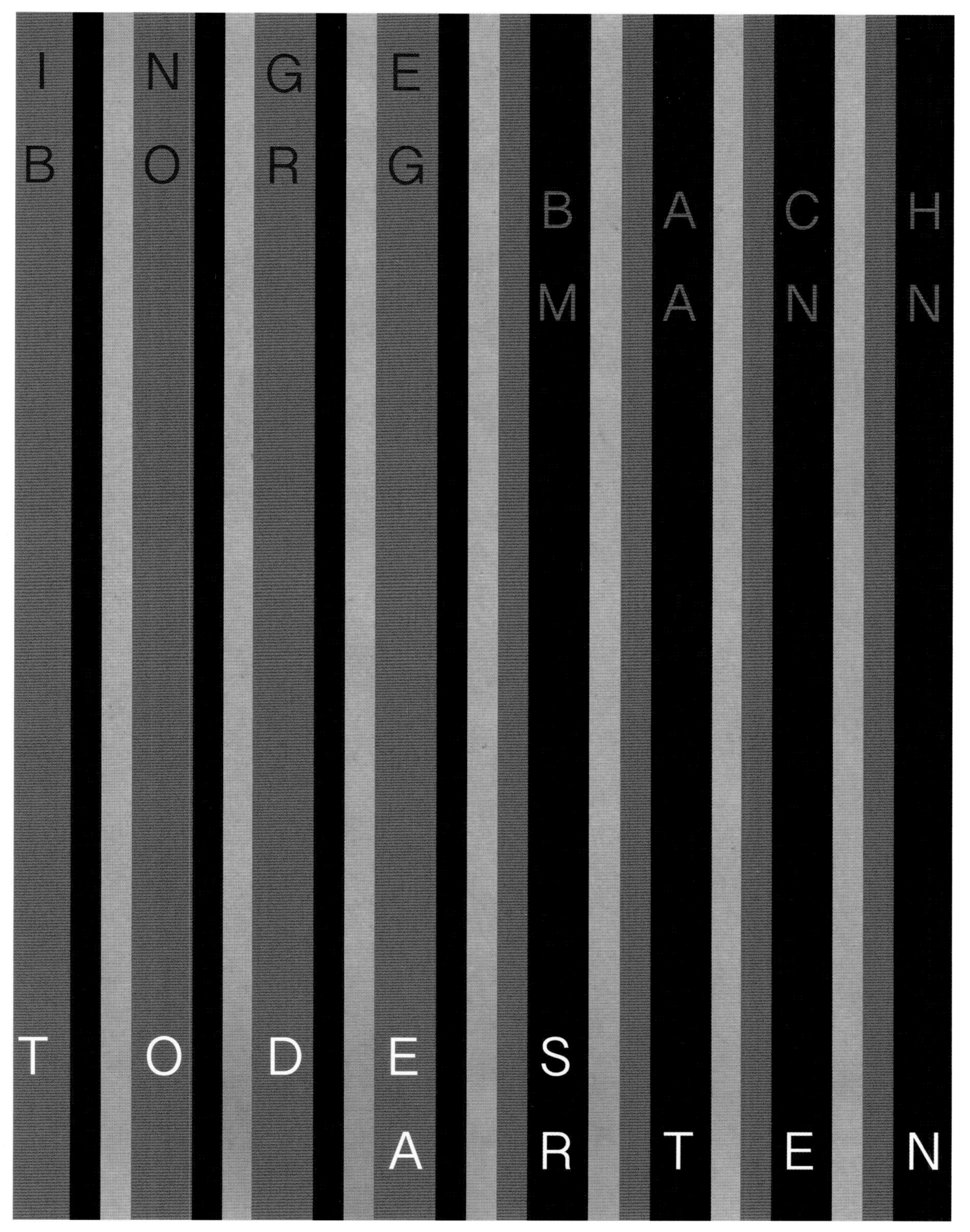

Cover: Claire Köster

SOME OF WHAT WE MISSED

The surviving fragment of *The Franza Case* concerns a Viennese psychiatrist who becomes obsessed with the Nazis and starts to practice some of their sadistic methods on his wife, Franziska. She escapes with her brother, Martin, to Africa, where she meets first a former SS captain and then a violent end. Meanwhile an appearance by Malina makes the reader wonder whether Martin really exists or is just a figment of Franziska's imagination. The book is partly a rumination on the significance of psychoanalytical theory (Vienna's main gift to the world) and partly expiation of war guilt.

The heroine of *Requiem for Fanny Goldmann* is an aging actress whose decline is a metaphor for the postwar decay of the Austrian capital. Her lifelong rival has been Malina's sister, Maria Malina. The work may reveal Bachmann's feminism, with great emphasis placed on the women's mutual antagonism and their social and financial dependence on men.

holding pen to paper. What we have of *Todesarten* is thus at least in part a meditation on the ways in which the banal and the fantastic interweave and interfere with each other. The book is also about the difficulties of drawing any meaningful line between people's external perceptions and their psychological interior worlds.

GRUPPE 47

Ingeborg Bachmann with two fellow members of this influential coterie: Martin Walser (left), author of *Marriages in Philippsburg* (1957) and Heinrich Böll (right), whose *Verlorenes Paradies* (*Paradise Lost*) is another notable unfinished work (see p.180).

DEEPER SIGNIFICANCE

But there is more to it than that. As the narrative unfolds, it becomes less and less clear whether the "I" and the Malina character (whom we at first take to be a man) are different people. "I am double," the former declares at one point, later adding that Malina created her as much as she created him. She even asks herself: "Am I a woman or something dimorphic?" This is meta-fiction—a genre that assumes that readers fully understand the novel form and thus licenses authors to take liberties with it. To fans of Bachmann's work, Ivan symbolizes the presence of absence. One critic has attached significance to the fact that "Malina" is an anagram of "animal" and almost an anagram of "anima," a basic concept in the psychological theories of Carl Jung. Another has interpreted the work as Bachmann's take on Christian theology, with the main characters comprising a spiritual trinity, like the Father, the Son, and the Holy Ghost. Textual interplay between Christianity and Judaism has also been remarked upon. Bachmann witnessed Hitler's takeover of Austria and Celan was a Romanian Jew who had spent the greater part of the Second World War in a Nazi labor camp. There's a lot of war guilt.

The narrator starts to question whether she should finish her story, which may be the fairy tale and may be *Todesarten* itself. Should she redirect her energies into the "beautiful book" that Ivan wants her to produce?

Such uncertainties—which may be perceived as metaphors for the dialectic of negativity and affirmation—are powerful enough but cumulatively they can prove exhausting.

THE PHILOSOPHY OF LANGUAGE

If we look even deeper we see what may have been Bachmann's real theme, her central preoccupation: language. If that is an accurate surmise, it would fit neatly with her background—she wrote her doctoral thesis on Heidegger and was a great admirer of Wittgenstein and his struggle to express the inexpressible. In a lecture delivered in 1959 at the University of Frankfurt, where Bachmann was the first professor of poetics, she observed that the problem with literature is that it "cannot itself say what it is." Perhaps *Todesarten* was her attempt to fill that gap, to reveal the hitherto unseen hand of the author.

> *"[Literature] cannot itself say what it is."*
>
> Ingeborg Bachmann

Malina concludes abruptly with a murder, an ending that has been interpreted as an echo of Carol Reed's *The Third Man* (1949), a British film noir set in Vienna. Or at least, *Malina* concludes abruptly with something that appears to be a murder. Is it a slaying in the accepted sense of the term, or some kind of figurative, psychological occurrence? Death prevented Bachmann from ever telling us—or, as at least seems possible, from not telling us.

Here is an author of whom a single lifetime's study might not suffice. For the determined few, however, there is a wealth of insight in Karen R. Achberger's *Understanding Ingeborg Bachmann* (1995), a work that raises the possibility that the structure of *Todesarten* was based on that of Arnold Schönberg's opera *Moses und Aron* (1957).

Readers of Bachmann may feel like lost travelers in a forest. Some find her work self-indulgent and willfully obscure. Others enjoy the relentless uncertainty, the constant suspicion that nothing is as it seems. The latter may lament the fact that the work is unfinished, but it is no obstacle to their enjoyment because for them the lack of clarity and conventional structure are part of the work's fascination. GL

WILL IT EVER HAPPEN?

5/10

On the one hand, there is no shortage of potential: the fragment Bachmann left is so open to interpretation that no continuator need feel constrained by a previously established plot. On the other hand, no addition could possibly be authentic: only the author knew where, if anywhere, *Todesarten* was headed and she took the destination board with her to the grave.

WHAT HAPPENED NEXT . . .

Two of Bachmann's projected *Todesarten* novels, *The Franza Case* and *Requiem for Fanny Goldmann*, were published as posthumous fragments in a single volume in 1999. In Werner Schroeter's film version of *Malina* (1991), Isabelle Huppert (below) played the narrator as a self-obsessed woman who is more the victim of her own psyche than of anyone or anything else. *The New York Times* described the movie as "terribly tedious," "heavily Freudian," and "often pretentious," but vouchsafed no opinion about whether it was faithful to the book on which it is based.

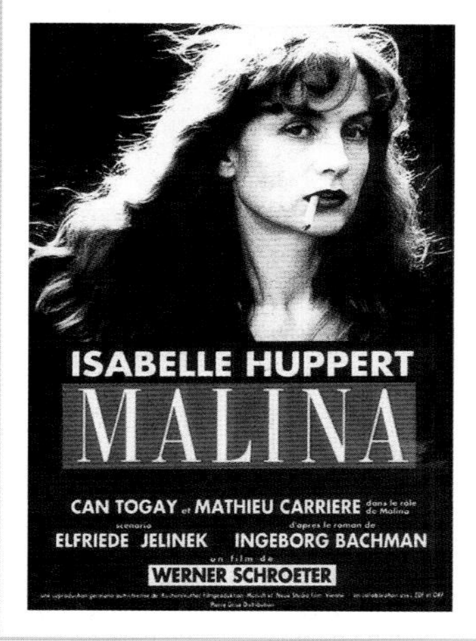

Chapter 6

Dalton Trumbo
NIGHT OF THE AUROCHS

THE COCKTAIL WAITRESS
JAMES M. CAIN
STEPHEN KING
The House on Value Street
The Original of Laura
Vladimir Nabokov
ANSWERED PRAYERS
TRUMAN CAPOTE

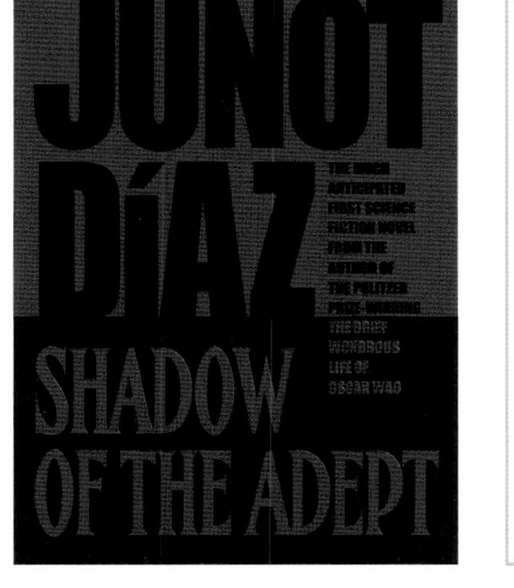

1976–Present

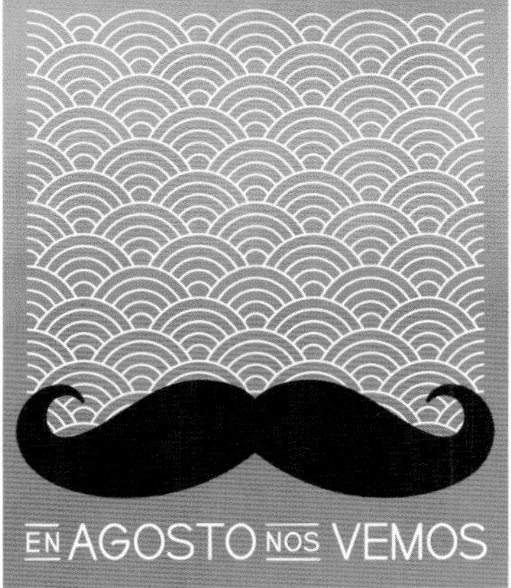

NIGHT OF THE AUROCHS

Author Dalton Trumbo **Year** 1976 **Country** United States **Genre** Novel

DALTON TRUMBO
Before the Second World War, Trumbo was one of the highest-paid scriptwriters in Hollywood. After his disgrace before the House Committee on Un-American Activities, he kept working, albeit at drastically reduced rates, but had to conceal his identity for many years. He wrote 30 scripts under pseudonyms.

The Book of Job states that "Man is born unto trouble, as the sparks fly upwards." Dalton Trumbo seems to have done more than most people to immolate himself in political fire. Wherever the zeitgeist was, he was always someplace else.

His anti-war novel, *Johnny Got His Gun* (1939), was published just as Hitler went on the rampage through Europe and Japan was contemplating a strike on Pearl Harbor. In 1946, he wrote a magazine article in which he expressed the view that, if he were a Russian (which he was not; he was of French extraction), he would fear the Americans even more than the Americans feared the Soviet Union. This was not a smart move at a time when the United States was entering the "reds under the bed" era, and it landed him in front of the U.S. House Committee on Un-American Activities—the McCarthy witch hunts—which denounced him as a communist and gave him an 11-month prison sentence. After his release, he was blacklisted—one of the Hollywood Ten—and for several years thereafter had to write under assumed names.

MAKING LIFE EVEN MORE DIFFICULT

Trumbo continued swimming against the tide throughout his life. In the 1970s, when Nazi leaders thought to be in hiding were being sought all over the world, he began work on *Night of the Aurochs* (an auroch is an extinct European bison). The main character of this novel is Ludwig Richard Johann Grieben, a fictionalized composite of the three commandants of Auschwitz. Many writers would have depicted a monster, but Trumbo treats him sympathetically, and has him draw plausible comparisons between his own position and that of Americans during the Civil War: both, in Grieben's view, were striving to keep the races separate and pure. His position is later compromised when he falls in love with a Jewish woman. Toward the end of the book, as the concentration camp is surrounded by Soviet troops, we see a broken man, whose life's work is about to be ruined and about whom no one will ever have a good word to say.

Dalton Trumbo was no more a Nazi in the 1970s than he had been a communist in the 1940s: examination of his work suggests that he was a contrarian who would assume perverse poses in order to test the strength of

Cover: Dean Martin

WHAT HAPPENED NEXT . . .
In 1979 Viking Press published *Night of the Aurochs* in the fragmentary form in which Trumbo had left it, together with his notes for the conclusion. The author was by then fully rehabilitated, and had been given due credit for his work in 1960 on the movies *Exodus* and *Spartacus*. It was badly received, not because it touched raw nerves but because it was judged to be ill-written. *Kirkus Reviews* described it as "didactic and heavy-handed" and giving "every indication" that it "would have been a dreadful book."

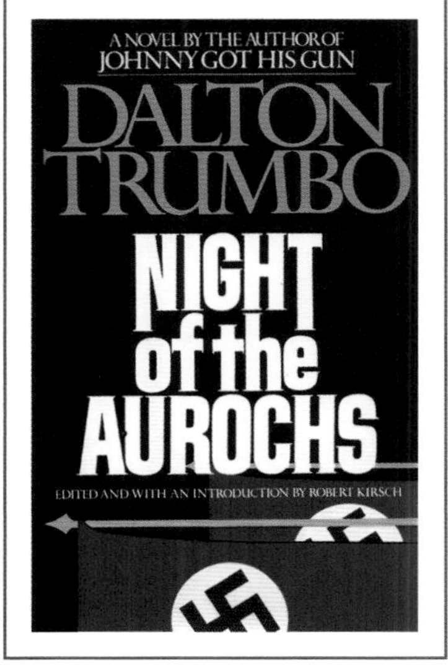

the prevailing orthodoxy. He was in a way like the method actors with whom he worked—one who liked to get "inside" his characters and "become" them, if only for the duration of the performance. He died before he could complete this work, and thus avoided being further traduced. GL

WILL IT EVER HAPPEN?

1/10

There's no discernible reduction in interest in the Nazi theme—any publisher will tell you that a swastika on the cover of a book will increase its sales—but neither is there any shortage of material: a host of writers across the seriousness spectrum, from William Styron (*Sophie's Choice*, 1979) to Robert Harris (*Fatherland*, 1992), have tackled the subject, and it is often easier to write something original than attempt to make a bad existing book good.

THE COCKTAIL WAITRESS

Author James M. Cain **Year** 1977 **Country** United States **Genre** Crime novel

JAMES M. CAIN
Maryland-born Cain served in Europe in the First World War and was managing editor of *The New Yorker* until the success of *The Postman Always Rings Twice* emboldened him to become a full-time writer of novels and screenplays.

James M. Cain hit the big-time in 1934 with his first novel, *The Postman Always Rings Twice*, which has since been adapted several times into movies. He followed this success with the novels *Double Indemnity* (1936) and *Mildred Pierce* (1941), both of which also became major Hollywood movies. Thereafter the law of diminishing returns began to apply to his work. None of his numerous subsequent thrillers—including some complete posthumous works—was anything like as successful as his first three.

In 2002, Charles Ardai, an editor at Hard Case Crime, publishers of pulp fiction, got wind of another novel, which Cain had almost completed at the time of his death in 1977. But he could find only fragments of it in the author's archive in the Library of Congress, so he asked around and eventually received from a Hollywood agent a typed manuscript of a novel entitled *The Cocktail Waitress*.

So far so good, but then it got complicated. Ardai soon discovered that this was not the only complete manuscript: it was one of several, none of which was dated and each of which differed substantially from the others, not just in the details but also in the running order. Ardai finally secured all the rights and worked on the text himself until he was satisfied that it was finished. The resulting version of *The Cocktail Waitress* was eventually published in 2012.

The first-person narrator is Joan Medford, a young mother who is left without a penny after her abusive husband is killed in an automobile crash. She delivers her son into the (she thinks temporary) care of her sister-in-law and takes a job as a scantily-clad waitress at a restaurant bar. Meanwhile the police suspect her of her husband's murder.

She soon becomes involved with two men: one a handsome scoundrel, the other a rich and sick old man. She wants them both—or, more specifically, she wants the best things about each of them. This is classic Cain territory: the frontier lands between lust and the love that is based on (and vitiated by) pragmatic self-interest.

Although the numerous versions of the work suggest that Cain died unsatisfied with parts of *The Cocktail Waitress*, it is hard to believe that he had any further work to do on Ardai's chosen ending, which crime novelist

Cover: Rebecca Richardson

Michael Connelly aptly described in *The New York Times* as "a gut-turning cosmic comeuppance." The route to this denouement is less satisfactory, however: there is too much signage along it, with several twists in the plot telegraphed to the reader before their due time.

It is charitable to assume that Cain, had he lived, would have ironed out these faults. So has Ardai honored the memory of the writer he venerates? It could be argued that publication was a service to Cain aficionados who welcome any relics or fragments of his achievement. Conversely, one could take the view that the only fair way to publish the work would have been a variorum edition containing every version. But such a volume would have been larger, and more costly to produce; it would have had less popular appeal and sold fewer copies. Art and commerce are seldom comfortable bedfellows. GL

WHAT HAPPENED NEXT . . .

Critics were unanimous that *The Cocktail Waitress* was good, but some remarked that, for all its merits, it was unworthy of comparison with Cain's best work of the 1930s and 1940s. Bookreporter.com observed that "Hollywood should take note: this is going to be a great film noir movie someday." However, at the time of publication of *The Greatest Books You'll Never Read* there were no known production plans.

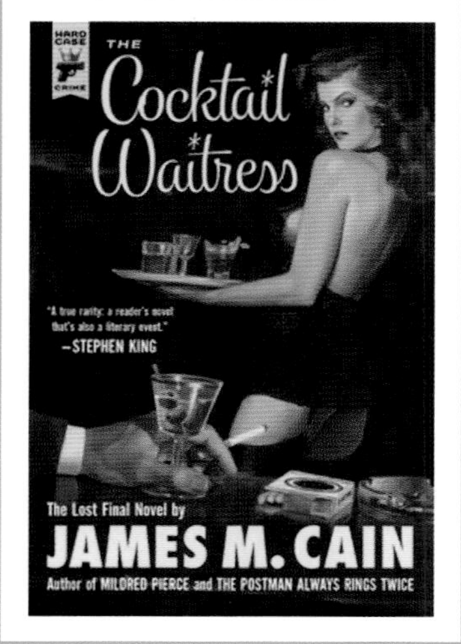

WILL IT EVER HAPPEN?

A scholarly edition that shows every one of Cain's arrangements of the material? Highly unlikely, in view of the decline in the publishing industry since the advent of the Internet. But not impossible: if the author maintains his current position with Dashiell Hammett and Raymond Chandler in the holy trinity of hard-boiled fiction writers, his works may become set texts, and that would shorten the odds against significantly.

THE HOUSE ON VALUE STREET

Author Stephen King **Year** 1977 **Country** United States **Genre** Novel

STEPHEN KING
The author from Portland, Maine, is widely credited with reviving the genre of horror fiction. To date his books have sold more than 100 million copies worldwide.

Stephen King came to prominence with *Carrie* (1974), an epistolary novel about a girl with telekinetic powers that in 1976 was turned into a movie directed by Brian De Palma and starring Sissie Spacek. He has since produced more than 50 horror, suspense, sci-fi, and fantasy novels.

After completing his third book, *The Shining* (1977)—later a film directed by Stanley Kubrick and starring Jack Nicholson—King started writing about one of the biggest news stories of the decade: the abduction in 1974 of American heiress Patty Hearst, granddaughter of newspaper tycoon William Randolph Hearst, by a revolutionary group called the Symbionese Liberation Army (SLA) and her subsequent apparent conversion to their left-wing cause.

He soon came up with a title—"The House on Value Street" (his fictionalized gang's hideout)—but when he got down to work on the text, he found that the facts inhibited his imagination. As he plowed on, his mind began to wander onto an older true-life story, about the Dugway Incident of 1968, in which the U.S. Army accidentally killed 3,000 sheep in Utah while testing nerve gas. Meanwhile, other things vied for King's attention. One was *Earth Abides* (1949), a novel by George R. Stewart in which a mysterious disease wipes out all but a few members of the human race. The other was a voice on a Christian radio station that he heard say: "Once in every generation the plague will fall among them."

Together, these elements stimulated King's creativity in a way that the story of Patty Hearst alone had failed to do. He abandoned "The House" after six weeks and wrote *The Stand* (1978), a post-apocalyptic fantasy novel. He didn't find this easy, either: it took him two years (much longer than his norm) and it was later described as his Vietnam, a conflict that he hated, but could not finish. However, he was pleased with the result, which he said "seems to sum up everything I had to say up until that point."

FEEDING DEMAND

Meanwhile, King's publishers had become so concerned about the non-delivery of the Hearst book that the author knocked out *Rage* (1977) under his pseudonym Richard Bachman and *Night Shift* (1978), a collection of short stories. What had seemed to be writer's block turned out to be the harbinger of one of the most productive periods of a prolific career.

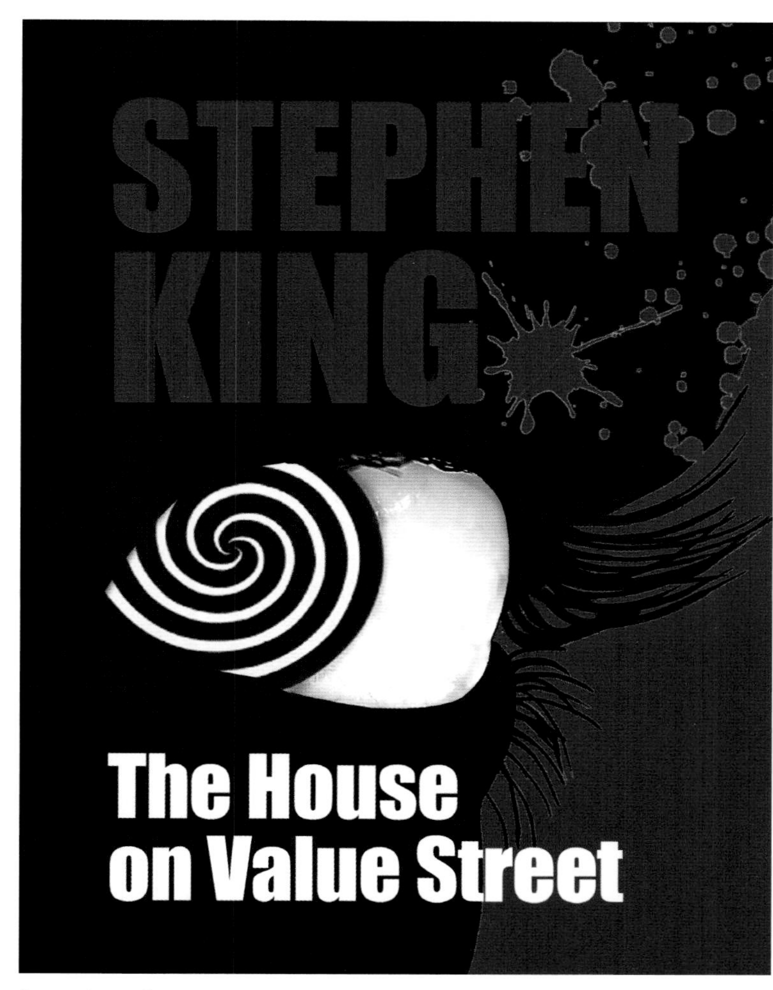

Cover: Jayne Evans

The House on Value Street was never published, but from the piles of screwed-up typescript pages in King's waste bin emerged one of his most memorable recurrent characters, Randall Flagg—also known as the Dark Man, the Walkin' Dude, and the Ageless Stranger, among other names—who was partly based on Donald DeFreeze, leader of the SLA. GL

WHAT HAPPENED NEXT . . .

Many of Stephen King's unpublished works are stored in the Fogler Library at the University of Maine. Some of them are available for public viewing; others may be accessed only with the author's permission. *The House on Value Street* does not appear in the current library catalogue. Donald DeFreeze was one of six members of the SLA killed in a police shootout in 1974. Patty Hearst served time in jail. Her subsequent memoir, *Every Secret Thing* (1982), co-written with Alvin Moscow, was republished in 1988 as *Patty Hearst: Her Own Story* to coincide with a movie version directed by Paul Schrader.

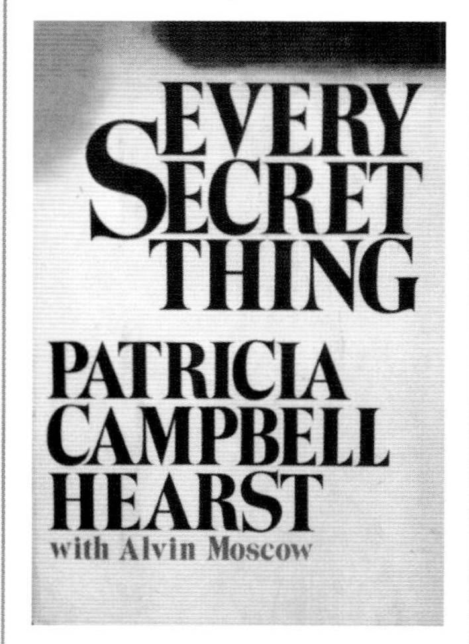

WILL IT EVER HAPPEN?

A tough call. If *The House on Value Street* is viewed as notes toward *The Stand*, probably not. Alternatively, if the work were to be regarded as the ur-*Stand*, it would almost certainly appeal to Stephen King's millions of fans. It is not known what happened to the manuscript of *The House on Value Street*, however, so for the time being any speculation is purely hypothetical.

THE ORIGINAL OF LAURA

Author Vladimir Nabokov **Year** 1977 **Country** United States **Genre** Novel

VLADIMIR NABOKOV
Born in 1899 in St. Petersburg, Nabokov was raised in a household that habitually spoke Russian, French, and English, linguistic skills that served them well when they were forced into exile during the communist revolution of 1917.

Best known for his novels *Lolita* (1955), *Pnin* (1957), and *Pale Fire* (1962), Vladimir Nabokov is a shining star in the firmament of novelistic experimentation and innovation. When he died in 1977 at the age of 78 he was working on a novel called *The Original of Laura*, with the alternative titles *Dying is Fun* and *The Opposition of Laura.* Nabokov was a perfectionist and requested that this work be destroyed after his death if he was not able to complete it.

PREOCCUPIED WITH DEATH

Nabokov first mentions his work on *The Original of Laura* in a diary entry of December 1, 1974. By the summer of 1976, he noted that the story was completed in his mind. But by then his health was failing rapidly.

The incomplete manuscript consists of 138 handwritten index cards, each one measuring 5 inches x 4 inches (12.7 x 10 cm), the equivalent of about 30 manuscript pages. Nabokov usually composed on index cards. He wrote in soft pencil, occasionally obliterating text with a grubby eraser. The story concerns a promiscuous young woman named Flora, who becomes the subject of a scandalous novel called *My Laura*. Flora is the daughter of Adam Lind (who photographs his suicide) and the ballet dancer Lanskaya, and granddaughter of a kitschy Russian artist. She is groped as a child by an Englishman called Hubert H. Hubert (echoing *Lolita*'s Humbert Humbert).

In the later, more fragmentary pages, Flora's husband Philip Wild appears. He is an enormously corpulent neurologist. Flora initially appealed to Wild because of another woman with whom he'd previously been in love, named Aurora Lee. Death, a subject that fascinated Nabokov from early on, is central. It is not clear how old Wild is, but he is preoccupied with his own death and sets about obliterating himself from the toes upward through meditation on a mental blackboard, a sort of deliberate self-inflicted self-erasure. There are many cards noting the business of imagined death, related to Buddhist concepts of nirvana, extinction, self-annihilation, and "absorption into the supreme spirit." Interestingly, the final index card resembles an entry in *Roget's Thesaurus* of words for erasure: "efface," "expunge," "delete," "rub out," "wipe out," "obliterate." One of the words has been eliminated by pencil scrawls.

Cover: Isabel Eeles

The novel contains multiple examples of Nabokov's curious style. It is clearly written by someone for whom English is not the first language. In some ways this can be refreshing, since it produces vivid novelties, as the author approaches expression from an oblique angle. And his vision is original too. Which other author would or could describe slippers sitting in their case as "located foetally in their zippered pouch"? Not to mention "pale squinty nipples," "prefactory contemplation," "librarious fates," "hypnagogic gargoyles," and "sporadic crucifixion." There is, however, a certain amount of strained wit: Flora's rejected suitor is named Rawitch, "pronounced by some Raw Itch, by him Rah Witch"; someone is said to have "taught thought."

". . . a brilliant, original, and potentially totally radical book . . ."

Dmitri Nabokov

In many ways Nabokov has ignored the stringent diktats of good prose, and ventured into realms in which poetic originality and irresponsibility are the order of the day. The result is a combination of brilliant creative decisiveness and stumbling naive incompetence, which can only be inevitably described as "Nabokovian."

SPEAK, POSTERITY

After Nabokov's demise, his widow, Vera, failed to carry out his wishes not, according to his son Dmitri, through defiance but through "procrastination due to age, weakness, and immeasurable love." Vera died in 1991, leaving Dmitri as the sole literary executor. In 2008, he took the manuscript out of the Swiss bank vault in which it had been stored and arranged for it to be published. When it appeared in print it was hailed by the BBC's *Newsnight* television program as "likely to be the literary event of 2009."

FOR PURPOSES OF COMPARISON

When *The Original of Laura* was first published, several reviewers made a great deal of the links they perceived between two of the main characters in the novel and two great female representations in Renaissance art: Titian's *Flora* (c.1515, left) and Giorgione's *Laura* (c.1506, right). Unfortunately, neither masterpiece is mentioned in the manuscript itself. It is therefore difficult to avoid the conclusion that the critics were merely clutching at the straws that they sometimes hope might save them when they are trying to make sense of works like this one that defy interpretation.

WHAT HAPPENED NEXT . . .

The edition of *The Original of Laura* that was published by Penguin in 2009 was designed by Chip Kidd and is an extremely handsome and unusual object. Subtitled "A novel in fragments," the book can be considered a collector's item. Each page reproduces one of Nabokov's index cards, with perforations round the edges, so that the reader can, if they wish, tear them out and rearrange them into an order of their choosing. The paper is dark grey and below each card is a transcription of the text—usually accurate, but not always. There are also some editorial shortcomings: Dimitri Nabokov fails to explain that John Thornton and William A.M. Smart, authors of *Human Physiology* (1926), are real people, and his introduction sometimes glides into fatuity and special pleading. Nonetheless, *The New York Times* described the format as "a model of how to publish a posthumous and unfinished manuscript."

Opinion remains divided about whether it should have been published, but at the very least it provides fascinating insights into the writing methods of this particular writer. Martin Amis commented: "When a writer starts to come off the rails, you expect skidmarks and broken glass; with Nabokov, naturally, the eruption is on the scale of a nuclear accident." This comment is a bit harsh from a disciple who had previously described the "Nabokovian essence" as "a miraculously fertile instability, where without warning the words detach themselves from the everyday and streak off like flares in a night sky," but perhaps not too wide of the mark.

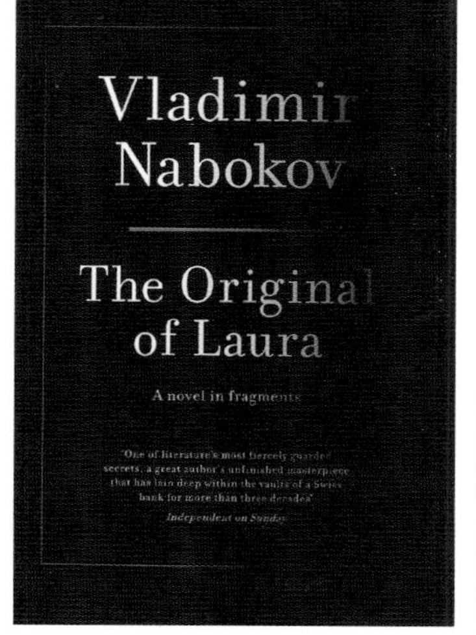

And in a sense it was, but for all the wrong reasons. Many critics thought it was a poor work, which should never have been printed. *The Wall Street Journal* described it as "the writer's version of a great athlete in decline: not . . . the glorious Lou Gehrig of 1927, but the feeble shadow of the same man, retiring at midseason in 1939." Dmitri was unrepentant, however, saying that although he felt bound to uphold his "filial duty" and grant his father's request, he felt that the novel, had it been completed, would have been "a brilliant, original, and potentially totally radical book, in the literary sense very different from the rest of his oeuvre." He reportedly added that "his father . . . or his father's shade," would not "have opposed the release of *Laura* once *Laura* had survived the hum of time this long."

The Original of Laura is not much more than an interesting assemblage of fragments—it does not have the confident trajectory of other works that have been left unfinished. It is often difficult to make sense of "framed" stories in disintegrating modernist texts that are supposed to be finished, and so nigh on impossible in something in inchoate form. BR

1/10

WILL IT EVER HAPPEN?

The work of Nabokov divides opinion. Some people—perhaps the majority, certainly now the more vocal party—extol his thematic daring, his linguistic pyrotechnics, and his modernism. Others find oblique expressions such as those quoted above rather tiresome, the writing of a foreigner whose heavy-handedness increases as he strives for lightness of touch. The one thing that both groups may agree on is that he is inimitable. Hence it would be impossible to complete this work without being "Nabokovian"—a double-edged term—and without descending into parody.

ANSWERED PRAYERS

Author Truman Capote **Year** 1987 **Country** United States **Genre** Roman à clef

TRUMAN CAPOTE
Capote told *People* magazine that he was constructing *Answered Prayers* like a gun: "There's the handle, the trigger, the barrel, and, finally, the bullet. And when that bullet is fired from the gun, it's going to come out with a speed and power like you've never seen—wham!"

A roman à clef (French for "novel with a key") is a work in which the characters are real but lightly disguised. The reader may derive enjoyment from knowing, guessing, or trying to work out their true identities. *The Carpetbaggers* (1961), for example, might be more interesting to readers who know that the main character is based on business magnate Howard Hughes than to those who labor under the misapprehension that "Jonas Cord" is a product of author Harold Robbins's imagination. Such works may be good for gossip, but one of the problems with them is that they blur the distinction between fact and fiction. At their worst, they make you wonder whether they're anything more than under-researched biographies in which the names have been changed to protect the authors from a shower of libel writs. *Answered Prayers* is an extreme case in point.

HE BIT THE HANDS THAT FED HIM

Truman Capote arrived on the literary scene in 1948 with an acclaimed debut novel, *Other Voices, Other Rooms*. He became established with *Breakfast at Tiffany's* (1958), about a fey young playgirl, the film adaptation of which was a major hit starring Audrey Hepburn. In 1966, Capote was paid a $25,000 advance for a novel that Random House publishers hoped would turn out to be the American equivalent of Proust's *À la recherche du temps perdu* (*In Search of Lost Time*, 1913–27).

However, in the meantime, Capote had drifted away from the semiautobiographical fiction with which he had made his name into journalism. *In Cold Blood* (1965), published shortly after he'd signed the big-money contract, was a "nonfiction novel" based on interviews with people involved in a multiple murder by a pair of psychopaths in Kansas.

This book brought Capote even greater celebrity, and the author wallowed in it, loving every minute of his involvement in high society. He soon appeared to be dividing his time between showing up at glitterati events and showing off about them on television: when, people wondered, did he find time to write?

In *Answered Prayers* he bit the hands that fed him and made the fatal error of publishing parts of the work in progress in serial form. Four chapters—"Mojave," "La Cote Basque," "Unspoiled Monsters," and "Kate McCloud"—

Cover: Damian Jaques

WHAT HAPPENED NEXT . . .
The chapters originally published in *Esquire* were reissued in book form in 1987 under the title *Answered Prayers: The Unfinished Novel*. In 2012, a further fragment, "Yachts and Things," was found among Capote's papers in the New York Public Library; it was published in *Vanity Fair* in December of that year.

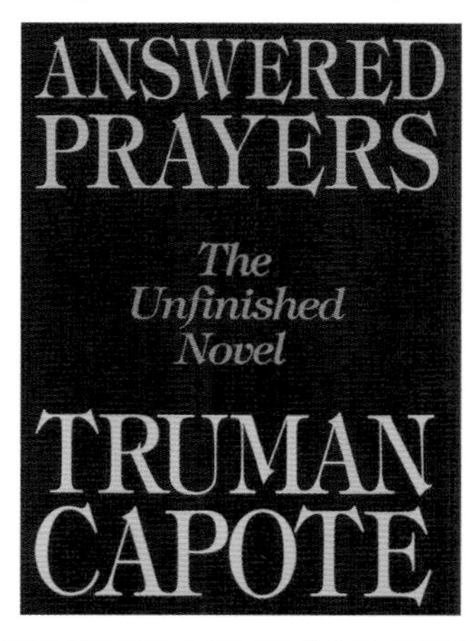

appeared in *Esquire* magazine in 1975 and 1976. When the rich and famous read his depictions of them they were justifiably offended and dropped him from their guest lists. His victims included Gloria Vanderbilt (reputed inventor of designer blue jeans), Katherine Graham (publisher of the *Washington Post*), Jacqueline Kennedy Onassis (widow of the assassinated U.S. president), Peggy Guggenheim (art collector), and William S. Paley (head of the television network CBS). Not people to get on the wrong side of.

After they shunned him, Capote declined into alcohol and drug abuse. In 1980 the publishers tried to revive his creative juices by upping his advance to $1 million, but even that failed to inspire delivery of the completed manuscript. In a 1971 television interview, Capote had described his difficulties with the work, telling Dick Cavett "either I'm going to kill it or it's going to kill me." Truman Capote died in 1984, aged 59, leaving *Answered Prayers* unfinished. **GL**

WILL IT EVER HAPPEN?
In favor of the possibility that it will finally be published is the fact that Capote left numerous unpolished outlines and notes, not all of which have been examined by scholars. Against it is the likelihood that future discoveries will be unworthy of publication: "Yachts and Things" is both stand-alone and unfinished—no more than a curiosity.

FOUNTAIN CITY

Author Michael Chabon **Year** 1990 **Country** United States **Genre** Novel

MICHAEL CHABON
As Chabon neared the end of his studies at the University of California, Irvine, his supervisor, the novelist MacDonald Harris, submitted his master's dissertation to a literary agent who responded immediately with a top-dollar offer for what soon became a hot literary property.

Success came early to Michael Chabon: he had a hit with his first work of fiction, *The Mysteries of Pittsburgh* (1988), at the age of 25 while still a university graduate student. The book became an instant best seller and was eventually turned into a movie starring Nick Nolte and Sienna Miller (2009); the author embarked on the follow-up, *Fountain City*, about an architect building a perfect baseball park in Florida.

Writers are popularly supposed to find their second novels tricky. The most common complaints are either that they repeat their original success in diluted, less inspired form or that they dry up. Chabon encountered a slightly different problem: he had no trouble with the words, but he could not get a grip on the structure. Among the characters were an Israeli spy and an AIDS patient, and the story touched on a range of subjects that included messianic Zionism, French cuisine, radical environmental activism, baseball, miniature-model building, and Japanese monster movies. At one point he sent a 700-page draft of the work in progress to his agent and editor, asking them what they thought of it so far. They both said it was terrible. Chabon eventually filled 1,500 pages—but still the work had given no indication of where, if anywhere, it was leading him.

IMITATION OF LIFE

After five years Chabon gave up and redirected his attention to another project. This turned out only seven months later to be *Wonder Boys* (1995), about a college professor who is struggling to write a follow-up to his first novel, which had been a runaway best seller. Art was imitating the life of the artist—Chabon later admitted that the lead character Grady Tripp was a "projection of my worst fears of what I was going to become if I kept working on *Fountain City*." Choosing to abandon *Fountain City* certainly spared him that fate: *Wonder Boys* received widespread critical acclaim, and Chabon's third novel, *The Amazing Adventures of Kavalier & Clay* (2000), won the Pulitzer Prize for Fiction in 2001.

The ghost of *Fountain City* had not entirely been laid to rest, however. In 2010 Chabon agreed to the publication of the first four chapters of the novel, with an introduction and footnotes intended, he said, to "deface the thing sufficiently to prevent anyone from thinking that I offered it with any

Cover: Heath Killen

THE PINK OF HEALTH
In the epigraph of *Brideshead Revisited* (1945), Evelyn Waugh wrote: "I am not I; thou art not he or she; they are not they." In *The Mysteries of Pittsburgh*, Michael Chabon made no such pre-emptive strike against readers who assume that authors are always writing about themselves, with the result that some reviewers, extrapolating from the sexuality of the hero, assumed that he was gay. He isn't, but he didn't mind because, he said, the story opened up a whole new audience.

kind of warranty of quality." Printed in the literary magazine *McSweeney's*, it was intended as a cautionary tale about the pitfalls of the creative process. According to one of Chabon's notes, "A book itself threatens to kill its author repeatedly during its composition"; in another he remarks that he could feel *Fountain City* "erasing me, breaking me down, burying me alive, drowning me, kicking me down the stairs."

The publication of the fragment was trailed as part catharsis, part postmodernist self-reference. Chabon makes no claim to be the only writer who's been through such a trauma, but he does chastise himself about the wasted years and the futility of the whole enterprise: "Often when I sat down to work I would feel a cold hand take hold of something inside my belly and refuse to let go. It was the Hand of Dread. I ought to have heeded its grasp."

> *"A book itself threatens to kill its author repeatedly during its composition."*
>
> Michael Chabon

TURNING A MINUS INTO A PLUS

Most—perhaps even all—writers have failures, works abandoned unfinished or rejected by publishers. They normally respond to setbacks in one of several ways: they abandon writing more or less altogether, as Harper Lee seems to have done (see p.202); they chalk their failure up to experience and get on with something entirely different, like Stephen King, whose decision to bin *The House on Value Street* catalyzed one of his most productive periods (see p.218); they salvage the good bits, if there are any, for use in subsequent undertakings, like Thomas Hardy with *The Poor Man and the Lady* (see p.94); they destroy their errors, like Nikolai Gogol with *Dead Souls* Part II

WONDER BOYS
Wonder Boys was made into a movie in 2000, directed by Curtis Hanson. Michael Douglas (right) plays the central character Grady Tripp, a novelist teaching creative writing at a university in Pittsburgh; Tobey Maguire (left) is the student whose talent he discovers.

WHAT HAPPENED NEXT . . .
Michael Chabon went from strength to strength. His subsequent publications have included *The Amazing Adventures of Kavalier & Clay* (2000), *The Yiddish Policemen's Union* (2007), and *Telegraph Avenue* (2012). In addition to his Pulitzer, he won a Hugo award in 2008. A great believer in cross-genre publication, Chabon is also a prolific author of short stories, screenplays, children's books, comics, and newspaper articles.

(see p.86), or at least ensure that they never see the light of day in their lifetimes, like Graham Greene with *The Empty Chair* (see p.148).

Chabon chose a different course: to hold the work up to public gaze and tell the world it should be pleased to have missed it. The failure to complete *Fountain City* had clearly been playing on his mind for many years, and at first glance this seems like a clever strategy toward compensating for the lost years that he spent on it. However, on further reflection, this whole approach can be brought into question: who says that a draft is wasted? Chabon himself has admitted to reusing parts of *Fountain City* in other works—the greenhouse in *Wonder Boys* was stolen "clean out" of it, and the plan to rebuild the Temple of Jerusalem resurfaced in *The Yiddish Policemen's Union* (2007)—which suggests that there were at least a couple of promising ideas contained within in it.

Ultimately, failure is as much a part of the creative process as success. In an interview with *The Atlantic* upon publication of the *Fountain City* fragments, Chabon demonstrated his awareness of this:

> "When I began annotating it, several years ago, I planned to go all the way through the thing, with the intention of figuring out, once and for all, what had gone wrong with it. I hoped that the experience might be useful not only for me but for millions of other failure enthusiasts and fans of ruination all around the world."

Ironically, he failed to complete this task, too. But in the course of annotating the novel he discovered that the process offered an unexpected side benefit: "the opportunity to recover, not the novel—irrecoverable as ever—but traces and fragments of the life I had led while writing it." Yet again, the unfinished work proved itself a useful source of inspiration.

The *Fountain City* fragments offer an interesting insight into a writer's perspective on an unpublished novel. In the end, he concludes, all that writers can do is "to pay attention to our failures, to break them down, study the tapes, conduct the postmortem, pore over the findings; to learn from our mistakes." **GL**

3/10

WILL IT EVER HAPPEN?
If Chabon were to complete *Fountain City*, he could no longer present it as an awful warning, and it would lose any appeal it may currently have to creative writing classes. Having converted the base metal fragment into gold, he will no doubt think it wise to leave it untouched. A continuator could not be hired without his permission. So no, probably.

SHADOW OF THE ADEPT

Author Junot Díaz **Year** 1996 **Country** United States **Genre** Science fiction novel

JUNOT DÍAZ
Díaz was born in Santo Domingo, Dominican Republic. He studied English at Rutgers and is currently creative writing professor at Massachusetts Institute of Technology (MIT).

Junot Díaz made his name with *The Brief Wondrous Life of Oscar Wao* (2007), a fictional account of the experience of Hispanics in the United States. This novel won him a host of awards, including a Pulitzer in 2008. One of the main attractions of the book was its use of words and expressions from the author's parents' native language: Díaz has been widely credited with doing for Spanglish what Saul Bellow did for Yiddish.

REACHING FOR THE STARS

Before he found success with *Oscar Wao*, however, he had spent time working on a science fiction novel called *Shadow of the Adept*. Díaz has a particular love of science fiction, citing authors such as Isaac Asimov, Arthur C. Clarke, Robert Heinlein, Ursula K. Le Guin, and particularly Ray Bradbury as important influences on his early reading habits. He was drawn to the genre by the questions that it asks about the nature of power, which resonated with his own experiences of dictatorship in the Dominican Republic.

Little is known about the plot of *Shadow of the Adept* other than that it is a post-apocalyptic nightmare set in the distant future. In a 2012 interview with *Wired* magazine, Díaz explained that the novel was part of a dual contract with his first book *Drown* (1996): in addition to this collection of short stories, he was contracted to write "a three-part science fiction and fantasy series that was intended to be a more 'popular' version of the Gene Wolfe *Shadow of the Torturer* books." Scheduled to come out a few months after *Drown*, it was going to feature a "Dying Earth-type setting."

However, it turned out to be much harder to write than the author had anticipated. And Díaz is, by his own account, a very slow writer. He managed to complete a rough draft of the novel, but was too unsatisfied with the result to go back and rework it, despite receiving encouraging comments about the overall concept from his publisher.

But the failure to complete *Shadow of the Adept* did not deter him from embarking on another science fiction project. Díaz has said that he wants to be a shapeshifter who writes alternately a high-flown, intellectual novel and a more populist work, and after completing *The Brief Wondrous Life of Oscar Wao* he sat down to write *Dark America*. Rather than wallow in the success of the former novel and produce more in the same vein, this was to

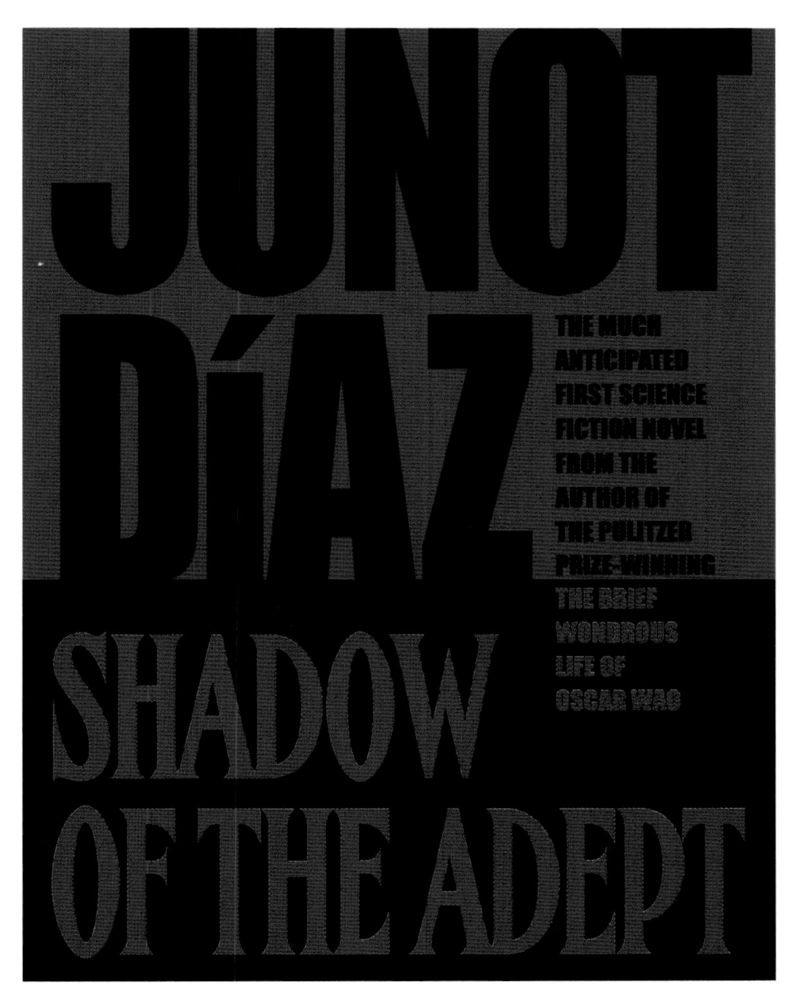

Cover: Emanuel Zahariades

be a "pseudo-*Akira*, pseudo-post-dirty-war novel about a young woman in a rebuilt city that had been blown up by some sort of strange perhaps-terrorist-psychic, perhaps not, and she was part of this whole historical recovery project." But it, too, proved unsuccessful: "The book was a disaster," Díaz told *Wired*.

One of his problems might have been that his own desire to diversify came into conflict with that of his readers for more of what had attracted them to him in the first place. This may at least partly explain his decision to return to the Spanglish vein for *This Is How You Lose Her* (2012).

Nonetheless, Díaz appears determined to fulfil his science fiction ambitions. In 2012 he released extracts from his novel-in-progress *Monstro*, which he has described as "a near-future story where these virused-up 40-foot monstrosities are going around eating people." GL

WHAT HAPPENED NEXT . . .

As *The Greatest Books You'll Never Read* went to press, Junot Díaz was still working on *Monstro*, which was partially serialized in *The New Yorker* in 2012. Characteristically, though, his progress is slow. He told *Wired* magazine: "I've got to eat a couple cities before I think the thing will really get going." Whether this work will be similar to or entirely different from the abandoned *Shadow of the Adept* and *Dark America* is unknown and possibly unknowable. He told Cressida Leyshon at *The New Yorker* that "all that remains is to see if I can cobble the courage together I will need to finish the book."

WILL IT EVER HAPPEN?

That's anyone's guess. For the time being it seems highly unlikely—while the author is focused on his latest science fiction attempt it is doubtful he will return to *Shadow of the Adept*. On the other hand, since Junot Díaz has been under contract to write it for more than 20 years, the pressure to deliver may one day force his hand. Meanwhile, it remains a talking point.

IF GOD WERE ALIVE TODAY

Author Kurt Vonnegut **Year** 2007 **Country** United States **Genre** Novel

KURT VONNEGUT
Vonnegut struggled for several years to establish himself as a writer. He was just about to give up when *Cat's Cradle* (1963) provided his breakthrough. He followed this success with *Slaughterhouse-Five* (1969).

Kurt Vonnegut, an American of German descent, served in the U.S. Army in the Second World War and was captured in the Battle of the Bulge (December 1944–January 1945). He was imprisoned in Dresden and witnessed the Allied firebombing of the historic city in February 1945. He survived the devastating attack probably only because his jail was underground in a disused abattoir, the German name for which—*Schlachthof-fünf*—he later adapted for the title of his most famous novel.

After his release at the end of the conflict he returned to the United States where he did blue collar jobs for General Electric while trying to become a writer. His first novel, *Player Piano* (1958), a dystopian account of an excessively automated world, was inspired by his experiences working on the production line. In his second, *The Sirens of Titan* (1959), about the nuclear attack on Hiroshima, he came closer to his major preoccupation: the inhumanity of war. In his sixth book, *Slaughterhouse-Five* (1969), he tackled the theme head-on. The novel is partly a memoir of Dresden, although the autobiographical content is to some extent filtered through the central character, Billy Pilgrim, an unreliable narrator.

SHADES OF REAL LIFE

The semi-autobiographical *Timequake* (1997) was the last work Vonnegut published in his lifetime. Shortly before it came out, in an interview for *Rolling Stone* magazine he had told Douglas Brinkley that he was through with writing: "I've given up on it," he was quoted as saying. "It won't happen. I've written books. Lots of them. Please, I've done everything I was supposed to do. Can I go home now?"

Vonnegut died later the same year. Among the unfinished papers he left behind was the partially completed *If God Were Alive Today.* This is a fictional biography of Gil Berman, a stand-up comedian who has been in and out of a psychiatric institution. Later on he hires a psychiatrist, called Dr. Klein. Berman hopes she will help him to deal with "life problems beyond mere substance abuse." Berman's father commits suicide and his mother has mental health problems. Vonnegut's own mother had mental health problems and committed suicide in 1944, and he himself suffered intermittently from depression. There are other similarities between the fictional character and the author: both their

Cover: Heath Killen

families are wealthy; there are talented people around them. Berman opts for drugs, and hopes that Dr. Klein will prescribe these.

The "what's real and what isn't?" dilemma—so prominent throughout Vonnegut's oeuvre—extends to other elements in this book. Gil Berman bears some resemblance to Shelley Berman, the American stand-up comedian.

The extant fragment of *If God Were Alive Today* is not easy to read because much of it is written as a long one-man show. Some of it is funny, or at least provocative. Berman is sexually a "neuter"; a strange term, the precise intended meaning of which is not made clear in the book. It does, however, lead to a joke: "Celibacy is like not lighting a cigarette."

Vonnegut's attacks on the media continue here as elsewhere in his writing: televisions are "erasers," wiping out people's memories of everything except the events of the last few minutes. Another joke reflects Vonnegut's disaffection with modern civilization: "The Martians have landed; the good news is they only eat homeless people and pee gasoline."

> *"Whoever told you a comedian is supposed to be funny?"*
>
> *If God Were Alive Today*

If God Were Alive Today is short—only 72 pages. The style is explanatory, telling us about a character and his place in the world. Many of the jokes are not funny, although it is possible to imagine that they might evoke laughter if they were spoken rather than written. In the book, a character asks Berman: "Whoever told you a comedian is supposed to be funny? . . . the great ones are heartbreakers."

This kind of writing also raises questions about the nature of storytelling. Why do we need to know these things? Many bits of information are dropped into the text, never to be followed up. Their purpose may have been to allow the author to attack some favorite targets, such as disgraced former U.S. President Richard M. Nixon. Alternatively, they may have been intended to

AMERICAN WRITERS AND WAR

American writers seem to have a unique relationship with war, perhaps a result of modern conflicts occuring at some distance from their home country, whether in Europe or the Far East (so far there has been little about the Middle East). American books and movies on the subject tend to be less earnest than their European equivalents—as evidenced in works such as *Catch-22* (1961), *M*A*S*H* (1970), *Apocalypse Now* (1979), and—at least the first among equals—Vonnegut's own masterpiece, *Slaughterhouse-Five*.

display solidarity with those of creative temperament: “Like ninety-nine point ninety-nine percent of great artists of every sort since the dawn of history, my dear mother, Magda, fell victim to audience shortages and a glut of talent.” Unfortunately, however, Vonnegut seems here to have forgotten the rule that being right doesn’t make you funny, and over the long haul the plethora of one-liners can become irritating.

A DEPRESSING READ

Vonnegut’s preoccupations include the gender divide, masculinity, and war. Many critics have referred to the author’s humanity and moral sense. When these are combined with a sense of the ridiculous, there can be humor, but in this book despair predominates. Berman is a recovering addict: “He sure missed drugs, and he was now terrified . . . of their puissance and ubiquity.” The despair is demonstrated by Berman’s suicide at the age of 45 in the year 2000, with a hint that his act has been triggered by the U.S. presidential election of that year, in which Republican George W. Bush triumphed marginally and controversially over Democrat Al Gore. Other plaintive moments include the use of the military acronym FUBAR (fouled up beyond all recognition) to refer to the effect of humans on the planet, and a description of money as a dehydrated form of mercy—“add tears and you find all sorts of people coming round.” The *Washington Independent Review of Books* described the work as “a full-on tirade of such manic indignation and gloom that after reading it, some readers may find they need a drink.”

Toward the end of *If God Were Alive Today* there is a story about Berman having to confirm to a mentally ill fan that he is Jesus Christ. Cod psychology might lead readers to the conclusion that Vonnegut wanted to die early, like Jesus, and that in some way he resented his own longevity. He seems to have not noticed anything good in the world, or if he did he keeps it out of his writing. Near the end of his life, Vonnegut had to leave his home because of a fire. Psychological help, a real Dr. Klein, might have made his final years more bearable than they turned out.

In the foreword to the published edition, Vonnegut’s daughter says the book is the “product of a slightly charred brain and the toxic circumstances of his life at that time.” In an obituary, Dinitia Smith wrote in the *Guardian*: “[Vonnegut] used humor to tackle the basic questions of human existence.” And so he did in his best work, but seldom in this book. BT

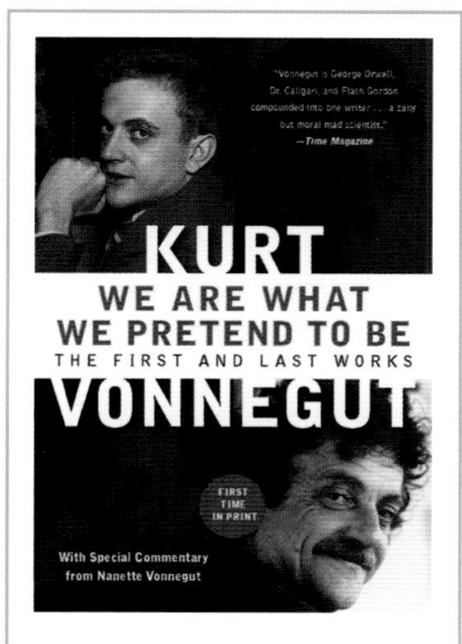

WHAT HAPPENED NEXT . . .

If God Were Alive Today was published in *We Are What We Pretend To Be: The First and Last Works* (Vanguard Press, 2012). This collection also contains “Basic Training,” a previously unpublished short story that is fresh and uncluttered and, according to his daughter Nanette, written when he was “at his happiest, before the war.”

5/10

WILL IT EVER HAPPEN?

Gil Berman dies of a morphine overdose in 2000, the year Nanette Vonnegut says her father started the book. This is not fertile ground for any aspiring continuator. If the story could be extended, we would be in heaven where God reassures Vonnegut that he is an atheist and didn’t die. Vonnegut’s chain-smoking and constant swearing provoke God into sending the author to hell, where he spends the rest of eternity as a third-rate celebrity judging infernal amateur dance contests.

EN AGOSTO NOS VEMOS

Author Gabriel García Márquez **Year** 2014 **Country** Colombia **Genre** Novel

GABRIEL GARCÍA MÁRQUEZ
Taking as his models two great American authors, William Faulkner and Ernest Hemingway, Márquez synthesized the former's intricate plots and the latter's muscular prose into a transcendent body of work in his native Spanish language.

The death of Colombian writer Gabriel García Márquez in April 2014, at the age of 87, brought tributes from authors, readers, and politicians around the globe. Latin America's best-known writer—his works have outsold everything published in Spanish except the Bible—he was described by British author Ian McEwan as "a one-off . . . one would really have to go back to Dickens to find a writer of the very highest literary quality who commanded such extraordinary persuasive powers over whole populations." Márquez's mastery of the genre of magical realism, a style that he made his own in titles such as *Cien años de soledad* (*One Hundred Years of Solitude*, 1967), *El otoño del patriarca* (*The Autumn of the Patriarch*, 1975), and *El amor en los tiempos del cólera* (*Love in the Time of Cholera*, 1985), saw him awarded the Nobel Prize in Literature in 1982. In his acceptance speech, he described the history of Latin America as a key influence on the genre:

> "A source of insatiable creativity, full of sorrow and beauty, of which this roving and nostalgic Colombian is but one cipher more, singled out by fortune. Poets and beggars, musicians and prophets, warriors and scoundrels, all creatures of that unbridled reality, we have had to ask but little of imagination, for our crucial problem has been a lack of conventional means to render our lives believable."

OLD MAN'S FANTASY

Following treatment for lymphatic cancer in 1999, Márquez turned his attention in later years primarily to autobiography and memoir. His last published novel is *Memoria de mis putas tristes* (*Memories of My Melancholy Whores*, 2004), about a 90-year old reporter who decides to give himself "a night of mad love with a virgin adolescent." When he first sees the chosen girl—a shy 14-year-old, whom he calls Delgadina—asleep and naked in a brothel, his life begins to change. He never speaks to her nor does he learn anything about her, nor she of him. Delgadina is the heroine of a medieval ballad that tells the story of the incestuous love of a king for his youngest daughter. To satisfy his desire she must be virginal in every sense: a blank, voiceless landscape, all geography and no history. Her presence reminds the nonagenarian of the other women in his life, all professional whores, but now

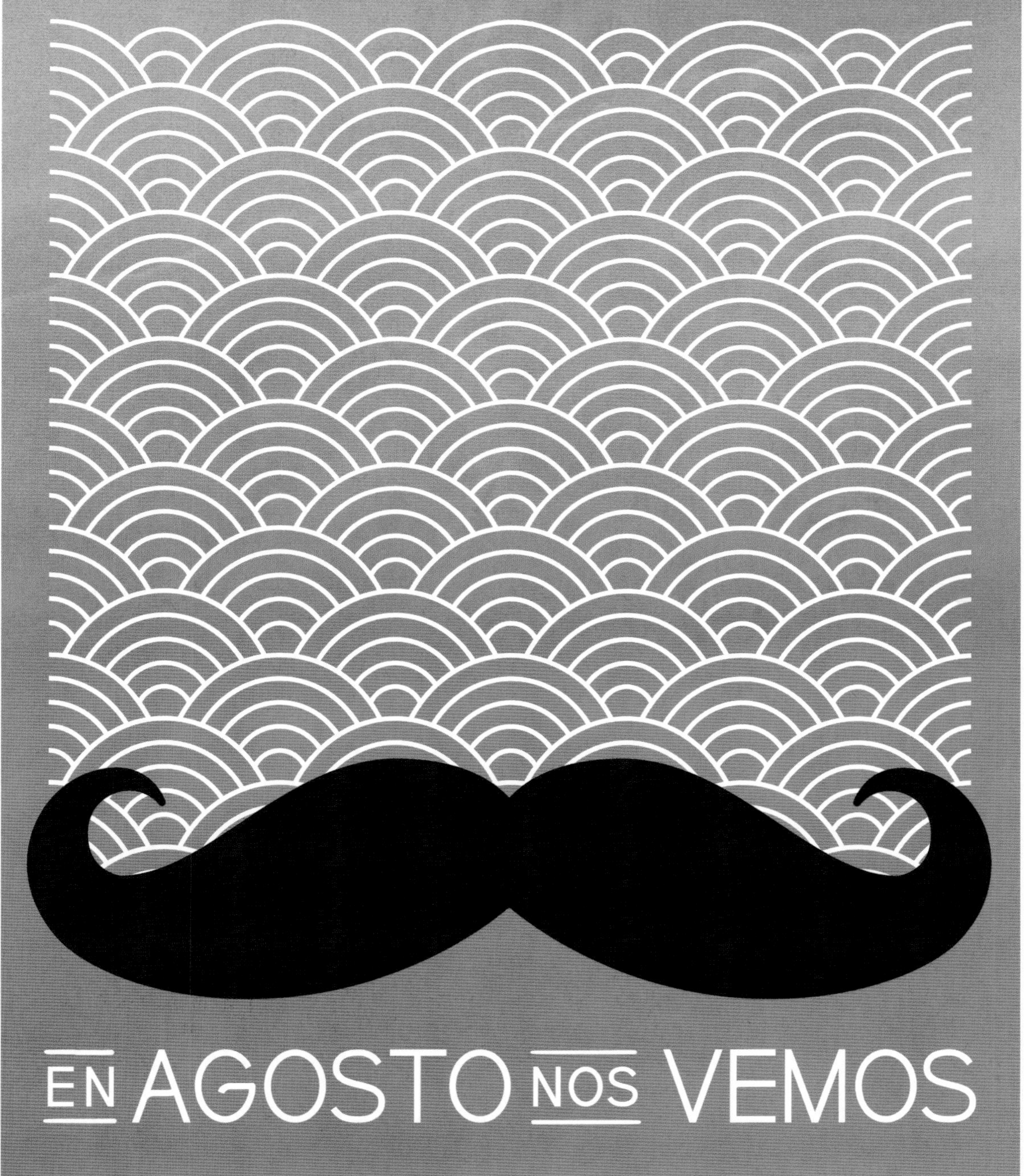

Cover: Isabel Eeles

he realizes that "sex is the consolation one has for not finding enough love." He celebrates his experience in a weekly newspaper column printing a series of love letters that "all people could make their own."

In 2010 Márquez's publishers, Random House, announced that he was working on a new novel called *En agosto nos vemos* (*We'll Meet in August*), but a publication date was never set for the work. It is still not certain whether the complete novel will ever be published, although extracts have appeared in the Spanish newspaper *El País* and in *The New Yorker*.

The story concerns a happily married 52-year-old woman who is undertaking her annual visit to her mother's grave on a Caribbean island.

> *"He didn't complete it because of the perfectionist that he was."*
>
> Claudio López

She has made the same trip for 28 years and every time stays in the same room of the same hotel. Each August 16th, at the same time of day, she visits the bleak cemetery so that she can place a bouquet of fresh gladioli on her mother's grave and relay to her the news from home. The woman's name is Ana Magdalena Bach, and she has recently celebrated the 23rd anniversary of her happy marriage. That evening she encounters a man in a white linen suit and a moustache, and offers to buy him a drink. She guesses that he is 46, but fails to guess which country he comes from or what his profession is. When the bar closes at 11 she feels that she has known him a long time, and invites him to her room. She wrenches off his clothes and has sex with

MAGICAL REALISM

Magical realism blends supernatural and other-worldly fantasy elements with the familiar and diurnal world in a matter-of-fact manner. Most commonly used as a literary genre, its traits can also be found in movies and the visual arts. The Argentine author Jorge Luis Borges (right) is regarded as a progenitor of the tradition, but Gabriel García Márquez also occupies an important and influential place in its invention.

The ubiquitous presence of the baroque in Latin America, especially in the continent's often rather strange architecture, has meant that the cultural environment there has been particularly hospitable to the intermingling of the disconcertingly marvellous and the mundane.

him. She feels fully committed to him, and yet does not explore an intimate emotional relationship. After an hour of trite conversation they kiss. He proves to be an accomplished lover who takes her to the heights of rapture. When she wakes during the night she taps her fingers on his back, but he fakes sleep in order to avoid making love again. She falls into a profound sleep. At dawn she is suddenly struck by the cruel realization that for the first time in her life she has had carnal relations with a man who wasn't hers. She turns to look at him over her shoulder and discovers that he is no longer there. At this point she realizes that she knows absolutely nothing about him, not even his name, and all that is left of her night of passion is a faint scent of lavender in the air. She picks up the book she'd left on the bedside table—Bram Stoker's *Dracula* (1897)—and discovers that he has left $20 between its pages.

UNCERTAIN FUTURE

En agosto nos vemos is currently in an almost unparalleled state of limbo. No one seems sure of the work's precise status. According to some commentators, the author gave up writing at least five years before his death. But Márquez himself was keen to deny such reports, telling the Colombian newspaper *El Tiempo* in 2009: "Not only is it not true, but the only thing I do is write." According to an interview with Claudio López Lamadrid, the Spanish literary director of Penguin Random House, Márquez was close to finishing the work. "But he didn't complete it because of the perfectionist that he was."

Neither is it certain whether the work was intended to be a novel. Márquez's biographer, Gerald Martin, said: "The last time I talked to Gabo about this story it was a stand-alone which he was going to include in a book with three similar but independent stories. Now they're talking about a series of episodes in which the woman turns up and has a different adventure each year."

In 2012, Márquez's brother Jaime revealed that the writer was suffering from dementia, and wouldn't be able to write the second part of his autobiography, *Vivir para contarla* (*Living to Tell the Tale*, 2002). It seems highly unlikely therefore, that he would have been able to write more fiction.

The truth may or may not be out there somewhere. What is unknown is whether, if this book ever appears in "finished" form, it will be in the final shape that Márquez intended. BR

WHAT HAPPENED NEXT . . .

Thousands of mourners paid tribute to Márquez at ceremonies in Colombia and his adopted homeland of Mexico. Outside the Palacio de Bellas Artes in Mexico City, a swarm of 380,000 yellow paper butterflies were released into the air, in reference to a motif used in *Cien años de soledad* (above). Speculation over *En agosto nos vemos* continues.

WILL IT EVER HAPPEN?

8/10

The popularity of Márquez's writing makes it highly likely that the novel will one day be published. Since his death from pneumonia, there has been almost incessant debate about the status of *En agosto nos vemos*: whether it's finished; whether it's supposed to be a novel or part of a collection of separate but interlinked stories; what the author intended. Such discussions have served to increase general interest, which will almost certainly make the work a sure-fire best seller when it eventually appears in whatever form.

NOT COMING SOON... A few more of our favorites

120 DAYS OF SODOM 1785
Marquis de Sade

When the Marquis de Sade was imprisoned in the Bastille, the notorious prison in Paris, France, he passed the time by writing a story of four male libertines who hold a four-month orgy in a castle. He wrote on a roll of paper nearly 40 feet (12 m) long (above).

At the beginning of July 1789, de Sade was transferred to an insane asylum. He hid his manuscript and left it behind in the jail, for fear that it might be confiscated. On July 14, the Bastille was stormed—one of the key moments in the French Revolution.

The author assumed that the work had been destroyed by looters. He died in prison in 1814, still lamenting its loss. But amazingly it survived and was eventually published in 1904. That it took so long to surface is mainly due to its horrific sexual content: it was a work that de Sade had hoped would shake the world to its foundations. The book is unfinished: it starts off as complete text but peters out at the end into notes. GL

THE WATSONS 1811
Jane Austen

The Watsons was abandoned by Jane Austen for unknown reasons, probably around 1811, when her father died. The 68-page manuscript of the unfinished novel was acquired in 2011 by the Bodleian Library in Oxford for over £1 million. There are some more pages in the Morgan Library, New York.

The Watsons is a promising and suggestive fragment, with plenty of Austen's characteristic wit, sharp observation, and good ear for dialogue. It's not easy to see where the novel is going on internal evidence, although Austen told her sister that Emma was to decline an offer of marriage from Lord Osborne.

Inevitably people have wanted to finish *The Watsons*; there was a version as early as 1850 by Austen's niece Catherine Hubback and there have been more since. A stage version is rumored to be in the pipeline by Laura Wade, the writer behind the *The Riot Club* (2014, based on her play *Posh*). BR

DUBROVSKY 1832
Aleksandr Pushkin

On his return from exile to his family's estate in Nizhny Novgorod, Pushkin hoped that Tsar Nicholas I's personal interest in his work would protect him from the censors with whom he had previously had so much trouble. But the Tsar's interference was, if anything, even worse than that of the imperial bureaucrats, who kept meddling anyway.

Nonetheless, the 1830s were his most productive period. Among the fruits of it were the short story collection *Tales of the Late Ivan Petrovich Belkin* (1831) and the comic poem *A Small House in Kolomna* (1830). In this flurry of activity, several other projects were abandoned, including *Dubrovsky*, a Robin Hood-like tale of a nobleman who responds to the confiscation of his property by a greedy aristocrat by robbing from the rich and giving to the poor. Pushkin never gave the novel a title, but it was later named for the protagonist when published after his death in 1841. GL

DENIS DUVAL 1863

William Makepeace Thackeray

Thackeray began writing *Denis Duval* in the spring of 1863. Following his death in December, only four installments of the planned eight appeared posthumously in *The Cornhill Magazine* (March to June 1864).

Denis grows up in the mid-18th century, in a colony of French refugees who have settled on the south coast of England. A French woman named Agnes de Saverne escapes from a tyrannical husband with the help of the sinister Chevalier de la Motte, who promises to be the villain of the piece. Denis falls in love with Agnes, but has to go to sea when he has exposed the smuggling activities of his family.

Henry James wrote an appreciative piece on the fragment in *English Hours* (1905), but confessed himself baffled as to which direction it might take. There are some working notes in the British Library. It seems that it would have been less skeptical and cynical than Thackeray's previous writings. BR

UNDER THE HILL 1898

Aubrey Beardsley

Beardsley is principally known as one of the most brilliant illustrators of the decadent 1890s. He died aged only 25 in 1898. This unfinished erotic novel is based on the legend of Tannhäuser, a 13th-century German poet-musician made famous in Wagner's opera of 1845. The first parts of it were published in the Aesthetic magazine *The Savoy* and then posthumously issued in book form by publisher Leonard Smithers in 1907. Smithers was ordered by Beardsley to destroy his obscene drawings after his death, but fortunately chose to preserve them.

The novel tells of the hero's sojourn to Venus's mountain for a year, spent worshipping the divinity. Filled with remorse he visits Pope Urban IV to seek absolution. Canadian writer John Glassco attempted a completion in 1959. Beardsley has remained distinctly marketable, so there are bound to be other attempts. We haven't seen the end of the *fin de siècle*. BR

STEPHEN HERO 1906

James Joyce

Joyce's *A Portrait of the Artist as a Young Man* (1916) is one of the great autobiographical novels of the 20th century, but—like many good literary works—it did not come into existence all at once and *Stephen Hero* represents the work in progress. Joyce threw it on the fire when it was rejected by publishers, but it was rescued by his wife Nora. What survived of it was first published in 1944, and it is a fascinating document in charting the forging of a novel. Its 383 pages correspond to the last 93 pages of *A Portrait*. Of great importance is that the Joycean doctrine of "the epiphany" is first outlined: "By an epiphany he meant 'a sudden spiritual manifestation, whether in the vulgarity of speech or of gesture or in a memorable phase of the mind itself.'" It would in theory be possible to reconstruct *Stephen Hero*, which would result in a low-key and detailed version of *A Portrait*. But what would be the point? BR

THE ASSASSINATION BUREAU, LTD 1916

Jack London

Jack London—the pen name of John Griffith Chaney—was a prolific American author of short stories and novels, the most famous of which are *The Call of the Wild* (1903) and *White Fang* (1906). *The Assassination Bureau, Ltd* is a thriller about a man who founds a secret assassination organization, but then finds himself at odds with his colleagues about the hit list, and soon discovers that he is on it himself. Having bought the plot of the novel from Sinclair Lewis, author of *Elmer Gantry* (1926), in 1910, London struggled to find a credible dénouement and gave up after 20,000 words. The work was completed in 1963 by Robert L. Fish, the author of *Mute Witness* (1963), which was later filmed as *Bullitt* (1968), starring Steve McQueen. Fish based his ending on an outline composed by London's widow. In 1969, *The Assassination Bureau, Ltd* was also made into a movie, directed by Basil Dearden and starring Curt Jurgens and Telly Savalas. GL

À LA RECHERCHE DU TEMPS PERDU 1922

Marcel Proust

It is easy to think that a towering work of literary genius is somehow monumental, and thus has the solidity and permanence of a building. Proust's *À La Recherche du temps perdu* (*In Search of Lost Time*) certainly towers, but investigation reveals that it is not as substantial and finished as might be thought. Proust worked on it for many years, and even on his deathbed was correcting proofs. Or rather, he was continuing to compose, for this is how he used his proofs. For decades editors have been pointing out errors and contradictions in the text, and have been uncovering sections that probably should be incorporated. The most famous of these is *Albertine Disparue*, discovered by Proust's niece in 1986 and first published in 1987.

So will the novel ever reach the state of being finished? Probably not. The fact that this is one of the major novels of the 20th century will probably deter all but the most foolish from attempting such an impossibility. BR

THE TEMPLE AT THATCH 1925

Evelyn Waugh

Waugh began writing *The Temple at Thatch* in 1924, during his final year at Oxford. The plot, according to diary entries, is largely autobiographical, based on the writer's experiences as an undergraduate, and dealing with themes of madness and black magic.

In 1925 he showed the manuscript to his aesthete friend Harold Acton, who later said: "It was an airy Firbankian trifle, totally unworthy of Evelyn, and I brutally told him so. It was a misfired jeu d'esprit." Waugh was so upset that he burned the manuscript, went down to the beach and started swimming out. In his autobiography Waugh said: "Did I really intend to drown myself? That was certainly in my mind." But not far from the shore he was attacked by a jellyfish and swam back. It is probable that he incorporated some of the material from the novel into his story "The Balance" (1925).

It is unlikely that anyone will reconstruct the novel. There is little to go on, and Waugh's wit and stylishness would be difficult to imitate. BR

THE BUCCANEERS 1937

Edith Wharton

The title of *The Buccaneers* conjurs up images of pirates, but in fact it continues the Henry James "International Theme" of impoverished Englishmen hoping to have their financial fortunes restored by injections of cash from rich American girls. This was a popular fictional motif in the early 20th century, influenced by marriages in the real world such as that of Consuelo Vanderbilt to the 9th Duke of Marlborough. These adventurous young women were known as "Buccaneers" at the time.

The novel was left unfinished at the time of Wharton's death in 1937. Marion Mainwaring finished it in 1993, a work that met with an adverse reception because of its clunking clichés. In 1995 Maggie Wadey wrote a version for a television miniseries, which involved a happy, Hollywood-style ending and was also heavily criticized. The "International Theme" remains alive in the popular television show *Downton Abbey*, so it seems likely that further writers will pursue the subject. BR

DIE BEKENNTNISSE DES HOCHSTAPLERS FELIX KRULL 1955

Thomas Mann

Thomas Mann won the Nobel Prize in Literature in 1929 and his novels *Der Tod in Venedig* (*Death in Venice*, 1912) and *Der Zauberberg* (*The Magic Mountain*, 1924) are often cited as required reading. He began planning this novel about a trickster in 1910. The first part of *Die Bekenntnisse des Hochstaplers Felix Krull* (*The Confessions of Felix Krull, Confidence Man*) was published in 1922 as a short story, but it was not until 1951 that Mann returned to project. When he died in 1955 it was still not finished.

A parody of Goethe's autobiography *Dichtung und Wahrheit* (*Poetry and Truth*, 1811–33), the novel tells the story of a clever swindler who makes his fortune by deception and ingenuity. He encounters a wide range of characters whose favor he wins by performing the roles they desire of him.

Mann's irresponsible sense of fun and impressive erudition would be hard to emulate by anyone attempting to finish the novel. BR

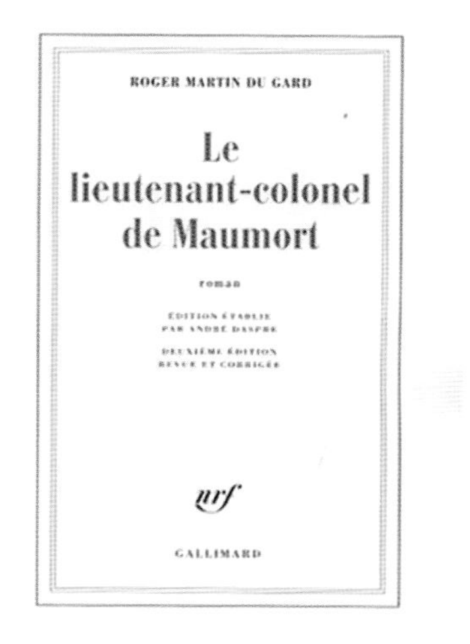

LE LIEUTENANT-COLONEL DE MAUMORT 1958

Roger Martin du Gard

Nobel Prize-winning French author Roger Martin du Gard wrote this novel over the last 18 years of his life. Intended only for posthumous publication, it was left unfinished at his death. It concerns the life of the title character, an aristocrat, soldier, and intellectual who is brought up according to the finest and most enlightened precepts, but whose conduct repeatedly betrays self-interest and moral lapses of a frequently disturbing order, especially when his mettle is tested during the First and Second World Wars. The question at the heart of the book is why do even people who are finely attuned to morality so often do wrong?

A quarter of a century elapsed between du Gard's death and publication of the work in French; the first English-language edition appeared in 1999. *Lieutenant-Colonel de Maumort* is an unfinished work that does not require completion as what we have is sufficient for total understanding; an ending might be neat, but it is not necessary. GL

PER FINE OUNCE c. 1966

Geoffrey Jenkins

Ian Fleming began writing James Bond stories in 1953. Ten years later, secret agent 007 had leaped off the page and landed profitably on the silver screen: *Dr. No* (1962) and *From Russia With Love* (1963) had both been huge global hits. A third movie, *Goldfinger*, was in production when Fleming died in 1964. His executors, accurately foreseeing that, with careful husbandry, Bond was a franchise that could run and run, sought a new author to carry on where the original creator had left off. They hired Geoffrey Jenkins, a South African whose first novel, *A Twist of Sand* (1959), had been a popular success. Jenkins produced *Per Fine Ounce*, about diamond smuggling, but Fleming's widow had reservations and the work was eventually rejected. All but 18 pages of the text are now believed to be lost.

Fleming has since had a host of authorized continuators: first Kingsley Amis (writing as "Robert Markham") with *Colonel Sun* (1968); later Sebastian Faulks and Anthony Horowitz. **GL**

THE ACTS OF KING ARTHUR AND HIS NOBLE KNIGHTS 1968

John Steinbeck

John Steinbeck had great success in his lifetime, and since his death in 1968 the critical response to his three major works—*Of Mice and Men* (1937), *The Grapes of Wrath* (1939), and *East of Eden* (1952)—has remained largely positive.

The author himself thought that this novel—based on Thomas Malory's *Le Morte d'Arthur* (1485), one of the books that most influenced him as a child—would have been his greatest. It was a retelling of the chivalric epic in which medieval derring-do is examined in the light of modern psychological theories. In 1959 Steinbeck told an interviewer that it would be his final work.

Unfortunately, he died of congestive lung disease before he could complete his valediction. It has an ending but it is unfinished. The extant fragment is so idiosyncratic a synthesis of ancient and modern that it is difficult to imagine even the most fearless continuator taking it on. **GL**

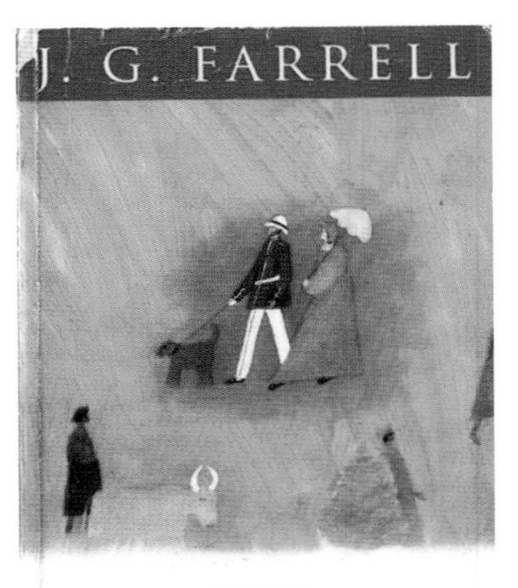

THE HILL STATION 1979

J.G. Farrell

In 1973, Farrell won the Booker Prize for *The Siege of Krishnapur*, about the Indian Mutiny of 1857–58. Thereafter he consolidated his reputation until he was swept from a seaside rock while fishing in Ireland. He was 44 years old.

The Hill Station, on which Farrell was working at the time of his death, would have been the final part of a tetralogy about colonialism. Although the novels were linked only loosely thematically, the main character of his last work, Dr. McNab, had been introduced in *The Siege*.

The final book was later completed by John Spurling and published in 1981. The poet D.J. Enright described it as "less dense, less effortful in the reading" than Farrell's previous works. Could it be that Farrell was on the brink of transition from promising talent into "one of the really major novelists of the English language," as Salman Rushdie predicted he would have become? We cannot tell: *The Hill Station* may be good, but it is not the whole work of the original author. **GL**

A RULING PASSION 1991

Joan Collins

In 1991, when British actress Joan Collins—star of the TV series *Dynasty*—delivered this 690-page novel, Random House publishers rejected it and demanded their advance back.

There followed years of legal dispute about the wording of the contract: could the term "complete manuscript" be taken to refer to quality as well as to quantity? In 1996, a New York court ruled that Collins could keep the money she'd already been paid.

During the case, lawyers repeatedly questioned—and sometimes pilloried—Collins's ability as a writer, but their criticisms did no damage to her popular appeal: her next three novels—*Too Damn Famous* (1995; retitled *Infamous* in the United States, where it came out in the following year), *Star Quality* (2002), and *Misfortune's Daughters* (2004)—took her career book sales in English and 30 other languages over the 50 million mark. Perhaps unsurprisingly, none of these hits carried the Random House imprimatur. *A Ruling Passion* has never seen the light of day. GL

L'ÉTUDIANTE 1993

Vanessa Duriès

Vanessa Duriès enjoys a cult status, furthered by her early death in 1993 in a car accident. Her first novel *Le Lien* (*The Ties that Bind*, 1993) tells the story of a young student who is initiated into the world of BDSM (Bondage and Discipline, Sadism and Masochism). It is based on her own experiences as a BDSM slave.

Her second novel, *L'Étudiante* (*The Student*), which she began writing in 1993, is also autobiographical, and continues along a similar theme. Duriès had written only five chapters at the time of her death. It was posthumously published in 2007, as a joint volume with *Le Lien*. The novel describes student life in Bordeaux, portraying in parallel the BDSM relationships of the heroine and the relationships of her contemporaries, whose love-lives are more conventional. She finds them both amusing and disturbing, using the contrast to analyze the BDSM milieu.

Will it be finished? Almost certainly. Any *succès de scandale* is bound to be followed by after-comers. BR

THE PALE KING 2008

David Foster Wallace

Wallace's breakthrough novel, *Infinite Jest* (2006), was a satire of American consumerism. Its rambling style and copious use of footnotes and endnotes drew praise and condemnation in comparable measure.

A lifelong depressive, Wallace took his own life in 2008 at the age of 46. Three years later, his editor, Michael Pietsch, completed *The Pale King*, on which the novelist had been working when he died. Set in an Internal Revenue Service office in Peoria, Illinois, its central theme is boredom—not the widely recognized kind of boredom that desensitizes and demoralizes, but the healthy kind that diverts people from their lemming-like pursuit of stimulation. For Wallace and his continuator, ennui is a welcome respite from strife.

Wallace's prose style was so distinctive, and his themes so far removed from mainstream thought, that it is hard to believe anyone could have made a better job than Pietsch of completing this novel. It is even harder to believe that anyone else would try. GL

BOOK COVER DESIGNERS

Angharad Burnard is a Cambridge-based illustrator who recently graduated from Cambridge School of Art. Her work has been published in Jack Zipes's *The Golden Age of Folk and Fairy Tales*, and she was highly commended for the Penguin Random House Design Award 2014.

Gareth Butterworth is the designer of several best-selling titles, including three unofficial Lego books. Outside of his work in illustrated non-fiction, he also designs album covers for local bands, infographics for London's mobile museums, and adverts for charitable social media campaigns. He is an infallibly splendid dinner companion.

Isabel Eeles is a London-based designer of illustrated reference books by day and a freelance creative by night. She achieved a first class honors in graphic design at Central Saint Martins. She contributed to both *The Greatest Movies You'll Never See* and *The Greatest Albums You'll Never Hear.* isabeleeles.com

Jayne Evans is a freelance artist, paper engineer, and graphic designer. Her work ranges from designing and making children's pop-up books and 3D models, to album covers and painting from her North London studio.
www.jayneevansart.co.uk

Gerry Fletcher is currently working as a UX & D designer for the BBC, in addition to working on illustrations for a number products, bands, and websites. He contributed several album cover designs to *The Greatest Albums You'll Never Hear*.

Hortense Franc was born in Paris and raised in London, and is currently a graphic design student at Central Saint Martins. She has worked on musicians' visual identity and in the movie industry, as well as undertaking various freelance projects.

Sarah Holland is a graphic designer who works for a small London-based design studio named Howdy. Her work covers print, illustration, identities, and websites.

Tom Howey is a book designer and typographer based in London. He is currently a PhD candidate at the Royal College of Art, investigating new forms for typography in spatial and multisensory contexts.

Damian Jaques trained in printmaking at Wimbledon College of Art and Portsmouth Polytechnic before becoming involved in graphic design. He was a co-founder and designer of *COIL, Journal of the Moving Image*, and designer of *Mute* magazine from 1997 to 2005. His work has been published in *Typography Now Two—Implosion, Mapping* (2008), and *magCulture: New Magazine Design* (2003).

Heath Killen is an Australian artist, writer, and broadcaster. Recently he worked as the editor of the popular design magazine *Desktop* and since then he has been working in a freelance capacity for a diverse roster of clients as a designer and consultant. Some of his current and previous clients include Paramount Pictures, Art Gallery of New South Wales, Powerhouse Museum, Golden Age Cinema & Bar, and the popular city guide series *The Thousands*. In 2015 he will be launching a new podcast series called *The Territories*, as well as a range of art and publishing projects under the banner Fort Street.
www.heathkillen.com

Claire Köster is currently studying Graphic and Communication Design at Central St Martins, London. Born and raised in Berlin, she is bilingual and interested in art, literature, and travel.
cl.koester@me.com

Joseph Bisat Marshall studied Graphic Design at Central Saint Martins, London. Book design, typography, and writing make up significant parts of his design practice. Marshall also works in theatre design—shows have included *Miss Saigon*, *The Phantom of the Opera*, and *Oliver!*—and works extensively with graphic designer Ken Garland.
www.josephbisatmarshall.co.uk

Dean Martin is a London-based graphic designer and illustrator.
deangmartin@me.com

Steve Panton, second-prize winner of the Penguin Design Award 2013, is a London based designer and illustrator with a very big passion for book covers, working with a variety of clients including HarperCollins, *New Scientist* and *Saga Magazine.* He currently works as an in-house Junior Designer at Profile Books and Serpent's Tail.
www.stevepanton.com

Josse Pickard is a graphic designer and typographer living in London. Since graduating from Central Saint Martins in 2013 he has worked on

CONTRIBUTORS

numerous books, including *Sci-Fi Chronicles*, *Garden Design Close Up*, and the *Making Sense* series, and other typographic freelance projects. cargocollective.com/jossepickard

Rebecca Richardson is a London-based graphic designer specializing in book design, with a complimentary interest in custom display typefaces. She enjoys developing her work to its most succinct form, creating considered designs that are both functional and aesthetically balanced. The result is work that has been described as clean and elegant.
www.rebecca-richardson.co.uk

John Round trained at Brighton University and Central Saint Martins School of Art and Design. After graduating, he learned book design while working with Martin Lovelock before establishing John Round Design. He has primarily been designing books for 20 years along with undertaking work within the field of education and exhibition design.

Emanuel Zahariades is a graphic and editorial designer from the sunny island of Crete, Greece. He loves magazines very much and can be often seen in Magma, trying to discreetly smell the pages of *Monocle* and *apartamento*. A Central Saint Martins graduate, he has worked for titles such as *men's file* and *The Spectator's Life*, while his freelance projects include work for clients ranging from the UCL Urban Laboratory to Hunter Boots. He likes (to design with) lines and lots of white space and firmly believes a good grid is the king of pretty much everything.
zahariades.co.uk

Helen Barr (HB) is Fellow and Tutor at Lady Margaret Hall, University of Oxford. Her publications include *The Piers Plowman Tradition*, *The Digby Lyrics; Socioliterary Practice in Late Medieval England*, and a wide range of articles on Middle English Literature. Her recently published *Transporting Chaucer* (2014) explores the traffic of Chaucer between medieval and early modern literature and material culture.

Claire Chandler (CC) is a London-based editor and writer with more than 20 years' experience in illustrated, academic and reference publishing. She has a degree in modern languages, and has studied translation and worked in Germany, Austria, and Belgium.

Reg Grant (RG) is author of more than 50 books on history and culture. He studied History and French at Trinity College, Oxford, and Social and Cultural Studies at Chelsea College, London.

Meredith Jones Russell (MJR) is a graduate of the University of Leeds and of London University's School of Eastern European and Slavonic Studies, She has lived and taught in Russia. In the West, she has translated and interpreted for movies, including *Kick-Ass 2* (starring Jim Carrey) and *Black Sea* (starring Jude Law).

George Lewis (GL) is an author and critic who works in publishing and runs courses on writing and editing. He studied English Literature at Brasenose College, Oxford, and believes that the two best writers in English are Shakespeare and Elmore Leonard.

Juliet Lough (JL) is an editor and literary translator who lives in London. She studied French and Italian at Exeter College, Oxford. Although she considers Dante to be beyond compare in Italian literature, Calvino holds second place in her heart.

Professor Bernard Richards (BR) was the Fellow in English Literature at Brasenose College, Oxford from 1972 to 1996. He is the author of *English Poetry of the Victorian Period 1830-1890* (1988, revised edition 2001). He has edited Henry James's *The Spoils of Poynton* and *The Princess Casamassima*, and is the author of more than 300 scholarly articles and reviews. He is currently an Emeritus Fellow of Brasenose College.

Dr. Liv Robinson (LV) teaches Medieval English Literature at Brasenose College, Oxford. She has published on the *Roman de la rose* and its Middle English translation, on the 15th-century French writer Alain Chartier, and on plays performed by nuns in medieval convents.

Brian Turton (BT) is a psychologist and was born in Manchester. He moved to London for romantic reasons many years ago and is now married and living in London. When not seeing patients, he focuses on the grandchildren, looking for things worth reading, and learning to play the piano.

Hazel Wilkinson (HW) is a research fellow in English Literature at Fitzwilliam College, Cambridge. She received her first degree from Christ Church, Oxford, and completed her studies with a PhD from UCL. Hazel has published articles on the 18th-century book trade, and regularly writes for *The Times Literary Supplement*.

INDEX

Page numbers in **bold** refer to illustrations

L

M

S

T

PICTURE CREDITS

Every effort has been made to trace all copyright owners, but if any have been inadvertently overlooked, the publishers would be pleased to make the necessary corrections at the first opportunity.

(Key: **t** = top; **c** = center; **b** = bottom; **l** = left; **r** = right; **tl** = top left; **tr** = top right; **bl** = bottom left; **br** = bottom right)

Front cover: © Images Source / STOCK4B

Back cover: Poodle Springs Josse Pickard **Das Schloss** Heath Killen **The Long Goodbye** Dean Martin **En agosto nos vemos** Isabel Eeles **Journals** Tom Howey **Willow** Steve Panton **Hero and Leander** Rebecca Richardson **Shadow of the Adept** Emanuel Zahariades **Prince Jellyfish** Heath Killen **Praeterita** Steve Panton **Hyperion** Angharad Burnard **The Crab and the Butterfly** Heath Killen

2 Lebrecht Authors **6** Michael Ochs Archives / GettyImages **12** © Roger Wood / CORBIS **15** PBL Collection **16** © Lebrecht Authors **17b** © culture-images / Lebrecht **17t** © Fine Art Photographic Library / Corbis **20** DeAgostini / Getty Images **22t** REX / JOHN DEMPSIE **24** Universal History Archive / Getty Images **26b** Heritage Images/Getty Images **26t** © Lebrecht Authors / Lebrecht Music & Arts / Lebrecht Music & Arts / Corbis **27** © Bettmann / CORBIS **28** Heritage Images / Getty Images **30b** © Lebrecht Authors **31** © Tristram Kenton / Lebrecht Music & Arts **36** © stefano baldini / Alamy **38** REX / Everett Collection **40** © Lebrecht Authors **43** © Lebrecht **44** Heritage Images / Getty Images **46** DeAgostini / Getty Images **50** © Lebrecht / ColouriserAL **52** Print Collector / Getty Images **53** Universal History Archive / UIG via Getty Images **54** Lebrecht Authors **56** Lebrecht Authors **58** Leemage / Lebrecht **62r** © Lebrecht Authors **64** © World History Archive / Alamy **70** © adoc-photos / Lebrecht Music & Arts **74** © Lebrecht Authors **76t** Grasmere, c.1830 (w/c on paper), Robson, George Fennel (1788-1833) / Wordsworth Trust / Bridgeman Images **76b** Dove Cottage, Grasmere, c.1806 (w/c on paper), Wordsworth, Dora (1804-47) / Wordsworth Trust / Bridgeman Images **78** Rischgitz / Getty Images **80** Sean Sexton / Getty Images **82** © adoc-photos / Lebrecht Music & Arts **84** © Lebrecht Music and Arts Photo Library / Alamy **86** © RIA Novosti / Lebrecht Music & Arts **88** © Gavin Parsons / Alamy **90** © Rue des Archives / PVDE **94** © Lebrecht Authors **96b** UniversalImagesGroup **98** © adoc-photos / Lebrecht Music & Arts **101b** © Lebrecht Authors **101t** © Lebrecht Authors **102b** Lebrecht Authors **103** IRST STANDARD MEDIA / THE KOBAL COLLECTION **104** © Lebrecht Music & Arts **107tl** DeAgostini / Getty Images **108** © adoc-photos / Lebrecht Music & Arts **114** Lebrecht Authors **116t** Hulton Archive / Getty Images **118** © INTERFOTO / Alamy **120** © Lebrecht Authors **122b** © The Art Archive / Alamy **122t** © Lebrecht Authors **123** Jt acquaviva / Wikimedia Commons / CC-BY-SA-3.0 **124b** Leemage / Getty Images **124t** BIOSKOP / WDR / GAUMONT / THE KOBAL COLLECTION / PIERRE, GEORGES **125** © The Art Archive / Alamy **128** Lebrecht Authors **132** © adoc-photos / Lebrecht Music & Arts **136** Fox Film Corporation **138** Mirrorpix / Lebrecht Authors **140t** © adoc-photos / Lebrecht Music & Arts **142** © IMAGNO / Lebrecht **144** Three Lions / Getty Images **145** © Daniel Bockwoldt / dpa / Corbis **146b** Courtesy of the Lask Collection **148** Popperfoto / Getty Images **150b** FILM Copyright © 1949 STUDIOCANAL FILMS LTD. ALL RIGHTS RESERVED / THE KOBAL COLLECTION **151** Rue des Archives RA / Lebrecht **152** Leemage / Lebrecht **154** © Lebrecht Authors **155t** Leemage / Lebrecht **155b** © De Agostini / Lebrecht Music & Arts **156** © Lebrecht Authors **158b** DEA PICTURE LIBRARY **158t** © CTK / Alamy **160** © Ullstein bild / Lebrecht Music & Arts **163** PARAMOUNT / THE KOBAL COLLECTION **164** © adoc-photos / Lebrecht Music & Arts **166t** © Oote Boe / Alamy **168** Leemage / Lebrecht **174** ABKCO FILMS / THE KOBAL COLLECTION **176** © Jeff Lowenthal / Lebrecht **178t** Numismatica Ars Classica NAC AG, Auction 46, 2008, lot 475 **178b** Keystone-France / Getty Images **180** Interfoto / Lebrecht **182** Photo by Emilio Ronchini/Mondadori Portfolio via Getty Images **184b** Mondadori / Getty Images **188** © Bettmann / CORBIS **189** © Vespasian / Alamy **190** Ralph Crane / The LIFE Images Collection / Getty Images **191** © David Howells / Corbis **192** © RA / Lebrecht Music & Arts **194** Everett Collection Historical / Alamy **197b** Archive Photos / Stringer **200** © Bettmann/CORBIS **201** © AF archive / Alamy **202** © Bettmann / CORBIS **203** © LARRY DOWNING / Reuters / Corbis **204** © Everett Collection Historical / Alamy **206r** © AF archive / Alamy **208** Nora Schuster / Imagno / Getty Images **210b** © Ullstein bild / Lebrecht Music & Arts **214** John Swope/The LIFE Images Collection / Getty Images **216** © CORBIS **218** © Alex Gotfryd / CORBIS **220** Louis MONIER / Gamma-Rapho via Getty Images **224** Mirrorpix/Lebrecht Authors **226** Ulf Andersen / Getty Images **228b** PARAMOUNT / THE KOBAL COLLECTION / CONNOR, FRANK **230** Essdras M Suarez / The Boston Globe via Getty Images **232** Leemage / Lebrecht **236** YURI CORTEZ / Getty Images **238** Ulf Andersen / Getty Images **240l** MARTIN BUREAU / AFP / Getty Images **240c** Lebrecht Authors **240r** RIA Novosti / Lebrecht Music & Arts **241l** Lebrecht Authors **241c** © Heritage Image Partnership Ltd / Alamy **242c** © adoc-photos / Corbis **242r** Hulton Archive / Stringer **243c** © MARKA / Alamy **244c** © Everett Collection Historical / Alamy **245l** Photo by Jason LaVeris / FilmMagic

The copyright for book covers is held by the designers who created them. However, for some of the covers, third parties supplied images that were incorporated into the designs: **47** Marcus Stone / Getty Images **95** Susan Trigg / Getty Images **109** Linda Steward / Getty Images **139** CSA Images / Mod Art Collection / Getty Images **153** CSA Images / B&W Archive Collection / Getty Images **225** © Javarman / Alamy

The quote on the *Poodle Springs* cover (page 191) is taken from *The Long Goodbye* (1953) by Raymond Chandler.